BANKING AND FINANCE DISPUTE RESOLUTION IN HONG KONG

This book examines the concept of 'naming, blaming, claiming' in the application of arbitration for private banking dispute resolution. The author focuses on examining this issue using Hong Kong as a case in point, blending theory and empirical evidence to unveil how disputes are resolved within the banking and finance industry, which will enable them to explore possible effective and efficient mechanisms to resolve financial disputes.

The book offers a comprehensive review of the laws and regulations governing the private banking industry in Hong Kong and selected jurisdictions, as well as how they are implemented. It examines the clients' perceptions through an innovative methodology for empirical studies. Describing how clients react to the laws and regulations and the potential adverse impacts to the stability of the banking industry, the author identifies possible factors that could trigger another financial crisis. Synthesising his analysis, the author proposes newly discovered self-corrective mechanisms embedded among clients and concludes with policy recommendations.

Directly relevant to banking practitioners, particularly legal and compliance departments, and senior management, the book is also written for legal professionals interested in the practices of dispute resolution in banking and finance. Additional readerships will include bank regulators, government officials, policy makers, researchers, and those involved in courses in banking and financial law, as well as Arbitration and Dispute Resolution.

Dr Sau Wai Law (Samuel) holds a PhD in Law from the University of Hong Kong. Before becoming a full-time academic in January 2021, he had more than 14 years of banking experience in Hong Kong, taking up roles in credit risk management, private banking, and strategic planning. His research interests are Dispute Resolution, Banking and Finance Law, Professional Ethics, Risk & Compliance, Financial Inclusion, and Virtual Banking. He is a trainer and course reviewer, on the Certified Banker Programme and the trainer and the study guide writer on the Enhanced Competency Framework in Operational Risk Management and Compliance at the Hong Kong Institute of Bankers.

PRACTICAL FINANCE AND BANKING GUIDES

Consumer Credit: Law and Practice
Second edition
Alexander Hill-Smith

Bank Regulation, Risk Management, and Compliance
Theory, Practice, and Key Problem Areas
Alexander Dill

Banking and Finance Dispute Resolution in Hong Kong
The Suitability of Arbitration in Private Disputes
Sau Wai Law

For more information about this series, please visit: www.routledge.com/law/series/PFBG

BANKING AND FINANCE DISPUTE RESOLUTION IN HONG KONG

THE SUITABILITY OF ARBITRATION IN PRIVATE DISPUTES

SAU WAI LAW

informa law
from Routledge

Designed cover image: Getty Images

First published 2024
by Informa Law from Routledge
4 Park Square, Milton Park, Abingdon, Oxon OX14 4RN

and by Informa Law from Routledge
605 Third Avenue, New York, NY 10158

Informa Law from Routledge is an imprint of the Taylor & Francis Group, an informa business

British Library Cataloguing-in-Publication Data
A catalogue record for this book is available from the British Library

ISBN: 978-1-032-52631-7 (hbk)
ISBN: 978-1-032-52633-1 (pbk)
ISBN: 978-1-003-40759-1 (ebk)

DOI: 10.4324/9781003407591

Typeset in Times New Roman
by Deanta Global Publishing Services, Chennai, India

CONTENTS

LIST OF TABLES

TABLE OF CASES

PREFACE

In the private banking industry, the use of Alternative Dispute Resolution (ADR) mechanisms is still uncommon, and even in some circumstances, the availability of such mechanisms is unknown. The need to explore a suitable ADR mechanism for banking disputes in Hong Kong is imminent. The private banking sector in Hong Kong is largely an unexplored area, and the insights aim to offer fresh perspectives of interest to a global audience given the unique status of Hong Kong as an international financial centre. This book rides on the naming, blaming, claiming model (NBC model) through the lens of the power differential theory and examines the suitability of arbitration for resolving private banking disputes from the client's perspective.

Content Analysis: The Role of ADR in Private Banking Disputes

The backbone of a successful ADR is a solid contractual relationship. The book starts with the current legal and regulatory framework of the private banking industry in Hong Kong and selected jurisdictions, covering two aspects. The first aspect (Chapter 2) focuses on understanding private banking businesses, and how the laws and regulations are being enforced and delivered by the banks to their clients using account opening forms as contracts. The second aspect (Chapter 3) focuses on unveiling the regulatory preferences on dispute resolution mechanisms in banking, examining how it may replace arbitration. It analyses the power balances between banks and clients through a comparative analysis of respective laws and regulations on private banks, dispute resolution mechanisms and the arbitral rules in selected jurisdictions, and a contextual analysis of account opening forms, websites from banks, and Financial Dispute Resolution Centre (FDRC) annual reports. Then, the findings are explained through the author's first-hand experiences of escalating a complaint directly to a bank and Hong Kong Monetary Authority (HKMA). The content analysis and insights are also validated from the first-hand observations which offer hypotheses to the research questions that clients might be unable to adequately name their grievances due to the power imbalance caused by a one-sided contract, hence arbitration might not be a viable option and is under-utilised. The pure contextual analysis lays down the background for the empirical studies for the content of the survey and interview questions.

Empirical Studies: Is Arbitration Suitable for Private Banking Disputes?

The book presents empirical findings to examine whether arbitration is suitable for private banking disputes in Hong Kong from the client's perspective, by assessing clients' knowledge of the laws and regulations governing private banks and investigating clients' experiences of their interactions with private banks. The empirical studies involve quantitative analysis of the data collected from the surveys, and qualitative analysis through adopting the NBC model, to study the insights generated from face-to-face interviews. The findings echo the implication from content analysis with closer relevance to private banking disputes. First, the grievances are unlikely to come from deviation of what is being agreed upon in the written contract. Second, clients rely heavily on their private bankers to fulfil their requests for banking services, regardless of contractual scope. Third, the function of the bank's internal dispute process puts clients in a passive position due to the lack of transparency in banks' processes. Fourth, probably due to the above, clients have most of the responsibility in managing their relationship with the bank to ensure nothing goes wrong. All these create a clients' perception of their weak power in a private banking dispute. To explain this under the NBC framework, grievances are not transformed into disputes due to the above reasons.

Theoretical Implications: Clients' Self-Corrective Mechanism to Eliminate Dispute without a Proper Resolution

The analyses are synthesised to explain why an arguably suitable mechanism is not utilised at all. The findings lead to a theoretical explanation that clients possess self-corrective mechanisms that work to eliminate, instead of resolve, disputes once a grievance starts to form. An in-depth analysis of the case studies from the four private banking clients has shown that clients believe that they had no choice but to eliminate their grievances internally with the bank or exit the relationship. Whether there exists a gap in terms of regulatory requirements and actual practice cannot be known for sure, as this would only be exposed to the regulators during a periodic review, rather than as specific situations arise. the findings hopes to achieve the following objectives: (i) derive theoretical implications of the role of private bankers who act as influential third parties in dispute transformation; (ii) identify any general factors which could make arbitration a viable option to resolve private banking disputes; and (iii) understand clients' behaviour in how they react to their grievances and any potential impacts to the general health of the financial system, especially when clients have no choice but to resolve disputes in their own way. Although arbitration could be a suitable process from the client's perspective, it is not always necessary and efficient due to unequal contractual relations, the perception of power imbalances due to lack of transparency of a bank's internal dispute resolution process, and active management by clients to prevent disputes. In light of this, banks should be required to provide further transparency of the complaint-handling process and to engage clients in this process. Regulators might consider taking a more active role in supervising the resolution of disputes. It is in the public interest to unveil disputes so that bank practices can be publicly scrutinised. Continuous improvement of bank operations triggered by disputes can contribute to the avoidance of larger problems if identified early. Currently, the tight regulation might agitate clients because banks can never be challenged due to the perception of strict regulations and compliance, and a regulatory preference to leave banks and clients alone to resolve the dispute themselves.

ACKNOWLEDGEMENTS

This book is originated from my doctorate studies at the Faculty of Law at the University of Hong Kong. I am grateful to the guidance from Ms Katherine Lynch during my studentship and subsequently from Professor Shahla Ali who took over the supervision and made my continued studies possible. I am also grateful for all the unfailing administrative support and advice provided by the faculty. I am also thankful to my family for their unwavering endorsement. I am grateful for the friendships and fellowships developed during this journey and to those who offered valuable insights for this work. Special thanks to the Routledge publishing team for professionally overseeing the review and publication process. I am thankful to the peer reviewers. All that is positive in this book reflects the support and guidance of all. All errors and omissions are my own.

LIST OF ABBREVIATIONS

ADR	Alternative Dispute Resolution
AIS	Authorised institutions
AML	Anti-money laundering
AMLO	Anti-Money Laundering and Counter-Terrorist Financing Ordinance (Cap. 615)
AUD	Australian dollar
BO	Banking Ordinance (Cap. 155)
CDD	Customer due diligence
CFT	Counter-financing of terrorism
CIETAC	China International Economic and Trade Arbitration Commission
CJR	Civil Justice Reform
CPWP	Certified Private Wealth Professional
FATF	Financial Action Task Force on Money Laundering
FDRC	Financial Dispute Resolution Centre
FIDREC	Financial Industry Disputes Resolution Centre Ltd
HKD	Hong Kong dollar
HKIAC	Hong Kong International Arbitration Centre
HKMA	Hong Kong Monetary Authority
HNW	High net worth
KYC	Know Your Client
NBC	Naming, blaming, claiming model/framework
P.R.I.M.E.	Panel of Recognized International Market Experts
PD	Practice Direction
SFC	Securities and Future Commission
SOW	Source of wealth
SPM	Supervisory Policy Manual

CHAPTER 1

Introduction

1.1 Background

1.1.1 From civil justice reform to private banking dispute in Hong Kong

Before the Civil Justice Reform (CJR), customers had several ways to handle banking disputes in Hong Kong (HK), which did not necessarily include mediation or arbitration. If customers failed to resolve their dispute with the bank directly, they could launch a complaint to the Hong Kong Monetary Authority (HKMA); however, the HKMA would not investigate or order action in particular cases (see Chapter 3, Section 3.2.2). Customers could also make a complaint to the Securities and Future Commission (SFC), where its internal Complaints Control Committee would conduct assessments of complaints to determine whether they would require further action, such as investigation, prosecution, and/or disciplinary action. The Consumer Council could offer financial assistance through its Consumer Legal Action Fund to eligible consumers to take legal action and offer greater access to legal remedies (Consumer Council, 2021a). This fund played a crucial role in complaints against financial services before the Lehman Brothers crisis in 2008. Nevertheless, it is noted that the Consumer Council was restricted to 'receiving and examining complaints and giving advice to consumers' (Consumer Council, 2021b). It also provides conciliation service but does not have the power to order compensation. Compensation remedies require consumers to submit their claims to the courts, such as the Small Claims Tribunal, if the disputed amount is less than HK$50,000 (at the time of the crisis, revised to HK$75,000 in December 2018) or to a higher court if the amount is higher. Customers can also report the matter to the police's Commercial Crimes Bureau to investigate the matter, and criminal charges are laid if they are substantiated. Yet it is important to recognise that before all of the above happens, Hong Kong regulators prefer customers to negotiate directly with the bank, with or without assistance from third parties. For example, a report on 10 December 2008 in the

 DOI: 10.4324/9781003407591-1

South China Morning Post showed that the Democratic Party announced that it assisted more than 60 investors in Lehman derivatives (Man, 2008).

CJR became effective on 2 April 2009 with six underlying objectives, namely: (a) to increase the cost-effectiveness of any practice and procedure to be followed in relation to civil proceedings before the Court; (b) to ensure that a case is dealt with as expeditiously as is reasonably practicable; (c) to promote a sense of reasonable proportion and procedural economy in the conduct of proceedings; (d) to ensure fairness between the parties; (e) to facilitate the settlement of disputes; and (f) to ensure that the resources of the Court are distributed fairly (Civil Justice Reform, 2021a). There are two features that are relevant for the purpose of this research: active case management and facilitation of settlement.

The feature of active case management refers to the greater case management powers given to the court to 'prevent tactical manipulation of the rules to delay proceedings' (Hong Kong Legislative Council, 2015) and to implement a more disciplined approach to conducting cases efficiently, such as through organising Case Management Conferences and fixing certain milestone dates. Amendments were also made to 15 primary and subsidiary legislations, which address the costs and other procedural matters to implement active case management (Civil Justice Reform, 2021b). In addition, there are 22 Practice Directions (PD) covering a wide range of substantive and procedural issues, such as personal injuries (*PD 18.1*), Employees' Compensation (*PD 18.2*), Construction (*PD 6.1*), Matrimonial and Family Proceedings (*PD15.12*), and procedural issues such as Appeals to the Court of Appeal (*PD 4.1*), Case Management (*PD5.2*), Interlocutory Summonses (*PD 5.4*), Costs (*PD 14.3*), Settling Draft Orders (*PD 16.1*), Sealing of Writ of Summons, Newspaper Advertisements, and the filing of documents (*PD 24.1*).

The objective to facilitate settlement is implemented through *PD 31*, which states that the court has a duty to encourage the parties to use ADR mechanisms and to help parties settle disputes. For example, *PD 31* has clearly stated that the parties and their legal representatives have the duty of 'assisting the court to discharge such duty' (Chief Justice, 2014). The parties should submit the case to the court only after they have made reasonable efforts to settle but have failed to reach an agreement. The refusing parties may be subject to an adverse costs order on the grounds of unreasonable refusal to mediate. Mediation is one of the highly advocated dispute resolution channels. There were a number of initiatives to facilitate ADR. On 10 July 2010, the Joint Mediation Helpline Office was set up to provide mediation referral services for disputants on a non-profit making basis (Joint Mediation Helpline Office, 2021). In 2013, Mediation Ordinance was enacted. In the same year, Hong Kong Mediation Accreditation Association Limited was founded as an industry-based, umbrella body for mediator accreditation in Hong Kong. PD 3.3 also sets out the provision for voluntary mediation in respect of petitions presented under s. 723 of the Companies Ordinances (Cap 622) and petitions for winding up on just and equitable grounds under section 177(1)(f) of the Companies (Winding Up and Miscellaneous Provision) Ordinance (Cap 32). This is used where the court 'wishes to encourage the parties to consider the use of mediation' if the disputes do not involve the interests of a creditor or if it is in the public interest. Also, Hong Kong became the first Asian jurisdiction to pass apology legislation in 2017.

It is obvious that a well-recognised ADR mechanism, serving the same purpose and owning the same public trust as the court, has become vital to the success of CJR, and lots of progress have been made. As of 28 July 2021, there were 707 corporations committed to the 'Mediate First Pledge' (Department of Justice (2021), but only five banks were signed up, namely: Taiwan Business Bank Ltd, Bank of China (Hong Kong) Limited, Bank of East Asia Limited, HSBC, and the Tai Sang Bank. If a bank is a member of the Financial Dispute Resolution Centre (FDRC), it must respond to the request of the mediation filed by a claimant (although the vice versa is not true, a bank cannot force clients to come to mediation or arbitration through FDRC). Whilst the CJR has made its impact on many industries in the use of ADR mechanisms, the financial industry has not been widely impacted and FDRC has not been widely adopted.

1.1.2 From Lehman Brothers' collapse to protecting individual clients

Prior to the launch of CJR, on 15 September 2008, Lehman Brothers went bankrupt (Editors, 2008). This subsequently triggered a vast number of complaints lodged by investors against the mis-selling of Lehman Brothers' investment products by banks, of which the Minibond caused the most concern: with the issuer gone and the collateral that was supposed to support the investment allegedly not existing, this led to massive losses for individual customers who had invested, involving an estimated 48,000 Hong Kong investors with HKD20 billion worth of investment assets in Hong Kong (Ali & Kwok, 2010, p. 165). It has been described as 'The Lehman Crisis'. The court appeared to be overloaded with cases: HKMA received over 21,000 complaints alleging fraud, misrepresentation, and/or misconduct related to bad advice from banks and bankers. Some complaints came from very agitated investors, and many went to protest or even occupied the street.

To resolve this, HKMA launched the Lehman Brothers-related Investment Product Disputes Mediation and Arbitration Scheme in October 2008 to handle settlement amounts ranging from HKD40,000 to over HKD5 million (Hong Kong Monetary Authority, 2008). The first mediation successfully concluded on 10 December 2008 and lasted for only five hours, with an overall 88% success rate. It became apparent that a permanent and independent mechanism should be established. Extensive research discussing how to incorporate ADR into the regulatory framework was conducted. Soo et al. (2010) assessed the characteristics and processes of the Lehman Brothers-related Investment Product Disputes Mediation and Arbitration Scheme and concluded that it was a success due to the good publicity associated with the high success rate in mediation (Soo et al., 2010, p. 152). Weixia (2011) advocated the need for the creation of the FDRC to ensure the city's ability to resolve disputes that 'arose from the under-regulation of sales by banks of particular high-risk financial products' (Weixia, 2011, p. 21). FDRC was later established in November 2011, aiming to provide a 'quick, simple or efficient means' to resolve disputes and to fill the gaps of regulators having the role of receiving complaints but having no power to adjudicate disputes or order compensation (Securities and Futures Commission, 2008). Ali and Da Roza (2012) reviewed the efficacy of the use of ADR and observed that the eligibility test for mediation and arbitration services should be expanded and a clear roadmap should be provided through the development of an 'in-house multi-tier dispute resolution system' where collective efforts from HKSAR Government, HKMA, SFC, and retail banks should be in place to introduce expert decisions at the first tier led by the HKMA, mediation at the second tier led by the FDRC, and the third tier being arbitration arranged by the FDRC (Ali & Kwok, 2010). The concept of 'mediation first, arbitration next' was planted as early as that stage. Yet these efforts have not been further developed in the financial industry, with the reasons remaining unclear.

1.1.3 Suitability of ADR for banking and finance

This section reviews the arbitration process and its suitability for banks by examining the merits, concerns, and possible models. Arbitration is not the only option available for private banking disputes, and perhaps more often it might indicate that the choice is progressive: if one channel does not work then the claimant can move on to the next option. The scope of this book focuses on arbitration, but it does not necessarily mean that other channels do not play their role in the dispute resolution process. More likely, other channels have been attempted before reaching arbitration and making the ADR process a progressive one. Different ADR mechanisms would play their role and are briefly mentioned below, although they are not directly related to private banking disputes. Further discussion with regard to the merits, concerns, and models for arbitration are described in Section 1.2.3 in this chapter.

Arner et al. (2010) discussed the impact of global financial crises on Hong Kong and the country's regulatory responses, and they provided a comprehensive review of the effectiveness of the available dispute resolution options triggered by the Lehman crisis (Arner et al., 2010, pp. 32–34). **Litigation** under a public adjudication system as an obvious choice may be commenced swiftly but, given the complexity of the Lehman crisis, the overlapping civil law and regulatory regimes, and the stringent standards applied to representative actions (if any), the costs and time required to resolve disputes through litigation are substantial. **Arbitration** is also adjudicative in nature, and it is argued that a fairer outcome may be achieved through the engagement of a subject matter expert acting as an arbitrator. Nevertheless, there are numerous shortfalls. First, it is difficult to find a suitable arbitrator who is capable of simultaneously dealing with the interacting regimes of civil law and regulations, the bank-customer relationship, and financial products. Second, arbitrating a class of complaints simultaneously makes the arbitration process time-consuming and may result in inconsistent awards/decisions. Among these concerns, Arner et al. also pointed out the confidential nature of arbitration and the fact that legal representation is dispensable in arbitration, with the potential of widening the 'information gap between distributors and complainants', keeping claimants and regulatory bodies in the dark as to important information relating to the 'reasoning and the range of compensation'. **Negotiation** is the least formal and expensive method, but it does not favour those vulnerable complainants who are disadvantaged by either their age, education level, financial literacy, or financial resources. They would go straight to the court instead of negotiating with the bank. The fact-finding process in an adversarial system or the lack of an inquisitorial process in a negotiation would lead to a disparity in treatment between the settlements offered by intermediaries. The diversity offered in these processes should help resolve private banking disputes, but somehow it does not happen in Hong Kong despite the success in resolving Lehman-related disputes during the global financial crisis.

1.1.4 A missed opportunity for banks to build a more resistant global banking system

The global financial crisis in 2008, CJR, and the success of the Lehman Brothers-related Investment Product Disputes Mediation and Arbitration Scheme sponsored by HKMA could have offered the perfect timing to set the tone for the use of ADR in the financial industry. In Hong Kong, numerous efforts have been made to promote ADR within business, commercial, and financial industries since the introduction of CJR in April 2009, which is expected to have contributed to the healthy development of the financial industry in Hong Kong. It has provided perfect timing to incorporate ADR into the regulatory framework to strengthen our current financial regulatory system. The SFC has proposed the establishment of an ombudsman for financial services and recommended the creation of a dispute resolution mechanism for the financial industry (Securities and Futures Commission, 2008, section 4.7.1), whilst the HKMA has similar proposals (Hong Kong

Monetary Authority, 2011, section 7.2.1). The SFC recommended that the Code of Conduct be amended to require client agreements to specify a right for clients to resolve their disputes through the newly established FDRC. It appeared to acknowledge the importance of embedding a well-structured and recognised ADR mechanism into the regulatory framework and to defend this value through building a proper ADR infrastructure alongside public confidence.

However, when compared to other industries in Hong Kong, the development appears slow. Alexander (2018) provided an update on the development of mediation in different industries which includes family, construction, commercial, financial, insurance, community, building management, school, victim-offender, and intellectual property conflicts. In the financial industry, the only development in promoting ADR appeared to be the establishment of the FDRC accepting claims with a threshold of HK$500,000 maximum claimable amount. The amount was subsequently increased to HK$1 million in 2017, which is nevertheless contrary to the original proposal of HK$3 million (FDRC, 2016). The progress of using arbitration in the financial industry has been even slower. Arbitration is not commonly used to resolve disputes between banks and their clients. For example, despite its overall success, the Lehman Brothers-related Investment Product Disputes Mediation and Arbitration Scheme has recorded no case of arbitration (Hong Kong Monetary Authority, 2008). There has also been only a very small number of cases of arbitration in the FDRC, with only eight arbitration cases between 2012 and 2020 versus 159 cases for mediation, significantly less than the 2,961 complaints received by the HKMA in 2021 alone (Hong Kong Monetary Authority, 2021).

Private banks are no exception in Hong Kong. A private bank is subject to more or less the same regulatory regime as other conventional banks, but they offer personal and exclusive services when compared to their retail banking counterparts. Although all licensees of the SFC and HKMA and member banks of the FDRC are obliged to comply with individual consumers' wishes to enter mediation and arbitration, the utilisation of the FDRC may not sound as impressive as first imagined. It can be argued that neither customers nor banks find the FDRC an obvious external choice for dispute resolution. In fact, as we shall see further in Chapter 3, the FDRC has revised the threshold to the maximum claimable amount up to HK$1 million (instead of the originally proposed HK$3 million), except when both parties consent to a higher amount. Except for parties' consent, FDRC has literally excluded most private banking disputes. Most private banking transactions have a minimum amount of USD200,000 (c. HKD1.6 million).

This resistance to arbitration in the private banking industry is also a global phenomenon. According to a 2016 ICC report, there exist issues of legal clarity, legal certainty, and public confidence that are risky to the stability of the private banking industry (see Chapter 3, Section 3.4.1). A common thought is that private banking clients have the financial capacity to challenge banks through open courts or to mobilise their resources to create social impact, such as hiring professional protestors to create noise consistently to damage the reputation of the bank.

This book aims to offer a theoretical perspective on this phenomenon to explain why arbitration is not widely utilised to resolve disputes between private banks and their clients. It also aims to examine the factors affecting the suitability of arbitration in resolving private banking disputes from the perception of private banking clients.

1.2 Literature review

This research draws on three major bodies of literature in addressing the research questions under study, namely, the theory of power and the NBC framework, as well as existing literature related to the suitability of arbitration in finance disputes. Whilst the power balance between parties often affects the decision of which mechanism to adopt, what comes before this is the need to understand whether disputes could be justifiably formed in the first place, affected by factors not just related to perceived power balances but also others named in the NBC model. Finally, existing literature on arbitration in banking and finance will be reviewed to explore existing arguments for and against this mechanism, whilst it is observed that these arguments might not have incorporated the views of disputants. There are no directly relevant studies for private banking, but relevance could be derived from similar research; the literature review suggests the potential inter-disciplinary approach to legal studies in order to gain a holistic view whilst controlling the scope of the research matter.

1.2.1 Could we win? Perspective from power theory

1.2.1.1 The source of power in ADR

Examining the role of power balance in the ADR process is critical in assessing whether disputants will engage in a particular dispute resolution process. The power dynamics between private banking clients and private banks are presumably different from those between mass retail clients and their own banks. Nevertheless, the underlying theories set a foundation for the analysis of clients' perceptions, be they wealthy customers or otherwise.

Dispute resolution processes can be defined as the full range of processes such as negotiation, mediation, conciliation, facilitation, independent expert appraisal, and arbitration with advantages in costs, timeliness, flexibility, consensual outcomes with party control, and widened scope in terms of claims and remedies. Astor and Chinkin (2002), in an Australian context, examined the issues of power imbalances in mediation and concluded that the fact that mediation is consensual creates a risk of producing an outcome that only reflects the power balance and relationship between the parties (Astor & Chinkin, 2002).

With regard to power, the assumption of rough equality between the parties within informal dispute resolutions has been challenged by Fiss (1984). Fiss argued against the proposal of advocating settlement as part of the new direction of legal education from Bok (1983). His central argument was that power imbalances between disputing parties could undesirably influence the settlement created in private informal dispute resolution processes in three ways, which is only a process of 'peace-making' but perhaps at the cost of justice. The first way is the lack of bargaining power due to the parties' different abilities to analyse information to predict outcomes in an intended litigation process; the less wealthy may be less able to 'amass and analyse' the information needed to predict the outcomes of the litigation, less able to wait for the judgment given they wanted to accelerate payment, and they may be forced to settle due to a lack of resources to finance a litigation process (Fiss, 1984, p. 1076). The second way is the temptation to get less than what is deserved in exchange in an immediate settlement. Individuals could be bound by 'the rule they generate' which 'impair their autonomy' and could lead to the absence of authoritative consent. This mostly impacts organisations, as it blurs who can speak on behalf of an organisation and groups where there is a lack of structural or procedural methods to form a stance (Menkel-Meadow, 1999). The third way is when the disadvantaged party may be forced to settle because they do not have the resources to finance the litigation in the fear that the wealthier party might manipulate the procedural mechanisms to prolong the process and impose additional expenses (Fiss, 1984, p. 1076). Mayer (1987) evaluated the choice of dispute resolution process as 'the vehicle through which a weaker party has to choose between two unfavorable outcomes… increases the power differentials, it should probably not be used' (Mayer, 1987, p. 78). Astor (2005) pointed out that an assessment of power poses a challenge to third-party neutrals, relative sizes, perceptions in the mediation process (e.g., whether mediation is voluntary or mandatory), and the person facilitating the dispute resolution process (e.g., mediator). There is other literature carrying similar analyses in negotiation and mediation in different disputes, summarised by Weinstein (2009). In *Brown v Board of Education* (1954) the court was of the view that cases with real equality should not be settled whilst tortious cases are better off settled.

Although Fiss acknowledged that power imbalances caused by a claimant's financial constraints may not apply to the financially wealthy (Fiss, 1984, p. 1077), financial strength is not the only source of power. To appreciate this argument, it is first noted that the source of power is not capable of being quantified but could be categorised in different dimensions, such as authority, habitual, resources, or morals (Mayer, 2012). Mayer (1987) defined power as 'the capacity to influence the behavior of others, their emotions, or the course of events' which comes from formal authority, expert power, associated power, resource power, procedural power, sanction power, nuisance power, habitual power, moral power, and personal power. Waldman (2011) described such power as reflecting the ability to shape the mediation process and outcome. The outcome of an adjudication is often a result of whether the process provides a level-playing field for parties to achieve what they need and their motivation for submitting a claim (Baylis & Carroll, 2005). The source of a power imbalance can come from resources, knowledge, merits in the eyes of the law, moral conviction, personal traits, the ability to inflict pain or irritation, and perception (Waldman, 2011). Identifying bargaining powers is critical in assessing customers' perceptions as to whether they would be affected by the factors identified or not identified in existing theories. Whilst this study relies on the factors identified in the NBC model, it is critical to evaluate how power plays its role in dispute transformation.

1.2.1.2 Power imbalance in ADR

The studies of ADR often concern studies of power. For example, concerning the role of a mediator to bring neutrality between parties of different sizes to create equality between parties (Astor, 2005) and identifying factors that can create a 'level playing' field when repeated players have more advantages given their familiarity with the process (Galanter, 1974). The environment might also play a role. Abel (1982) studied the possibility of interventions due to a reduction in coercion and costs in mediation, where intervention can act as a 'good cop' in a 'good cop, bad cop' interrogation. He argued that a state-controlled court might attract more cases because the informal setting of ADR may impose an inferiority setting where the 'privileged class' would not submit their cases, resulting in only the poor and underprivileged members of society submitting cases, as noted in the US and the UK. Also, whilst ADR neutralises conflict, it may erupt in a form that is 'unacceptable to the state' with its need to maintain law and order, if the result is a compromise rather than a real solution to 'genuine grievances', such as with discrimination (Galanter, 1974). The factors identified by these studies could impact clients' perceived power in other dispute resolution channels, which deserve crucial analysis in different situations before the ADR process is started. For example, the issue of one-sided contracts and the demand for a tailor-made arbitration process for private banking could not be properly explained without incorporating the features associated with power imbalances.

The dynamics of power are complex and are less one-way between private banks and private banking clients. The power could exist in many forms, for example, from formal authority when a bank imposes rules in accordance with laws and regulations. It could also manifest in the form of expert or information power when bankers provide advice based on experiences their clients might not have, or in terms of resources when banks might have more resources to defend cases in court or to settle them by using money. Private bank clients have certain varieties of power too – for example, associated power when clients might be associated with other important businesses of the bank. They have certain sanction power if they decide to stop their relationship with the bank, or in extreme situations they will ask their associates to exit any relationship. On the other hand, the restraint is that a bank may exercise procedural power by imposing controls to onboard or exit a client.

Therefore, both parties could consider out-of-court processes when private banks and their banking clients are in dispute. Davis and Salem (1984) claimed that mediation is conducive to redressing power imbalances: given the fact that it is voluntary, disputing parties will take responsibility to work on their own solutions (Galanter, 1974). This can be coupled with facilitation from a 'respectful behaviour' that treats the parties with dignity and equality and fosters an open exploration of the issues, instead of the mere exercise of naked power. Moore (2014) even argued that a stronger party will support a productive exchange that will benefit both parties, although its practicality comes into question if the number of cases is substantial, limiting its potential to resolve systemic social problems (Moore, 2014). These power imbalance analyses mainly study the negotiation/mediation processes but rarely examine the arbitration context.

Both formal and informal channels in facilitating dispute resolutions are necessary. Informal justice has been examined by voluminous amounts of literature that aim to connect ADR to formal justice through institutionalisation. For example, judicial promotion of settlements such as the CJR in HK advocates how the public interest is served by reducing public spending in resolving otherwise private matters. However, this does not come without its own challenges, arising mainly due to a lack of transparency in such a process: little is known about how mediation or arbitration is proposed, scheduled, organised, and evaluated. Little evidence on how these processes are perceived by disputants and studies often rely on disputants' memories and might not offer a comprehensive view that can be validated. In arbitration, although there are published awards, their applicability to wider society is often un-tested and can be difficult to use as precedents. The use of precedent is non-binding and usually lacks public scrutiny. The shift from litigation to settlement in many legal systems has made the role of the legal position more prominent, for example in the use of the term 'litigotiation' by Galanter and Cahill (1993), where the process of 'maneuvering and bargaining' happens 'in the shadow of the law' (Mnookin & Kornhauser, 1978). Whilst this shadow is always here, institutionalising the ADR process could make ADR part of the judiciary system, with people aiming to settle in fear of going to court. This form of institutionalisation, as described by Sander (1976), often represents a very crucial way to promote a settlement and creates a 'multi-door courthouse' (Sander, 1976, p. 111). These reflect the social aspect of the justice system where formal and informal justice interacts and becomes part of the judicial system where private institutions could also perform adjudicating duties. Therefore, it triggers the need to examine the adjudicating role in a complaint-handling process managed by private institutions such as banks and its impact on the choice of an external adjudicating channel such as arbitration.

1.2.1.3 The roles of power balance in choosing an ADR platform

Existing literature has led to the question of whether private banking clients perceive themselves to be in a weaker position in contractual relationships with private banks due to one-sided contracts. A weaker position with terms and conditions imposed on clients would make arbitration not a viable option to resolve disputes and hence arbitration would be under-utilised. Power balance/equality between disputing parties affects the perception of the dispute resolution process and outcomes. Although unequal contractual relations creating power imbalances between contracting parties are believed to exist in dispute resolution processes, empirical research has not been conducted to examine the issues in the banking industry. The driving factors identified in the existing literature might not be relevant in engaging in arbitration in private banking disputes.

Notably, the studies of power and choice of dispute resolution focus on the procedural difference with litigation and the effects on expected outcomes of dispute resolution, particularly to the perceived weaker party. The key interest of this research project extends the scope of existing studies by explaining how the perceived power imbalance, created at the contract formation stage, affects the choice of dispute resolution mechanism. In a banking relationship between clients and banks, a one-sided contract could lead to a 'take it or leave it' situation where clients have no choice but to engage with the banking service in a term totally determined by the bank. Yet under such circumstances, a client could find resolving a dispute with the bank to be totally meaningless. This research project relates the above phenomenon to the decision-making process of whether to engage in arbitration, by examining the impact of clients' perceptions of power balance that are created before the dispute resolution process, before a dispute is formed, or due to dominant control by the bank in the complaint-handling process. The theorisation of this could be built through adopting the 'naming, blaming, claiming' model, which describes the dispute's transformation starting from grievance.

1.2.2 Could grievance be transformed into dispute? The 'naming, blaming, claiming' framework

The NBC model is the core theoretical framework that will be used to assist the critical analysis in this empirical study. This section, under the backbone of the power theory, lays down the basis of this model and explains how the model provides a framework to examine the suitability of arbitration and to answer the research questions. The NBC model has inspired the hypothesis of this book that arbitration is under-utilised because clients actively eliminate grievance and distort dispute transformation. This model also contributes to the research questions by providing a theoretical framework and structured guidance in the disputing process. It allows for a systemic assessment at different dispute transformation stages in the context of private banking disputes. It allows us to study the status before a dispute is formed. It also allows for empirical observations to be analysed in relation to how power perceptions impact the formation of a dispute and the choice of a particular dispute resolution process.

The NBC model first emerged from studies of dispute transformation and it became more popular when the Civil Litigation Research Project (or CLRP) was launched in the 1980s.[1] Since then dispute has not only been a 'found object' to be processed and resolved through the legal system (Albiston & Sandefur, 2013, p. 106) but also an issue as part of the social landscape before entering the legal system. CLRP surveyed the experience of potential legal problems from ordinary households arising from contract disputes, injuries, or discrimination (Miller & Sarat, 1980). A key finding was that many more potential legal disputes existed much earlier before reaching the courthouse and did not always end there (Miller & Sarat, 1980, p. 561). This had huge implications on resources and the social meanings of a legal problem and broadened dispute studies from being legal-only to being a wider non-legal social construct. It was then acknowledged that there might only be a few disputes that would make it in front of the courts (even though the courts might have already been overwhelmed by court submissions). This expanded scope became the backbone of transformation studies of Felstiner, Abel, and Sarat A (1980), that dispute transformation processes leading to injurious experiences have *three* stages before litigation commences (Felstiner et al., 1980, p. 636). The first stage is ***naming***, which occurs when an unperceived injurious experience is perceived or recognised as being an injurious experience or grievance. Naming an event as harmful provides the impetus for future

1 The CLRP addressed, at the time, the need for civil justice planning, theory, and empirical analysis for court reform in the US. It has adopted the behavioural approach to generate hypotheses about the reasons different disputants make different types of dispute decisions. For results and commentary of the Civil Litigation Research Project. See Grossman, J. B., and Trubek, D. M. (1980). Special issue on dispute processing and civil litigation. *Law & Society Review, 15*(391), 395–399.

action (Lind et al., 2000, p. 557). It may not be easy to be identified due to a lack of information, internalised oppression, or other factors (Felstiner et al., 1980, p. 633). The second stage is called ***blaming***, where a person attributes an injury or grievance to the fault of another individual or social entity (Felstiner et al., 1980, p. 635). Blaming provides a target for subsequent remedial action. The third stage is ***claiming***, which occurs 'when someone with a grievance voice it to the person or entity believed to be responsible and asks for some remedy' (Felstiner et al., 1980, p. 635). The transformation is influenced by factors identified in individuals' attributional processes, such as the number of people exposed to potential harm and availability of relief from alternative sources (Felstiner et al., 1980), experience in past conflicts (Bruce, 1988), or expected positive outcomes in a legal action (Lind et al., 2000, p. 580).

The notion that 'transformation perspectives suggest that there may be too little conflict in our society' (Felstiner et al., 1980, p. 651) is of relevance to this book because there are very few court cases we see, in particular within private banking. The NBC model could assist in understanding why, presumably, a vast majority of disputes are deemed to be settled in the industry. This observation is aligned with the proposition of Felstiner et al. (1980). If such a proposition applies to the private banking industry, a notion that there is no need for arbitration as either the disputes could be too small for this platform or too big to be ignored could be valid.

1.2.2.1 The theoretical framework of naming, blaming, claiming

The NBC framework is developed in response to the need for further study of the capacity of people to tolerate substantial distress and injustice, particularly the 'everyday occurrences of trouble, problems, [and] personal and social dislocation' (Felstiner et al., 1980, p. 633). The three NBC stages help explain how these experiences can be escalated and transformed into a dispute. A few important observations need to be made. First, only a small fraction of injurious experiences ever mature into disputes and most of the attrition occurs in the early stages (Felstiner et al., 1980, p. 636). Second, institutional patterns restrict the options open to disputants (Felstiner et al., 1980, p. 636). Third, the processes through which disputes emerge, or through which people decide to lump them, are 'subjective, unstable, reactive, complicated, and incomplete' (Felstiner et al., 1980, p. 637). It has been argued that a domain of civil justice is more of a cultural, instead of legal, occurrence which happens in everyday life, with lawyers playing key roles to either alleviate such grievances to discourage or accelerate them to encourage disputing (Sarat, 2000, p. 427).

The study of dispute transformation involves identifying what is being transformed (the subject) and what the transformation (agent) does. It is not a simple matrix. Table 1.1 summarises the substance of each factor and illustrates that each factor can be both subject and agent and some may not

Table 1.1 Factors that identify the subject and agent of dispute transformation

Factors	*Subject (what is being transformed)*	*Agent (what does the transforming)*
Parties	Identity of parties, number of parties, type of action (collective or individual), personality of the parties, relationship and interaction between the parties, anticipation of the next moves	
Attributions	Perception of the experience, who to blame, new information, logic, insight, experience, adversary response, other processes (e.g., counselling) that could drain the dispute of moral content and diffuse responsibility for problems; degree and quality of blame	
Scope (or relevant disclosure about grievances and claims)	Identity of the participants, tactic uses, outcomes that become feasible	Objective, disputants' behaviour; processual characteristics of dispute institutions; context and circumstances of dispute
Choice of mechanisms (e.g., court, administrative agency, mediator, arbitrator, psychotherapist)	Objective, rules of relevance, cast of actors, costs, delays, norms, remedies	'whims' of the court clerks (p. 642), lawyers' preferences
Objectives sought	How much disputants can concede, choice of mechanisms, disputing experience	Availability of new information, partys' needs, adjusted rules, costs, delay, frustration, despairs
Ideology (sense of entitlement to enjoy certain experiences and be free from others)	Campaign type, legal change, legal victory broadcast encouraging more voice of grievances	
Reference groups	Individual or collective action, legal procedures or economic/political struggle, subculture of the audience influenced by social structural factors	Interaction with audiences or sponsors, formation of union/association, whether members are related to each other, influence from subordinate
Representatives and officials (such as lawyers, psychotherapists, union officials, social workers, government functionaries, and other agents and public officials)	Professional service providers who define the needs of consumers to accept or reject requests, and furnish information about choices and consequences; enforcement personnel (police, prosecutors, regulatory agencies) seek disputes to advance public policy or generate caseload. They may systematically 'cool out' clients even if they had legitimate grievances	

(*Coninued*)

Table 1.1 Continued

Factors	*Subject (what is being transformed)*	*Agent (what does the transforming)*
Dispute institutions (the norm and process in court, psychotherapy, mediation, arbitration, administrative hearings, and investigation)	Processes and discourse, substantive and procedural norms, burden of pre-trial procedure, remedies offered, the attitude of lawyers, time commitments, and delay due to overload or foot-dragging	

Source: Felstiner et al., 1980, pp. 639–649.

be categorised due to the dynamic interrelationship within the same factor (Felstiner et al., 1980, pp. 639–649). The most common agents identified in each factor are family, friends, co-workers, employers and organisations, resources, and social meaning, which shape the respondents' view of their experiences and evaluate their options for action. Also, factors could be reciprocal with each other. For example, between the 'objective sought' and 'choices of mechanisms' factors, the disputant's objective will affect their preference to where a complaint is escalated, but the function of such a channel might change the objective of the disputants (pp. 642–643). Recognising the indirect and inter-related relationship between activity, litigation, and decision aids the qualitative analysis by putting the insight collected from empirical research into a theoretical framework. It tests and contributes to existing empirical studies such as those of Caroline Harris Crowne (2001) in the evaluation of the Alternative Dispute Resolution Act of 1998 (Crowne, 2001); Lonny Sheinkopf Hoffman on the role of presuit investigatory discovery (Hoffman, 2006); Cynthia Estlund on mandatory arbitration (Estlund, 2017); and Resnik et al. (2020) on the accessibility of arbitration.

The framework and the study of dispute transformation are relevant to this book in the following ways: first, it enables an examination of un-institutionalised disputes relating to how an individual responds to perceptions, grievances, and conflicts. Second, given the individual attitudes, standards, and judgments, it helps evaluate the effectiveness of different forms of dispute processing. Third, it allows researchers to move away from the methodology of asking disputants to recall past events, which could be difficult to remember, and their responses may be coloured by the consequences already chosen. Through contemporaneous studies' motivations and interactions, perception can be formulated and catalogued. Fourth, it facilitates documentation of negative shifts and develops hypotheses about the chances of a dispute occurring (Felstiner et al., 1980, pp. 649–652). It also enables us to study whether people are slow to perceive injury, reluctant to make claims, or fearful of disputing. With a focus on private banking, the competence, habits, and culture of dispute processing agents and institutions can be explored.

1.2.2.2 Application of the framework

This model has been widely examined in different areas of disputes, on the subject/agent factors, the elements in each transformation stage, and their implications to law and society. Sarat (2000) unveiled the hidden domains of civil justice through the social, psychological, cultural, and professional dimensions involved in the emergence and transformation of disputes. Analysing different characters in 'The Sweet Hereafter', a movie based on real events,[2] Sarat observed that contingency and variability are necessarily part of the process of naming, blaming, and claiming (Sarat, 2000, p. 415), and that litigation is not an invariant social phenomenon covered by the law alone. The law has its own limitations, such as its inability to disentangle private needs from public roles. Hence the desire for alternative responses to loss and suffering due to grievances should always be contrasted with the perception that litigation or the law is the irresistible channel to resolve disputes (Sarat, 2000, p. 451). This has been echoed in various literature, for example, Resnik (2014) pointed out that the number of cases, measured by court-based filings, could not provide the actual number of occurrences of injuries because individuals often lack the capacity to 'name, blame, and claim'.

The framework has also been applied to examine political environments. Orsini (2002) looked at the collective action pursued by victims of hepatitis C-contaminated blood in Canada. Changes in the political opportunity structure, often defined as the external/political environment, which are consistent but not necessarily formal, permanent, or national (Pakulski, 1995), influenced the nature of their political action. Their action can be grouped within the NBC model. Each stage is interlinked. The naming stage affects claimants' ability to pursue the blaming and claiming stage (Orsini, 2002). Wiethoff (2003), through analysing a campaign in Maine on civil rights protection of gay men and lesbians, demonstrated how the argument patterns created consistent narratives that were appealing to disparate audiences through the naming, blaming, and claiming strategy. It has been used as a powerful rhetorical tool 'for those who seek to encourage a voting audience to take specific action against a target group' (Wiethoff, 2003, p. 78), but only to the right audience. Influencing the right audience is vital, as new

2 'The Sweet Hereafter' is a 1997 Canadian drama film inspired by the 1989 Alton, Texas, bus crash. A school bus hit a patch of ice and ran through a barrier and crashes into a lake, killing 14 children. The grieving parents are approached by an out-of-town lawyer who persuades them to file a class action lawsuit against the town and bus company for damages. A few surviving witnesses are coached to say the right things in court, and it involves subsequent influences from parents and lying in front of the court. See: https://en.wikipedia.org/wiki/The_Sweet_Hereafter_(film) (accessed: 22 April 2021).

information and counter-arguments usually have a small role for those with strong fundamental commitments in response to absolute authority. Harper (2014) observed that despite the fact that the law has empowered participants who confronted ableism, there were factors that reduced their preparedness to make claims. On top of limited resources, limited prospects of success and the fear of victimisation could also impact. There also existed a gap between the range of parties who caused disablement in society and the way in which anti-discrimination laws attributed duties. This was illustrated by the fact that only a limited number of regulated relationships were subject to discrimination laws and the failure of the law to attribute responsibility for equality to all parties that caused such disablement.

The framework has also been adopted in politics and policy, where politically named grievances are anticipated, invented, and paternalistically ascribed and expressed. Mamdani (2007) showed how 'naming' an object in a certain way has powerful political consequences, justifying interventions, reconstructing social and political differences, and thereby reinforcing patterns of domination' (Mamdani, 2007, p. 9). Brake and Grossman (2008) examined the 'rights-claiming' system for non-discrimination rights and uncovered that its failure was due to a lack of consideration of the social process reflected in addressing employees' needs, such as protection from retaliation. Hyman (2018) evaluated and identified the complexities of designing policies that identify bad doctors and prevent them from doing harm. In particular, the blaming stage may be distorted by the subjectivity of the complainants, whilst the complaints would find that it takes more effort to make a claim, as is evidenced by a very small number of claim cases (Hyman, 2019). Schritt (2020) argued that political actors also questioned the legitimacy of their opponents using 'naming, blaming and claiming' in their speech, by analysing radio debates about the prospects of Niger's oil refinery in 2011, which was an existing and well-structured political area that did not cause conflict.

Albiston et al. (2014) proposed a *dispute tree* metaphor to replace the dispute pyramid in the NBC framework. Instead of a linear process, grievances could be resolved through many branches in both legal and non-legal ways often at the same time. It does not categorise the steps in forming a dispute but instead describes the possible routes disputants might pursue when the grievance starts. It is one of the notable alternatives to the NBC framework. However, it has two limitations: first, there is no clear structure provided for empirical analysis. Second is the lack of description of what represents the root of the tree. These two limitations may restrict the structural analysis of empirical data. Nevertheless, it will enrich the theoretical context that contributes to the debate of legal consciousness (e.g., Campos et al., 1996; Silbey, 2005, Engel, 2016), which focus on the doctrinal changes, technical statutory reforms, and minutiae of rules and regulations (Campos et al., 1996, p. 2). It guides the theoretical discussion of the book to be depicted throughout the book.

1.2.2.3 Extended version of the framework

The framework has been further extended or adjusted to different types of disputes for different classes of disputants (see also Section 2.5.4, Chapter 2).

Rule-making, monitoring, and enforcement/implementation: Morgan (2017) studied the rights and regulations in a socio-legal context illustrated by reference to gender inequality. The claiming stage is then further extended by the stage of rule-making, monitoring, and enforcement/implementation, where parties involved will gather to establish the rule to resolve the situation for subsequent monitoring and enforcement. These stages are generated from the perspective of the 'relationship between the concrete institutional forms that each of the rights and regulation take' (Morgan, 2017, p. 12). Sarfaty (2017) approached the issues of complementarity between institutions and regulation, the salience of the structure of rule-making, and the monitoring and enforcement for fleshing out rights' capacity that could forcefully 'name, claim, and blame'. Larson (2017) stressed an inverse complementarity, where naming, blaming, and claiming can foster new structures of rule-making, monitoring, and enforcement. The claims for indigenous rights in the global arena partially transformed the tendency for the model to be nation-state centred, and the capacity of the agenda and sense of identity forecasts by rights-claiming activities are also linked.

Halting, altering, and agreeing: Price (2010) argued that the bankruptcy process under Chapter 11 of the Bankruptcy Code in the US experienced another disputation transformation mechanism, called halting, altering, and agreeing. This substantially different process has accomplished many of the goals of ADR and has avoided its pitfalls (Price, 2010, p. 20). Once a filing of bankruptcy occurs, the interactions among different stakeholders in the procedure can be termed in the following stages: the first stage of filing for bankruptcy is in essence an operation of ***halting*** all actions against the debtor (Price, 2010, pp. 7–9). The second stage is that debtor becomes a 'debtor-in-possession', in essence ***altering*** the subject company to a new entity which would hence own all associated fiduciary duties to its creditor (Price, 2010, pp. 9–10). The third stage of ***agreeing*** is the processing of disclosing relevant information and implementing a mechanism to process the debt, which is often less adversarial and allows for more flexibility in its contents and orientation.

Problem-definition continuum: Riskin and Welsh (2007) addressed the focus, in the context of mediation, that a problem can be defined into the following four issues: litigation issues, business/economic issues, personal core issues, or community issues (Riskin & Welsh, 2007, pp. 884–892). 'Each point on the problem-definition continuum may offer opportunities for addressing different dimensions of conflict – behavioural, cognitive, and emotional – depending on the circumstances of the case and the needs of the participants' (Mayer, 2010, pp. 98–100). The first, and a narrower continuum, is the litigation issue, which is the most explicit focus for mediators, defendants, and lawyers. The dispute will then be transformed by the professional handling the dispute on behalf of the party in a form so that his/her own expertise would be appropriate for its resolution (Felstiner et al., 1980, pp. 645–646).

Lumping: Engel (2016) observed that in the US, most injury victims do not seek legal remedies, but would lump it. Lumping appears to be an alternative to each stage of dispute transformation from unperceived injuries, naming, and blaming, to claiming; injured victims would have often found lumping as an alternative (Engle, 2016, pp. 25–33). These are common in tort cases where the victim's decision to lump is affected by eight key factors from social, political, and cultural environments (pp. 171–176). This analysis offers another theoretical direction to the study of the utilisation of a dispute resolution mechanism, as clients might not opt for a resolution in the first place.

These theories could have further described what is being transformed and what the transformation does (Table 1.1). In these studies, the transformation of grievances has been affected by mainly external factors such as professionals, institutions, or legal requirements. Potential blockers at each transformation stage have not been the focus, and very few of these reflect the disputants' own perspective in the process of these transformations. The NBC model can cover private banking disputes to examine clients' perspectives on each transformation stage, as well as how they affect the choice of dispute resolution mechanism.

1.2.3 Merits, concerns, and possible models of arbitration for banks

1.2.3.1 Merits and concerns

The arbitration process offers disputants autonomy to handle their disputes. It includes the adoption of specific procedural rules, choice of an ad hoc or institutional arbitration, the selection of arbitral seat, choice of law, appointment, and delegation of specific powers of arbitrator and control over privacy and confidentiality. Yet, in a client-banking relationship, autonomy is illusory under one-sided contracts. Arbitration matters should be agreed upon beforehand in the arbitration agreement. Hence the autonomy does not come from arbitration itself but from the contract, which very much depends on bargaining power at the contract formation stage. Whilst the arbitration process is often regarded as a form of informal justice to affect better social change, reduce bureaucracy, and introduce professionals to resolve disputes, the public might challenge these merits given the process is also unofficial and non-coercive, rendering it dependent on rhetoric rather than force, and it is non-bureaucratic, decentralised, relatively undifferentiated, and non-professional. The substantive and procedural rules have been criticised for being 'imprecise, unwritten, demotic, flexible, ad hoc and particularistic' (Abel, 1982: Ch 1). Arbitration may not necessarily be more efficient than litigation due to similarities in their procedures (Noyes, 2006). Administrative and arbitrators' fees can be high (Noyes, 2006, pp. 585–588). Confidentiality may lead to more disparities or unpredictable outcomes, as the procedures and awards issued are less subject to scrutiny (Noyes, 2006, p. 589). In addition, the court might not enforce the award (Noyes, 2006, p. 593). Hence, arbitration might not be understood by the disputants in terms of its function, availability, value, and merits (Ali, 2013, p. 174).

In banking, arbitration does earn its place given the support from the judiciary in different jurisdictions (Welsh, 2001, p. 850). William Park (1990) identified how arbitration facilitates the resolution of conflicts within the banking and finance industry since the 1990s. His analysis focused on how the terms and conditions of specific transactions (including guarantees, documentary credits, debt rescheduling, public sector lending, and securities brokerage) are interpreted. Despite questions on enforcement, costs, time, availability of summary judgment procedures, and issues arising from lender liability and punitive damage claims (Park, 1997), Park also identified five merits for arbitration for banks, namely: neutrality of the arbitrator, flexible handling of multi-lateral treaties, the ability to ignore foreign exchange control, the ability to avoid the risk excessive American jury awards, and the ability to seek experts to adjudicate (Park, 2000, pp. 7–13). He pointed out that arbitration clauses must be interpreted distinctively with each credit agreement (Park, 1990). His studies featured credit transactions with entities of specific transactions without a general rule of thumb to make arbitration efficient, and hence the factors identified could not be incorporated into arbitration agreements. The scope of his work is more applicable to corporate borrowers where arbitration clauses could have been embedded in the lending agreement. Be that as it may, since the private banking industry involves investment activities, the factors identified could still be relevant.

The suitability of arbitration has also been assessed by Hanefeld (2012). After summarising the literature and comparing sample clauses and arbitration rules from institutions which established rules designed to cater for resolving finance matters, she advocated for arbitration as a preferred dispute resolution method for banking disputes given its ability to handle complex transactions with an international dimension and its ability to offer parties practical benefits if there is the flexibility of choosing the arbitral seat and governing laws (Hanefeld, 2012, pp. 924–926). The complex nature of the deals makes a self-appointed arbitrator preferred as parties can assess arbitrator(s)' background before inviting the arbitrator(s) to adjudicate in disputes (Hanefeld, 2012, p. 928). The privacy offered also ensures that the parties can resolve their disputes in the most preferred process without losing autonomy (Hanefeld, 2012, p. 928). Nevertheless, Hanefeld raised two challenges that lead to unclear arbitration handling. First, there is a lack of legal certainty in outcomes due to different interpretations of the laws and regulations in different jurisdictions (Hanefeld, 2012, pp. 935–937), and second is the unclear approach to handling industry-specific mandatory rules (Hanefeld, 2012, pp. 937–939). However, the wider use of Hanefeld's findings is limited because she focused on disputes between commercial entities, which are mainly lending-focused. Yet the factors she identified could be assessed empirically in the context of private banking disputes, such as when examining the issue of legal certainty and regulation and their impacts on the perception of the suitability of arbitration.

Whilst the works of Park and Hanefeld identified key benefits and areas of focus for arbitration to be properly engaged in resolving banking and finance disputes, these benefits might not be applicable to other banking-related disputes, such as those within the private banking sector. For example, whilst Hanefeld regarded confidentiality in the arbitration process to facilitate the autonomy of disputants (Hanefeld, 2012, p. 928), Noyes regarded it as a problem because it prevents access to documentation and subsequent court protection (Noyes, 2006, p. 589). Also, the scope of their studies is defined in the disputes between two corporate entities, where the disputes are usually not caused by complex or ambiguous contract terms and therefore arbitration may appear as an 'unnecessary invitation to a split the difference award.' In this regard, William Park recognised that there is no one-size-fits-all arbitration model for disputes between banks and corporate borrowers, but instead, each arbitration must be responsive to its own situation (Park, 1990, pp. 1347–1348). Clauses must be interpreted distinctively with each credit agreement and its own arbitration clause (Park, 1990, p. 1339). This section has clearly illustrated that there is no general rule of thumb to make arbitration efficient for all industries. As such, specific studies are essential. Hence, there are three features associated with private banking disputes that should be noted. First, clients and private banks have unequal bargaining power due to the lack of meaningful consent in the agreements. Second, disputes of the same nature may involve influence from other non-contractual parties, in our case the private banker who manages client relationships on behalf of the private bank (see Chapter 5, Section 5.2.3). The nature of the disputes is more often related to a dispute between the private banker and the clients when the private banker acts contrary to the bank's policy. This is quite often different from the cases of disputes between institutions. Third, the terms and conditions written in the account opening form may be perceived as favouring the private bank given the fact that it is prepared in a one-sided fashion by the private bank itself.

1.2.3.2 Possible models of arbitration for banks

Ali (2013) offered insights in her comparative work on global ADR mechanisms to resolve consumer financial disputes. The handling of the post-Lehman crisis provided evidence that regulatory intervention is most effective in driving settlements in consumer financial disputes (Ali, 2013, p. 163). Yet arbitration might face further complexity when dealing with consumer financial disputes. These difficulties include identifying capable arbitrators, resolving high volumes of complaints simultaneously, narrowing the information gap between distributors and complainants, obtaining the reasoning and the range of compensation given the confidential nature of arbitration, and determining the arbitrability where regulatory issues are involved (Ali, 2013, p. 165). A survey in the same study of nearly 100 legal practitioners around the world on their views on the benefits, challenges, and suggestions on the arbitration process in resolving consumer financial disputes had further suggestions (Ali, 2013, pp. 169–175). Whilst the findings generated from these views might not directly explain the perception of clients, they can help build the content of the survey. Nevertheless, one must observe that, in Hong Kong, the use of ADR clauses is restricted in consumer-related contracts under section 15 of the Control of Exemption Clause Ordinance. This is to ensure that consumers will not be denied access to justice by one-sided contracts. This literature provides further guidance to the empirical studies within this research project and offers a potential theoretical background to my observations.

The empirical studies of Relis, although not centred on banking and finance, might also offer insights as to how this issue is approached. Relis analysed 131 semi-structured depth interviews, questionnaires, and observation files of plaintiffs, defendants, lawyers, and mediators in 64 mediations of medical injury disputes.[3] She adopted descriptive statistics to assess the proportions of particular responses and to evaluate the strength of any associations between certain variables. Relis reported that the findings justify the common theoretical debates on formal versus informal justices,[4] arguing that

3 The data is collected from three self-regulating institutions where mediation is held. They are ADR Chambers, Mandatory Mediation Programme, and through 'College of Physicians and Surgeons mediation', which were viewed by many complainants as precursors to litigation even though the organisations have no power to order financial compensation. See: Chapter 1: Introduction Relis, T. (2009). *Perceptions in litigation and mediation: lawyers, defendants, plaintiffs, and gendered parties*. Cambridge University Press.

4 There are various literatures debate whether formal or informal channels to resolve disputes would offer justice. Bentham viewed settlement as compromises (p. 35, Bowring, J., and Mill, J. (1843). The Works of Jeremy Bentham, vol. 6 onwards (Edinburgh: William Tait). Fiss argues court has measures to lessen the impact of distributional inequalities (Fiss, O. M. (1984). Against settlement. *Yale Lj*, *93*, 1073.). Auerbach posits that social justice through ADR is possible only if there exists shared commitment to common values between individuals and their community (Auerbach, J. S. (1983). *Justice without law?: Non-legal dispute settlement in American history*. Oxford University Press.). Abel asserts that ADR focuses only on process

formal channels of public court adjudications provide justice better than that obtained through more informal channels. The study had three important riders to this justification: first, both the court and out-of-court system can provide fairness, with litigation being no more likely than alternative methods to produce complete fairness under the observation of the phenomenon of 'litigation romanticism' (Menkel-Meadow, 1994, p. 1173). Second, lawyers might be incongruous with disputants' understandings and goals during dispute resolution processes (Relis, 2009, p. 240). Third, it may not be realistic for the legal system to handle disputants' extralegal needs (Banakar, 2003, pp. 7–8; 74). Relis challenged the third rider that the legal system should address disputants' extralegal needs and urged for a re-think of the objectives of the civil system. Banakar argued that the law is more than a system of legal rules, decisions, and doctrines (Banakar, 2003, pp. 134–135). it should also be understood as a field of practice or an ongoing process. Yet the role of the law has been widely argued from a public interest perspective. For example, Merry argued that the legal system should cater for the concerns of the public that do not relate to individuals to avoid catering to unrealistic desires (Merry, 1990, p. 179). Menkel-Meadow posited that the traditional adversary system caters only for legal implications and ignores emotional, interpersonal, and moral concerns (Menkel-Meadow, 1996, pp. 5; 7; 14; 19; 21–27; 42). Palmer cited the Chines model where wider social issues are considered during dispute resolution processes, which promotes social unity, stability, and the restoration of harmony between disputants (Palmer, 1987, pp. 240; 224; 259).

Ali and Huang (2012) identified several practical and court-related factors that could make arbitration generally preferred over litigation for securities-related disputes, which also explained the under-utilisation of CIEAC. First is the familiarity of arbitration, and second is change to the interpretation and understanding of the securities law: requesting parties' explicit consent to arbitration has negatively influenced case intake, the lack of arbitration agreement, and created difficulties in ensuring overall quality and integrity. Finally, there are concerns about the fees in arbitration. It is argued that whilst most of the factors identified could somehow be related to private banking disputes, the overall quality and integrity factor appears to be more influential. This could be due to the lack of precedent and understanding of arbitration, as will be illustrated in Section 4.3.2 of Chapter 4 of this book.

1.2.3.3 Relevance of these factors to private banking disputes

The literature suggests that arbitration is not perceived as a viable option to resolve disputes because disputants are not familiar with the arbitration

---

but not outcome (pp. 294, 308, ABEL, R. L. A., and Abel, R. L. (1982). The contradictions of informal justice, the politics of informal justice.)

process and there are potential costs associated with arbitration. It has identified what works and significant contributions have been made in terms of illustrating appropriate guidance. Nevertheless, this literature is mainly based on an assumption of comparing arbitration with litigation and hence unavoidably might ignore the clients' perspectives, as well as how dispute transformation could impact the choice of dispute resolution mechanism. Clients make the final decision in choosing the dispute resolution mechanism and hence their perspectives are vital in assessing the suitability of arbitration. Also, the relevance of these to the private banking sector is not assessed due to relatively few studies examining this subject.

1.3 The research gap and research question

1.3.1 The research gap

The literature review outlined above has shown that the suitability of arbitration can be explained by perceived power imbalances in the bank-client relationship, level of familiarisation of the arbitration process and uncertainty of the outcome due to a lack of precedent and a lack of due process. Nevertheless, arguably some of these features exist in litigation procedures. Besides comparing the adjudicating processes between court and arbitration, there are areas that need to be examined further – in our case the clients' perspectives at the pre-dispute stage through an NBC framework of dispute transformation, where clients' perspectives can be examined through the impact of various subject and agent factors. Specifically, they are elaborated upon below:

1.3.1.1 The impact of the power balance in dispute formation

There is a theoretical gap where the NBC framework has not been explicitly examined with power balance in the context of private banking disputes in assessing the suitability of arbitration. Although there has been a number of Lehman brothers' related studies, their findings focus on mediation due to the availability of empirical observation and on mass retail clients, and hence might not be applicable to private banking clients. For example, the assumption of power imbalances between institutions and retail banking clients might not be applicable to private banking clients given their complex business and personal relationships, as well as the financial strength of private banking clients. The source and use of their power in the relationship between banks and private banking clients require further examination. Hence, the research gap can be presented as the following: first, the factors affecting the perception of power balances between banks and private banking clients; second, any examination of the perception of power balances and its effects on the choice of dispute resolution mechanism; third, the factors affecting such power perception between banks and clients before a dispute emerges. This leads to the need to test the hypothesis that if clients find themselves in a weaker position in a bank-client relationship due to an uncertainty of their legal position, engaging in arbitration will not be considered by clients.

1.3.1.2 Clients' perspectives

There is an evidential gap where the literature on the merit of arbitration has mainly focused on its similarities and differences with court litigation and the utilisation of out-of-court informal channels. The perception of clients' needs to be examined systematically in relation to the viability of arbitration. It is hypothesised that the viability of arbitration is also related to how a dispute is (or is not) transformed in the first place. The merit of arbitration can be examined further through understanding the dispute transformation through the NBC model, in this study through using the private banking industry as a case study.

The dispute formation process could be related to clients' perceptions. Their decision-making could be affected by their mental status at different stages of their interactions with the bank before disputes are formed. Existing empirical studies have also focused on participants who have experienced dispute resolution processes already but may not have explored those who had not experienced such processes. Such differences are important to explain why clients choose the court rather than other ADR processes, as many clients have experienced neither court process yet still prefer the court. In terms of dispute resolutions between institutions and individuals, previous works have tended to focus mainly on mediation but lack an examination of arbitration. The studies on arbitration in banking disputes have mainly focused on disputes between institutions. Hence the gap appears to lie in a lack of perspectives from individual clients in the context of arbitration. Therefore, there is a need to examine how clients' perceptions of their dispute impact their perceptions of the viability of arbitration.

1.3.1.3 Impact from non-contractual parties in under-utilisation of a dispute resolution process

There is an evidential gap where the suitability of a dispute resolution channel has assumed that dispute is an exogenous factor. The nature of the dispute is not explicitly examined in relation to the choice of mechanisms made. The transformation of a dispute could be affected by third parties. As shown in this book, notably it is the regulators and private bankers who have created an impact. Their attitudes, preferences of which mechanism to use for dispute resolution, and influence when a grievance is being formed could ultimately impact the disputants' choice of dispute resolution mechanism. This book focuses on the role of the regulator in this aspect. In this book, particularly the role of non-parties in a dispute (such as the regulator), might have contributed to whether a particular method of dispute resolution mechanism is being utilised. The impact of the regulator needs to be examined to investigate whether it has contributed to the choice of dispute resolution channel. There is a need to examine the hypothesis that the under-utilisation of arbitration has been negatively impacted by the influence of third parties in the contractual relationship – in our case the regulator.

1.3.1.4 The issues of power imbalance, perception of viability, and under-utilisation of ADR in Hong Kong

This research study provides a theoretical framework for systematically assessing private banking clients' perceptions about engaging in the process of arbitration to resolve private banking disputes; through a structured survey, followed by open interviews with private banking clients concerning their experiences with private banks and dispute resolutions, including public courtroom adjudication and private arbitration. There is a need to explain how existing theories of power imbalances in the Hong Kong private banking sector by adopting the NBC framework developed by Felstiner et al. (1980–81), in order to identify how these transformation processes may impact private banking clients' choice of dispute resolution.

1.3.2 The research question

The aim of this study is to provide clients' perspectives about the suitability of the arbitration process to resolve private banking disputes and to examine their own assessment of the perceived power imbalance between themselves and their private banks in the arbitration process using the theoretical framework of 'naming, blaming, claiming'. Specifically, the following three interrelated questions are to be addressed:

- **Sub-research question 1:** How are banking clients' perceptions about engaging in arbitration shaped by clients' understanding of the power imbalance between the client and the bank?
- **Sub-research question 2:** To what extent is arbitration perceived as a viable dispute resolution option by private banking clients in Hong Kong?
- **Sub-research question 3:** To what extent do such perceptions explain the under-utilisation of arbitration in the private banking context in Hong Kong?

A private banking dispute is any dispute arising during the provision of banking services to private banking clients (Securities Industry Conference on Arbitration, 1994). A full definition can be referenced from the *Uniform*

Code of Arbitration, referring to customers believing that they have been wronged by a private bank. More specifically,

> all controversies which may arise between us, including but not limited to those involving any transaction or the construction, performance, or breach of this or any other agreement between us, whether entered into prior, on, or subsequent to the date hereof, shall be determined by arbitration.
>
> *(Speidel, 1996, p. 1339)*

Private banking clients are defined as those who have an account in a private bank.

In terms of the suitability of the arbitration process to clients, this relates to whether such a process can fairly 'deal with the legal and extralegal needs of the disputants' (Relis, 2009, p. 11). Extralegal needs include the motivation (that is the legal needs) or underlying motivation (that is the non-legal needs) of clients when they submit a commercial or legal claim and get a just result (Vidmer, 1984). Clients' subjective perceptions of fairness in the arbitration process can be broadly categorised by the following four elements, adopted from studies on social psychology by Welsh (2004):

- The process provides a chance for disputants to voice their concerns to a third party.
- The disputants perceive that the third party considers these concerns.
- The disputants perceive that the third party treated them in an 'even-handed' way.
- The disputants feel that they were treated in a dignified and respectful manner.

This research focuses on private banking clients' subjective perceptions about the private and confidential arbitration process, and their involvement in using the arbitration process to resolve their private banking disputes. It also assesses how private banking clients perceive the subjective perceptions of the strength of their bargaining power in an arbitration process. Previous research studies have acknowledged the importance of subjective perceptions where people who believed themselves to be treated in a procedurally fair manner are more likely to conclude that the outcome was substantively fair, even if that outcome was unfavourable (Hensler, 2006). While substantive (or distributive) fairness of a dispute resolution process cannot be readily measured, especially when the process is confidential and outcomes are not transparent (Schneider & Honeyman, 2006), the subjective perception of fairness is critical because even assuming objective fairness, the system cannot function well if it is perceived to be unfair or unjust (Sternlight, 2002). In this book, the shifting and unstable relationship between business and law associated with arbitration will be studied in a cumulative way, with the perceptions of private banking clients being examined in the above-mentioned inter-related dimensions (Dezalay & Garth, 2011, pp. 15–17).

This book explores whether arbitration is a suitable platform to resolve disputes arising from private banking transactions (i.e., private banking disputes). The choice of dispute resolution process contains many facets, such as court adjudication, extra-judicial methods, and out-of-court arbitration, but there is no single dominating process. In the private banking industry in Hong Kong, this study is particularly interested in how the legal and regulatory knowledge and perception of private bank clients play a role in making this decision. Whilst it is acknowledged that there are many other factors affecting this decision, such as the purpose of adjudicating disputes by a third party, expected outcomes, impact on industry norms, time involved and potential costs, the focus in this research is on the following three angles: firstly, the legal relationship between private banks and private bank clients; secondly, the role played by the regulators, namely the HKMA and SFC; and thirdly, whether the arbitration process would address specific needs for the resolution of private banking disputes. These factors might render arbitration not suitable for private banking disputes because it may put questions on how arbitration could ensure the awards are properly issued, as well as highlight the proper handling of mandatory rules governing the industry. These are paramount factors to gain public confidence. This book adopts an empirical approach to study existing regulatory requirements under the HKMA and SFC and assesses such regulatory knowledge and actual experiences of private banking clients to re-examine whether it is practical to incorporate arbitration as part of the regulatory framework governing the private banking industry. Since private banking clients are the wealthiest class of banking customers, they are capable of initiating litigation on disputes that could have been resolved otherwise through private forums. It is paramount to explore the perspectives of this group of clients considering the business nature and the perception of the people involved to utilise a private forum to handle their dispute.

1.4 Research design and methods

1.4.1 The research designs

The methodology employed is original and innovative, and I believe it deserves a detailed elaboration to appreciate its potential to study similar topics whilst acknowledging its limitations. The three-stage approach utilises empirical methods including surveys and interviews and draws upon my own first-hand experiences. This approach encourages and incorporates the personal touch derived from a systematic methodology, which would bring further insights from the data collected.

1.4.1.1 The three-stage approach

A well-structured research design seeks to address the five issues of any research study: the goals, conceptual framework, research questions, methods, and validity (Maxwell, 2012, p. 216). The goal is to identify trends and commonalities from the responses that could address the research questions and test hypotheses. The conceptual framework is that the data collected will allow for an analysis of the research questions using the 'naming, blaming, claiming' framework. The participants will not be directly asked to respond to the research questions to avoid receiving fake and perceptibly desirable answers. Instead, this study adopts a three-stage approach where the survey questions were set based on the results of content analysis, and interview questions were set based on the results of both content analysis and survey results. In this way it was believed that a more comprehensive approach will ensure that the right questions were asked but to still allow for flexibility in answers.

This research process was divided into three stages. The findings from a prior stage facilitated the research in the subsequent stages. Stage 1 consisted of an analysis of the content of private bank account opening forms and the legal and regulatory requirements issued by the SFC and HKMA (Annex III). Stage 2 assessed the legal and regulatory knowledge of private banking clients through a self-administered questionnaire built from the content identified in Stage 1. Stage 3 used the results of Stage 1 and 2 to conduct in-depth interviews with selected private banking clients. The account opening forms were obtained by making requests to private bankers, while the HKMA and SFC regulations were publicly available online. I invited private banking clients to participate through my own personal network and took measures to avoid potential bias within the selection process.

1.4.1.2 The use of mixed methods and an empirical approach

The research method is to adopt a mixed methods approach of conducting a content analysis on relevant documents and, based on the findings from the content analysis, conduct further empirical research on private banking clients' perceptions through assessing their knowledge and experience. The empirical research is conducted through both surveys leading to quantitative analysis, and face-to-face interviews leading to the qualitative analysis. The scope of the research is limited to Hong Kong only but should generate a good indication to the global trend given the special status of Hong Kong as an international financial centre.[5]

Empirical research studies are becoming more common in the legal community (Epstein & Martin, 2014). Stipanovich and Vasconcellos (2016)

5 Subject to potential limitation, see Section 1.4.6.3 for a description of how these potential limitations could be mitigated.

summarised three different empirical approaches. First is the mining of arbitration-related data from public and private sources, from multidisciplinary research approaches to structured studies (Stipanovich & Vasconcellos, 2016, p. 473). Second is the organisation of workshops or facilitated discussions for targeted participants to 'provide data, share perspectives and explore potential solutions' (Stipanovich & Vasconcellos, 2016, p. 473). Third, more commonly, through surveys or personal interviews with different stakeholders (Stipanovich & Vasconcellos, 2016, p. 473).

Surveys have been proven to be useful in contributing different points of view from different sources to collect, locate and generate data of the target population. They also facilitate the coding and summarising of data (Epstein & Martin, 2014). They are often widely applied; examples can be found within the ICC Commission report (2018) where a survey was used to interview 50 banks globally, consisting of both open and closed questions to gather views and experiences of arbitration for various types of agreements. The annual International Arbitration Survey organised jointly by the Queen Mary University of London School of International Arbitration and private law firms such as Fulbright & Jaworski (Queen Mary University of London, 2021). In their surveys, questions were asked in a format which required specific answer such as 'yes' / 'no', a rank of preference, and open questions to record respondents' views. There are however challenges with the use of surveys. Stipanowich and Vasconcellos (2016) mentioned that the survey results might be inadequate, or the responses might be compromised as the interviewees might be too busy. The questions in a survey may lack the depth and breadth to provide a meaningful, clear, and unambiguous response. It might be difficult to identify the right participants and the lack of representative group might make it difficult to provide meaningful conclusions. The participants might provide fake and perceptibly desirable answers, and the results could be hugely subjected to interpretation. These limitations could be offset by careful drafting of the survey with a balanced approach between a rigid and broad framework, as mentioned above. This would allow us to collect both qualitative and quantitative information related to the perception of private banking clients (Stipanowich & Vasconcellos, 2016, p. 478).

The balance between a flexible framework to obtain maximised outcomes and a systematic approach to facilitate presentation of the findings has been discussed in Dezalay and Garth (1996) in their sociological research on international commercial arbitration (Dezalay & Garth, 2011, pp. 15–17). They recognised that whilst a rigid framework allows for precision in the outcomes, a broad research domain facilitates the shifting and unstable relationship between business and law. Interviewees can produce self-representations reflecting what was in their minds and allows them to speak freely about what they felt about their experiences in the domain of law, instead of trying to produce desirable answers in response to a definition. Nevertheless, since this research is related to law, some boundaries should be set to avoid the participants faking their responses or exaggerating their own experiences (Dezalay & Garth, 2011, pp. 15–17). In this regard, some definitions and details of practice should be provided to the participants. To conclude, the balance between a rigid and broad approach can be achieved systematically through inference. This justifies the use of a qualitative approach to examine human experiences. This approach has been adopted by scholars such as Ellickson (1991) and Relis (2009), who aligned and borrowed methodologies from social sciences, economics, and sociology.

Given that private banking clients do not necessarily have the legal background to address the laws and regulations of the private banking industry, when obtaining their views, the interviewer provided the most relevant statements for them to respond and express their views freely in response to questions regarding the law, regulations, and practice. Considering the above approaches adopted in the studies of arbitration, my research adopted a mixed methods approach consisting of: (a) contextual analysis; (b) structured survey; and (c) open-end interviews with private banking clients. The research did not adopt a rigid framework but still provided some boundaries to facilitate analysis and presentation of the findings. A structured framework facilitates the collection of relevant facts, data and opinions in a confined scope. Specifically, as I aimed to let interviewees speak freely, some variation in the content and flow in each interview was unavoidable given the open-ended nature of the interviews. The consistency of information collected was catered through drawing the interview questions based on findings from the structured surveys. For example, if the structured survey showed that clients do not read the terms and conditions in the account opening forms, I proceeded to ask the interviewee whether they had read the terms and conditions before signing the forms and explored further as to their reasons why.

Adopting a mixed methods approach in my research was deemed essential in order to set necessary boundaries and a framework for participants, who might not have the legal background, to freely express their views in a controlled environment. A mixed methods approach has often been adopted in the research area of ADR. I have taken reference from two empirical studies for my own research.

Ali (2013) evaluated the effectiveness and fairness of financial dispute resolution frameworks in seven jurisdictions. She adopted a mixed methods approach consisting of secondary academic research, on-site data collection and surveys, which later facilitated a twofold analysis. Firstly, and principally, by comparing the corresponding structure of financial dispute resolution centres in seven jurisdictions, particularly the ombudsman, arbitration and multi-tier processes. Secondly, the study adopted the 'triangulation' structure to compensate for any bias arising from comparative studies.[6]

Relis (2009) adopted both qualitative and quantitative approaches to collect empirical evidence. Relis studied how 'diverse professional, lay, and gendered actors understand and experience case processing leading up to and including mediation in legal disputes' (Relis, 2009, p. 1), with a particular focus on recovering actors' understandings and meanings affecting their actions. The research methodology was based mainly on the qualitative paradigm and included 131 semi-structured interviews, questionnaires, and observation files of plaintiffs, defendants, lawyers and mediators in 64 mediations related to medical injury disputes (Relis, 2009, p. 26). Quantitative analysis was also undertaken although the sample population may not have been random to allow for full regression or multivariate analysis. Descriptive statistics were utilised to assess the percentage and proportions of particular responses and to evaluate the strength of any associations between certain variables. Normally, data is also analysed by segmentation on the basis of natural groupings by ages, gender, education and prior experiences in mediation, although often these factors may not be relevant (Gaskell & Bauer, 2000). Nevertheless, it was observed that only one out of 17 plaintiffs had general mediation experiences and it was related to commercial disputes (Relis, 2009, p. 29). The data was collected from three main institutional frameworks, namely ADR Chambers, Mandatory Mediation Programme and through the College of Physicians and Surgeons Mediation, a self-regulating body of the medical profession which is viewed by many complainants as precursors to litigation although those organisations have no powers to order financial compensation (Relis, 2009, pp. 29–31).

The research methodologies of the studies discussed above offer insights that support my adoption of a mixed methods approach using various sources. One note is that my research may not involve segmentation analysis because it is unlikely to be relevant to split the data into natural groupings given that the small sample of private banking clients. Data collected should also be analysed with caution because data collected from survey could be supported by findings from interview. Particularly it is noted that the data collected can be distorted by non-random selection of the sample as it depended on the researcher's own knowledge of identifying suitable participants. Given the small sample size may render the findings not representing the general

6 'Triangulation' is generally used by geological surveyors in cases where direct measurement of physical heights or spaces is impossible. Multiple research techniques can hence compensate for each other's deficiencies and provide a broader foundation for critical analysis, see Cook, J. A., and Fonow, M. M. (1990). Knowledge and women's interests: Issues of epistemology and methodology in feminist sociological research, JM Nielsen (Ed.), Feminist research methods: Exemplary readings in the social sciences (pp. 69–93). Cited in: Ali, S. F. (2013). *Consumer Financial Dispute Resolution in a Comparative Context: Principles, Systems and Practice*. Cambridge University Press.

pattern but rather an ad-hoc response to specific circumstances or come from same experiences from same group of bank or bankers. The interviewees may not have had the legal knowledge to address some questions and could have exaggerated or self-reported their responses, which I was not be able to independently verify. Clients may have self-reported the fact or, in some situations may immediately have responded to an incident rather than giving it careful thought. It is also difficult to verify the impartiality and fairness of the facts provided (Lande et al, 1993). Finally, as I have worked as a private banker between 2012 and 2019 in Hong Kong responsible for client relationships in various private banks related to loans, deposits and more often, investment advice and execution, the views collected in my research could be biased towards my own exposure and experiences in the industry.

1.4.2 Stage 1: Content analysis of law, regulations, account opening forms, and arbitral rules

Three sets of documents were studied and analysed. First, the private bank account opening forms and associated documents were collected through direct enquiries from private bankers working for private banks. Three private banks were selected: BANK A, BANK B, and Bank C (see Chapter 2). Second, SFC codes and HKMA Supervisory Policy Manual (SPM) regulating HK private banking industry are publicly available on the related websites (Annex III). Third, is the Arbitration Rules from selected Arbitration Centres worldwide, focusing on finance disputes. The findings were compared and cross-examined with the content of the account opening forms to identify any existing gaps between the two. Specifically, I examined whether the account opening forms included terms that were perceived to be unfavourable to private banking clients, or vice versa. Analysing account opening forms and regulatory requirements helped to identify relevant facts to be assessed in the survey at Stage 2.

1.4.2.1 Laws and regulations

The major source of laws and regulations are the Hong Kong Ordinances, SPM issued by HKMA, and various codes and guidelines issued by the SFC. They will be described more thoroughly in Section 2.3.2.1 of Chapter 2. An overview of these sources can be found in Annex III.

1.4.2.2 Account opening forms

Account opening forms from BANK B, BANK A, and Bank C bank were selected and compared. These forms collect information from clients to facilitate the onboarding process, which mainly facilitates the regulatory requirements of anti-money laundering (AML) and Counter-Financing of Terrorism (CFT) requirements, requests clients to make necessary disclosures (particularly clients' tax status and risk appetite information), and lists the terms and conditions of private banks for clients to accept. The information requested and disclosed were summarised and categorised into the four business stages, namely: (a) account opening; (b) understanding clients' product knowledge and risk appetite; (c) communication channels between bank and client; and (d) dispute resolution channel (see Chapter 2, Section 2.2.2). The content of the forms, including the number of terms and conditions, and client's declaration statement to exempt bank liability, were then compared and analysed.

1.4.2.3 Arbitration rules

The FDRC is the starting point for any study into the arbitration process. FDRC is non-profit-making organisation limited by guarantee and handles financial claims in accordance with the Terms of Reference (FDRC, 2018). Upon receiving a claim submitted by individuals, small enterprises,[7] or financial institutions, they are obliged to attend mediation or arbitration arranged if they are a member of the Financial Dispute Resolution Scheme (FDRS). I studied the 'FDRS Mediation and Arbitration Rules' and made reference to Mediation and Arbitration Rules from institutions who were known to have specific rules dealing with finance disputes, which includes arbitral rules adopted by the FDRC, The Financial Industry Disputes Resolution Centre Ltd (FIDReC), the China International Economic and Trade Arbitration Commission (CIETAC), the Panel of Recognized International Market Experts (P.R.I.M.E.), and Hong Kong International Arbitration Centre (HKIAC).

1.4.3 Stage 2: The use of surveys and conducting quantitative analysis

Stage 2 involved identifying trends and providing further context for the face-to-face interview questions. It involved an analysis of the survey results that unveiled the experiences and legal or regulatory knowledge of private banking clients. Clients were asked to respond to a set of questions relating to conduct with private banking clients. The questions were drafted based on the findings from Stage 1. Multiple-choice questions consisted of three answers: Yes/No/Unsure. The business conduct is based on four different stages of private banking business, namely: (a) account opening process; (b)

7 It means a limited company or a partnership, and in accordance with SE's or its group's latest financial year end statement has: (1) an annual turnover not exceeding HK$50 million; and (2) gross assets not exceeding HK$50 million; and (3) not more than 50 employees in HK. See Section A, 2.1, Financial Dispute Resolution Centre (2018), 'Term of Reference for FDCR in relation to the FDRS' Jan 2018, available at: https://www.fdrc.org.hk/en/doc/FDRC_ToR_Full_2018_en.pdf (accessed: 7 Sep 2021)

clients' declaration of investment product knowledge; (c) protocol of communications between bankers and clients; and (d) the availability of a dispute resolution mechanism. Clients were asked to answer two questions for each stage: whether (i) it complies with internal HKMA and SFC laws and regulations and (ii) whether they have experienced such conduct previously with their private bankers. The questions of the online survey were drafted based on selected clauses from the *Banking Ordinance (BO), Securities and Futures Ordinance (Cap. 571)*, as well as various codes issued by the Securities and Futures Commission. Those related to investment are the Code on Unit Trusts and Mutual Funds; Code on Investment-Linked Assurance Schemes; Code on Pooled Retirement Funds; SFC Code on MPF Products; and Advertising Guidelines Applicable to Collective Investment Schemes Authorized under the Product Codes. **Annex III** details the other sources of laws and regulations which indirectly affected the survey questions.

This analysis aimed to reveal perception versus reality. It revealed the relevant legal and regulatory knowledge of private banking clients in the private banking industry. It also assessed clients' awareness of their rights, or bank's obligation, with their private banks. It also considered whether clients' experiences with private banks are in line with regulatory requirements. The results offer a holistic picture of private banking clients' perceptions on the laws/regulations and a provide more accurate picture of how private banks or private bankers conduct their business, compared with what is written in the account opening forms. The discrepancy between their understanding of the laws and regulations and their actual experiences could be due to many reasons. For example, clients may mis-interpret the regulations, or they may be served inadequately by private banks. To avoid guessing, clients could answer 'unsure'.

The target participants were private banking clients who have or used to have private bank accounts in Hong Kong. Finding clients to participate had its limitations. The sample selection could have been limited by my experiences within the private banking industry, in that I could only invite private banking clients I knew personally and their referrals, and which affected the ability to collect a larger sample size. Participants may not have answered the surveys seriously due to the low stake nature of the survey, as they were no negative consequence for giving out fake or wrong answers. However, this stage still generated an overall assessment of clients' knowledge and helped to identify the gaps between their perceived knowledge and their actual experiences. Statistical methodology may be used to describe and analyse the data if the sample size is large enough (i.e., more than 30).

1.4.3.1 Designing survey questions

The survey questions were derived from the content analysis in stage 1 described in Chapters 2 and 3. Table 1.2 shows the extracts of laws and

Table 1.2 Extracts of law and regulation of HK private banking industry

Category	*Codes/policy*	*Section*
Account Opening	Treat Customers Fairly Charter for Private Wealth Management Industry	Principle 1
	Section III: Code on Investment-Linked Assurance Schemes	Annex Ai
Communication	Advertising Guidelines Applicable to Collective Investment Schemes Authorized under the Product Codes	Content of Advertisement
	Treat Customers Fairly Charter for Private Wealth Management Industry	Principle 3 Principle 5
	Section III: Code on Investment-Linked Assurance Schemes	7.8, 7.9, 7.10, 7.13
Product Knowledge	Treat Customers Fairly Charter for Private Wealth Management Industry	Principle 2
	Section III: Code on Investment-Linked Assurance Schemes	5.1
Complaint	Treat Customers Fairly Charter for Private Wealth Management Industry	Principle 4
	HKMA Supervisory Policy Manual (IC-4) Complaint Handling Procedures	All

Source: See Annex III.

regulations of the HK private banking industry, from which the questions were drafted. Table 1.3 shows the correct answers to each question, along with the regulatory source. The questions were not found in the content of account opening forms. The purpose was to assess clients' knowledge and experiences of their own rights and a bank's legal duties. The results indicate whether clients were able to name their grievance.

The online survey is divided into three parts as shown in **Annex III**. Part I is 'Understanding and experience of law and regulation governing the private Bank / Private banker'. It contains 20 questions grouped under four categories based on the four business stages (Chapter 2, Section 2.2.2). They are:

- Account opening (hereinafter referred to as 'Qa', Qa1 to Qa5)
- Product Knowledge and Risk Appetite of the Client (hereinafter referred to as 'Qb', Qb6 to Qb10),
- Communication Channel between Bank and Clients (hereinafter referred to as 'Qc', Qc11 to Qc15),
- Dispute Resolution Channel (hereinafter referred to as 'Qd', Qd16 to Qd20).

Table 1.3 The correct answers to each question and its regulatory source in the survey

Business stages	*Whether the conduct complies with law and regulation by HKMA/ SFC (Yes – complied; No – not complied; Not regulated – this conduct is not regulated by HKMA or SFC)*		*Source*
(a) Account opening	Qa1: You are asked to prove how you generate your wealth.	Yes	Guideline on Anti-Money Laundering and Counter-Financing of Terrorism, Ch. 12.3
	Qa2: The private banker explains to you the terms and conditions in the account opening forms.	Yes	DTC Association – Code of Banking Practice Chapter 1 – Relationship between Institutions and Customers – 5.1
	Qa3: The bank amends the terms in the account opening forms without your consent, but simply send you a letter that said the terms and conditions will change one month later.	Yes	DTC Association – Code of Banking Practice Chapter 1 – Relationship between institutions 5.9, 6.3, 6.4
	Qa4: Private banker requires to see your ID card for account opening.	Yes	s.2(1), section 4.1., Sch. 2, 4.1.3Guideline on Anti-Money Laundering and Counter-Financing of Terrorism,
	Qa5: You sign the blank account opening forms; the private banker fills in the details after.	Not regulated	N/A
(b) Product knowledge and risk appetite of the client	Qb6: Private bank explains the key product features and risks associated before placing an order.	Yes	Treat Customers Fairly Charter for Private Wealth Management Industry, Principle 2

(*Continued*)

Table 1.3 Continued

Business stages	*Whether the conduct complies with law and regulation by HKMA/ SFC (Yes – complied; No – not complied; Not regulated – this conduct is not regulated by HKMA or SFC)*		*Source*
	Qb7: Private bank discloses a conflict of interest before your investment order is executed.	Yes	Paras. 8,9, PWMA, Code of Ethics and Conduct, A. General Principles, Fairness and Conflict of Interest
	Qb8: A private banker offers you his own view of an investment.	Yes	Para. 6, PWMA – Code of Ethics and Conduct, A General Principles Honesty; section 107, Securities and Futures Ordinances Offence to fraudulently or recklessly induce others to invest money
	Qb9: You are asked to update your product knowledge and investment risk appetite regularly.	Yes	Para. 5.2 of the 'SFC Code of Conduct for Persons Licensed by or Registered with the Securities and Futures Commissions.'
	Qb10: You are asked to explicitly say you understand the product features before you place an investment order.	Not regulated	N/A
(c) Communication channel between bank and client	Qc11: You receive a letter to inform you that your private bank account is opened.	Not regulated	N/A

(*Continued*)

Table 1.3 Continued

Business stages	*Whether the conduct complies with law and regulation by HKMA/ SFC (Yes – complied; No – not complied; Not regulated – this conduct is not regulated by HKMA or SFC)*		*Source*
	Qc 12: Your private banker is registered as a Certified Private Wealth Professional (CPWP) certified by the Private Wealth Management Association (PWMA).	Not regulated	N/A; note however that HKMA **encourages** registration. See HKMA Press Release (Enhanced Competency Framework for Private Wealth Management ('PWM') Practitioners ('ECF') 24 Jun 2014)
	Qc13: You are asked to place an investment instruction through email.	Not regulated	N/A
	Qc14: The bank sends you written advice after an investment is executed.	Yes	section 36, Chapter 3, Code of Banking Practice
	Qc15: The investment product brochure shows expected future performance.	No	Para. 10, Advertising Guidelines Applicable to Collective Investment Schemes Authorized under the Product Codes, Content of Advertisement, Performance Information
(d) Dispute resolution channel	Qd16: You send a complaint letter to the private bank but get no reply.	No	HKMA SPM IC-4 Complaint Handling Procedure 3.2.2
	Qd17: Your private banker tells you that the private bank has no complaint-handling department.	No	HKMA SPM IC-4 Complaint Handling Procedure 2.1.1, 2.2.1, 2.2.2
	Qd18: You receive compensation directly from the private banker to resolve a dispute.	No	HKMA SPM IC-4 Complaint Handling Procedure 1.2.2

(*Continued*)

Table 1.3 Continued

Business stages	*Whether the conduct complies with law and regulation by HKMA/ SFC (Yes – complied; No – not complied; Not regulated – this conduct is not regulated by HKMA or SFC)*		*Source*
	Qd19: The private bank says they are not obliged to tell you how you can complain against the bank internally.	No	HKMA SPM IC-4 Complaint Handling Procedure 2.3.1
	Qd20: Your private bank tells you that your complaint can only be written in a letter can be followed up.	No	HKMA SPM IC-4 Complaint Handling Procedure 1.1

Source: See Annex III.

The respondents were asked to answer the same question twice: The first set of answers relates to **experience (Set A)**. Respondents should indicate 'yes' or 'no' as to whether they had experienced the described conduct from the private bank/private banker. Set A does not have any designated answer. To avoid wild guessing, the question was set in a way that correct answers contain 'yes' and 'no'. The field 'not sure' was also available.

The second set of answers relates to **knowledge (Set B)**. The respondents were required to indicate whether the described conduct complies with the regulation. The answers are either 'yes', 'no', 'not regulated by HKMA or SFC', or 'not sure'. There are correct answers (see Table 1.3). For example, Qb8 asks 'A private banker offers you his/her own view in an investment (question 8, Table 1.3)', if a respondent answered 'Yes' in Set A, it meant that the respondent did hear a private banker offering the banker's own view in an investment. In Set B, if the respondent answered 'Yes' it meant the client believed that this conduct complied with the respective laws and regulations, which is generally a correct answer subject to further requirements.

Part II is 'Your experience in private banking and arbitration'. There are six questions to identify the clients' experiences in private banking and arbitration. The clients were separated into two groups by the following characteristics, namely the number of private bank accounts they had, the amount of assets in each account, their years of experience in using private banking services, and whether they had experienced disputes and arbitration with their private bank.

Part III is 'Your preference on Arbitration Process to resolve private banking disputes'. There are ten questions extracted from respective arbitral rules (see Table 3.3, Chapter 3). Part III enquired clients' preferences in an arbitration process. The respondents were required to give either the answer of 'prefer', 'not preferred', or 'no preference'.

1.4.3.2 Sample selection and data collection

The online survey was posted on Survey Monkey. Respondents were invited personally by the researcher through mass email and instant messaging. In addition, the respondents were encouraged to further send the survey to their contacts of those who own/owned a private bank account. The researcher personally invited 200 individuals. The respondents consented to join this research project by signing an informed consent form before filling in the survey. The respondents' identities remained anonymous, so there should have been no external constraints for them to address the questions honestly. The survey was opened for one month and received responses from 58 respondents with 32 completed survey responses, 25 partially completed survey responses, and one incomplete survey response. There are overall 32 valid data-points. Admittedly, the sample size is only marginally acceptable, but it still enables the extraction of useful insights for preliminary analysis.

The preference of dispute resolution of the respondents is as shown in Table 1.4. All respondents are tallied towards one end except for Question 3 – the number of years the respondents had been banking with the private bank – with around a 70% and 30% split. For others, nearly all respondents had fewer than three private bank accounts (91%) and had a total asset value of less than HK$100million (91%). Only one respondent (3%) had disputes with their private bank. This presents two implications: first, the data only indicated that the clients' perspectives are mainly from their instinct without actual experience. Therefore, there is a need to conduct further empirical study (Chapter 5). Second, the data might indicate that it may not be meaningful to analyse the demographic of the sample due small sample size on one group.

1.4.3.3 Overview of descriptive analysis and its limitations

Statistical analysis was conducted to systematically study and summarise the patterns and to obtain insights. Responses were presented in simple proportions and descriptive analysis was adopted to study the pattern of the responses. If the descriptive analysis is not conclusive, further analysis might be needed.

Section 4.2 of Chapter 4 analyses clients' knowledge (Section 4.2.1), experiences (Section 4.2.2), and contains a descriptive comparison between the two (Section 4.2.3). It assesses whether the clients had the knowledge or

Table 1.4 Clients' experience in private banking and arbitration

Questions	*Answers*			
1. How many private bank accounts do you have?	**Less than three**		**Three or above**	
	29	91%	**3**	9%
2. On average, how many assets are banked in each private bank?	**Less than HK$100 m**		**HK$100 m or above**	
	29	91%	**3**	9%
3. How many years have you been banking with your private bank?	**Less than five years**		**Five years or above**	
	22	69%	**10**	31%
4. Have you been a disputing party in an arbitration before?	**Yes**		**No**	
	1	3%	**31**	97%
5a. If you have been a disputant in an arbitration before, was it related to a private banking dispute?	**Yes**		**No**	
	1	3%	**1**	97%
6a. If you have a choice, will you use arbitration as a channel to resolve your dispute with the private bank?	**Yes**		**No**	
	28	88%	**4**	13%
6b. Key reasons for not using arbitration to resolve the dispute(s)	I will settle that with the bank I will talk to the private bank or private banker directly.			

Source: Online Survey conducted by the researcher, Oct 2020.

experienced the correct bank's conduct. Specifically, there are four possible scenarios identified in the descriptive analysis:

- Scenario I: Clients answered most questions in Set B correctly, and their experiences matched the regulatory requirements. Based on this outcome, the clients were aware of their rights and banks have operated properly.
- Scenario II: Clients answered most questions in Set B correctly, but their experiences did not match the regulatory requirements. This outcome is in contrast to the phenomenon of low occurrence rate of disputes. The reasonable explanation to this condition is that the clients might have turned a blind eye and chose not to report any non-compliance.
- Scenario III: Clients answered most questions in Set B incorrectly, but their experiences matched the regulatory requirements. In this outcome, banks might have conducted their businesses according to the laws and regulations, despite the clients not being aware of or even have wrong perceptions about it.
- Scenario IV: Clients answered most questions in Set B incorrectly, and they experienced conduct that did not match the regulatory

> requirements. In this outcome, it is deduced that the financial literacy of the clients was considered low and there could be possible exploitation of the clients' interest by banks.

Section 4.2.3 of Chapter 4 will show that most responses fall largely in line with scenario I.

Section 4.2.4 of Chapter 4 describes the clients' preferences for the arbitration process. The data are described based on process(es) that is/are:

- Preferred by the majority.
- NOT preferred by the majority.
- That have a split view in terms of preference.

Section 4.2.4 of Chapter 4 will show that out of 12 major procedures, seven are preferred by clients, two were not preferred, and three items have split views.

There are three limitations. First, is that the data described are purely limited to the above listed choices of answers and the survey offered no option for free text answers. It may not be easy to explain why clients had good or bad knowledge or had certain experiences relating to the relevant laws and regulations. Second, only one out of 32 respondents had experienced arbitration, which may imply that the responses from Part III were pure instinct without actual experiences in arbitration. A third limitation is the potential selection bias: clients may have experienced some other conduct which might not be covered in the survey. Lastly, there is insufficient data to describe the results based on clients' experience in private banking and arbitration since the number in each group is too small.

1.4.4 Stage 3: Case studies and qualitative analysis

1.4.4.1 Theoretical basis of case studies through interviews

To explain the findings from stage 1 and 2, it was important to interview private banking clients and obtain insights from their actual experiences through personal interviews. The results of Stage 2 helped to provide context to conduct one-on-one structured interviews with private banking clients. It allowed them to unveil the actual practices based on clients' understanding of the HKMA and SFC regulations governing private banks. This was done by asking them to share their opinions and experiences. Part of the questions in the interviews were inspired and extracted from the survey results by requesting interviewees to explain, rationalise, or rebut certain phenomenon revealed in the surveys. Although public information such as news report or court cases are available, it is not always ideal to rely on second-hand information as it may lacs the details required for our purposes. Therefore, face-to-face interviews with the clients were conducted. I interviewed 12 private banking clients, thought processes and their experiences when dealing with private banks. As formerly a private banker in Hong Kong, I identified potential interviewees using my own personal network, which is often called a 'snowball' approach, meaning seeking referrals from my interviewees in order to generate a large enough sample size for the research (Dezalay & Garth, 1996).

Caution was exercised in the following two ways when designing the interviews. Firstly, interviewing my own ex-clients created some level of embarrassment, since they may not have wanted to appraise my own conduct in front of me. However, it is not always desirable to interview a stranger as the interviewee may not be willing to openly reveal sensitive information. Secondly, I am deemed to have my own personal views or insider knowledge due to my prior experiences in working with private banking clients, which turned out to be constructive for the interviews as I was able to ask the right questions to get insightful answers. In this case, caution was exercised to avoid prejudices or pre-mature conclusions in interpreting their responses. To mitigate any potential bias, the interview questions were set based on the results of Stages 1 and 2. When asking questions, I did not offer my own interpretation, clarification, nor elaboration. I mainly listened to their responses and asked follow-up questions. Since I knew some of the interviewees personally, during an interview I specifically requested them to remain anonymous when describing their experiences, and the interviewees followed that instruction. Also, by the time I approached them for an interview, I was no longer a private banker which helped to mitigate potential conflicts.

I have also adopted my own experiences. I was a private banker between 2012 and 2019 in three different international private banks in Hong Kong. This period working in different banks allowed me to generate relevant observations and reflections to underpin this project. These insights were collected during my own observation as a participant (Kawulich, 2005), enabling me to build grounded theory (Glaser & Strauss, 2017). This is a recognised way to collect data about people, processes, and cultures in qualitative research, in the following four ways (Kawulich, 2005, para. 19), where an observer:

- Is a complete participant where his/her identity is concealed to the research group.
- Is a member of the group. S/he does not participate but only collects data.
- Is NOT a member of the community, but is with the group only to collect data.
- Is a complete observer can also work within research when the subject group does not know about the existence of the observer.

My experience as a client-facing private banker allows me to access to a wider range of private banking clients, but it may also mean that my participants and subsequent analysis might be undesirably impacted by my own insider bias. The use of participant observation as a data collection method aims to help address this issue in qualitative research. Researchers sometimes get into the community as one of their own, with other members in the community knowing, or not knowing, the true identity of the researcher. Hence, I am a complete participant where my identity is concealed to the research group. As a matter of fact, I did not know at that time that I was the researcher. My own identity as a researcher was only be revealed after I became engaged in this book, which relied on my reflections afterward. Therefore, whilst it is very difficult to ignore my own voice in this research process, I have adopted that voice to facilitate the process and also address the research questions.

To discover theory grounded in data through a systematic and inductive process, breaking with the assumption that there are general patterns of cause and effect that can be used as a basis for predicting and controlling natural phenomenon (or positivistic persuasion), there are a number of important processes (Berthelsen et al., 2017, p. 415):

- Classical – Mainly **involves the 'why' questions** to discover why the participants act the way they do and thereby form a theory on what their main concerns are.
- Constructive – **Pose the 'how' questions** to describe 'what is happening' in the field and aims to explain how the participants act.

These two processes can be merged with the theoretical framework of 'naming, blaming and claiming' to help assess whether the model can explain, complement, or contradict the responses from the participants and my own experiences as a banker.

1.4.4.2 Conducting interviews

The purpose of the interviews is to explain the results of the online survey through private banking clients' own experiences and perceptions. The participants were asked to not only state their experiences but also explain the reasons behind each decision made when interacting with their private banks. There are three possible scenarios: (i) clients' experiences are aligned with the observations from the survey; (ii) clients' experiences are not aligned with the observations of the survey; and (iii) clients have not experienced the situation described in the survey. Seeking open comment from clients directly allows us to further understand clients' perception on how they interact with their bank, especially in the event of a dispute. This section will describe how each case was selected, collected and the associated limitations.

1.4.4.3 Case selection

The case selection occurred using three main related factors. First, the interviewees had first-hand disputing experiences with their private bank.

With their observations backed up by their own disputing experiences, their insights would be more reflective to the phenomena under study (Hamel et al., 1993, p. 23). In this study, our interviewees had either filed a formal complaint to the private bank, handled a complaint from a client on behalf of the private bank he worked for, or filed a claim in court against the private bank.

Second, the selected case should be representative enough to offer sufficiently in-depth insights so the responses from participants could be detailed and thoroughly explained (Hamel et al., 1993, p. 36). This is particularly important for this study due to the small sample of four private banking clients, although a combination of their in-depth descriptions from diverse backgrounds offers evidence to support the arguments offered in this study. The level of detail in describing a case study would also secure representativeness in a clearly defined manner with clear explanations of the subject being investigated. This is achieved by referring to the specific personal disputing experiences of each interviewee.

Third, they must have had a common base for comparison of similarities and differences. We compare members of the same class to allow in-depth understandings of the case that supports associated explanatory theories, to reflect 'important facets of the case' (Esterberg, 2002, p. 130). In this study, their similarities are that they are all private banking clients with more than one private bank account in HK and had personal disputing experiences with the private bank. Their differences in professions, their roles, the bank they dealt with, and different ways to handle disputes provide further dynamics to explain the data collected and support the analysis.

1.4.4.4 Data collection

As we have seen, this book adopts two approaches to collect clients' perceptions. First is through the online survey and the second is through face-to-face interviews. This section describes how the data of the face-to-face interviews were collected.

There are a few sources that guide what kind of data is necessary. The first source is the factors associated with the 'naming, blaming, claiming' model, which are the factors that have been relied on and that have helped the questions to be framed in a way that could generate theoretical insights. The second source is the findings of the content analysis and online survey, which generated some insights presented in the further chapters of this book. This allows us to form relevant interview questions and decide how the questions should be asked. The third source comes from my own experiences as a private banker. I was a private banker for nearly seven years at different international private banks in Hong Kong – my own experiences and insights could contribute, with caution made, to avoid insider bias.

By adapting both flexible and rigid frameworks of interviewing, these questions were not robotically asked but, instead, the interviews aimed to facilitate dialogue, with interaction and follow-up questions that helped express the views of the interviewees. This aimed to provide the benefits of both having a rigid framework so that participants were able to express their views without constraints but also allowed participants to express themselves freely through follow-up questions. The sample questions are in Annex I.

1.4.4.5 Content of the interview questions

Private bank clients interact with their bankers directly. Clients' legal knowledge and their awareness of clients' rights and banks' obligations will affect these interactions. The richer the knowledge, the greater the scrutiny to which their bankers are likely to be subjected. On the other hand, clients' expectations would also direct the conduct of their bankers. Also, it is common that private banking clients would have banking relationships with more than one private bank. Their descriptions present a wider spectrum of industry practice and the behaviour of private bankers from different private banks. When appropriate, the findings from stage 2 were shown to the clients to seek their feedback and immediate reactions.

The questions listed in Annex I: Sample Questions for Interview are split into four parts. The first part is the '*Introduction*', where clients were asked about their experiences of disputes with their private bank. The purpose of asking this question was first to recall their dispute memory before the dialogue went further to ask more reflection questions. It also confirmed their dispute experiences with the bank. The second part is 'in relation to the contractual relationship with the private bank' which refers to the basis of the bank-client relationship (Chapter 2, Section 2.3.1). The third part is 'in relation to the arbitration process' (Chapter 3, Sections 3.2.1 and 3.3), and the fourth part is 'in relation to the role of HKMA in a dispute' (Chapter 3, Section 3.2.2) to seek a response directly to arbitration and dispute resolution for private banking disputes. The questions set also attempted to follow the theoretical framework of 'naming, blaming, and claiming'. In brief, questions such as 'do you usually read all the terms and conditions of the account opening documents' aimed to understand how well clients were equipped to handle the situation when they were wronged. Questions such as 'how would you feel if it is mandatory to arbitrate your disputes with the private bank' relate to the claiming stage. Except for 'blaming' stage, there is little width in the banking context as to who is to blame, as it tends to be always the bank.

One important feature of the content is the importance of follow-up questions. The questions stated were only the guidance of what would follow when the participants were asked to elaborate further. The interactions allowed for more revelation of what happened behind the scenes and the rationales associated with those situations. As will be revealed, the blaming stage and the issue of power emerged after asking follow-up questions. These questions could not be pre-set as they depended on the answers provided by the participants. Nevertheless, the responses still largely adhered to the results of stages 1 and 2, such that the dialogues remained rigid and structured.

1.4.4.6 Identifying and interviewing private banking clients

The identification of interviewees is to a large extent a random process through my own knowledge of who was a private banking client and who was willing to be interviewed. In this context, it was a random process but practically, I utilised my existing relationships to make it easier to start a dialogue. Although the search process was to a large extent reactive and based on who was available and willing to share, all interviewees experienced unpleasant experiences with their private banks, such that their insights came from actual experience. One interviewee had experienced 'arbitration' before, which created a dynamic in their views of what might work and not work in arbitration. There are features which further add colour and make this analysis more representative.

Approaching individual clients is extremely difficult. From experience, clients would not just make themselves known to be private banking clients, and even if they are known to be using private banking services, they probably would not disclose information freely. I was only able to use my personal relationships (i.e., my ex-clients) and ask for referrals through a snowball approach. The snowball approach has been adopted by other legal dispute research studies, such as those from Sara and Felstiner (1997), where they used their own contacts to get contacts in their community. Hence, the selection process was not random, but this process ensured the interviewees were qualified to speak on the record for this research. It should be noted that it is common for clients and private bankers to have personal relationships and hence their answers might not only have come from a legal perspective, which could be fundamental when analysing the findings and assessing the legal relationships between private banks and their clients.

With the above constraints that only a limited number of available clients were willing to be interviewed, to improve the representativeness of the research I have incorporated my own observations as a participant in the observations. Participant observation is a recognised way to collect data about people, processes, and cultures in qualitative research. There are mainly four ways of doing it. First, the observer is a complete participant where his/her identity is concealed from the research group. Second, the observer is a member of the group, but s/he does not participate but only collects data. Third, the observer is *not* a member of the community but with the group only to collect data. Fourth, a complete observer within a subject group does not know the existence of the observer. The advantage of this is that the group will not be disrupted, but the research may lack objectivity and the group members may feel distrustful (Kawulich, 2005, para. 19). My past experiences could be regarded as a form of participant observation as a complete participant and any reflections associated with it.

It is also important to discover theory grounded in data through a systematic and inductive process, breaking with the assumption that there are general patterns of cause and effect that can be used as a basis for predicting and controlling natural phenomena (or positivistic persuasion). There are both classical grounded theory and constructivist grounded theory in participant observations. The classical grounded theory mainly involves the 'why' questions to discover why the participants act the way they do and thereby form a theory on what their main concerns are. The constructivist grounded theory would pose the 'how' questions to describe 'what is happening' in the field and aims to explain how the participants act (Berthelsen et al., 2017, p. 415).

The data have been collected from interviewees at different channels. They all offered their consent to the interview. Most were interviewed either face-to-face or via an online device (i.e., Zoom) with the exception of one who responded to the questions and follow-up questions via email. All interviews were conducted in English and were recorded and transcribed into English, to minimise any issue of translation. The data have been stored in a secured data-storage location and will be destroyed within three years after the research is completed. To seek the most genuine answers, I established ground rules before conducting an interview. They comprised principles of confidentiality, avoiding using real names, and not referring to others that could lead to the identification of that individual, for example, which bank s/he has worked for. It could also avoid embarrassment in case they were talking about my own conduct.

1.4.4.7 The interviewees

Following these three criteria, I interviewed 12 private banking clients, but only four allowed me to make recordings and cite them in this book. The remaining eight clients had signed confidentiality agreements. Nevertheless, their responses were somehow repeated by the four interviewees and therefore their experiences could somehow be representative for the purposes of our book. A comprehensive description of each participant's background is given here. Pseudonyms have been used in place of real names for confidentiality.

1.4.4.7.1 Mr Peterson (not real name)

Our first case, Mr Peterson, is a retired private banker who had been managing private bankers at a senior level in HK for over 20 years prior to retirement. He received and handled complaints directly caused by his staff.

Mr Peterson was my first supervisor when I first became a private banker in 2012, then later he left the bank and subsequently retired. I moved to another private bank as a client-facing banker, and he became my client in 2017. Whilst he does not have dispute experience himself as a client, he has handled numerous client complaints and was involved in setting up bank policy, so in this regard, his observations are representative of the perception of private banking clients, private bankers, and the private bank at the time. From Mr Peterson, we can see how he has assisted himself to ensure disputes would not happen. In the interview, he used the word 'pre-empt' a number of times, which reflects that he was very determined to handhold the process.

1.4.4.7.2 Mr Young (not real name)

The second case, Mr Young, is an entrepreneur whose business is also engaged in banking services. He has experienced two heated disputes, each with a different private bank, and has explored multiple possible channels to bring the matter to the attention of others, including writing a complaint letter to the bank, reporting to the regulator, employing lawyers to represent him, engaging in arbitration, and submitting claims to the court. This case study describes his background, the two incidents that occurred, and the major factors that describe how his grievance was transformed and finally eliminated. Mr Young was the sole owner of a small company doing metal trading and recycling. Once he recycled the metal, he categorised and sold it to his clients, usually in Japan and Australia. Hence, his business involved a large amount of foreign exchange as he would use Hong Kong Dollar (HKD) to buy the metal and received euros or Australian dollars (AUD) upon selling it. His business and his own personal life are not separable, because banks usually bank with his business only with his personal guarantee. He often had multiple banking relationships within the same bank. He was my private banking client from 2013 when his account was transferred to me. Whenever I moved between banks, he followed me to the new one, and every time I moved to a new bank, I opened a business account for his business as well. Mr Peterson relied quite heavily on bankers' advice. Every time he made an investment decision, he would always ask for my advice and information first, and then he would 'disappear' for a while, and then come back with an investment order. I later found out that he was seeking a second opinion from a different private banker before he decided to act after he had had two very unhappy incidents with his prior banks. From Mr Young, we can see how he also blamed himself when a dispute occurred. He repeatedly expressed that 'it is also my fault' to trust the banker or the bank so much, indicating his high awareness of his own obligation to ensure the business relationship ran smoothly, and he also blamed himself for not reading the contracts he signed before engaging in the deal.

1.4.4.7.3 Ms Emily (not real name)

The third case, Ms Emily, is a trained solicitor in corporate finance who later became an investment banker. She filed a complaint to the private bank as a client adversely affected by the merger of two private banks. Claiming happens when disputants ask for a remedy from someone responsible, and if this fails, the case is transformed into a dispute. Ms Emily nevertheless shows us another solution – to leave.

Ms Emily is an investment banker who was once a practising corporate lawyer specialising in drafting lending agreements between banks and their debtors. She had a frustrating experience when her existing private bank (Bank A) was acquired by another private bank (Bank B). During the interview, she referred to me, but I did not reveal this relationship in the entire interview in an attempt to maintain the impartiality of the process and avoid embarrassment.

Ms Emily had three company accounts with Bank A, and the owner of those companies was a trustee registered in a particular jurisdiction (Country C). She and her husband had inherited a significant amount of wealth, and they hoped to segregate these assets for their children. Two years after setting up this trust, she opened three bank accounts for these three companies with Bank A and was then told by her banker that their bank policy no longer accepted company accounts owned by companies registered in Country C. She was asked to either close the account or change the trustee. She was extremely unhappy about this, but at that time there were very few options for her because she was only given two months to make the change. Reluctantly, she went through the paperwork and changed the trustee of these three companies to Country D. Two months later, Bank A was acquired by Bank B. The banker in Bank B told Ms Emily that she had to go through the 're-papering' process where she would need to acquire all the company-related documents (e.g., identity documents, certificate of incumbency) again and she would need to provide details of her Source of Wealth.

> But I have just gone through that in Bank A! 2 months ago.
>
> *(Ms Emily, the interview)*

She questioned the banker from Bank B (referred to as 'Banker B' going forward) and said that it was extremely frustrating to go through the same process again, and it did not make sense due to this duplicated effort. This time, she was ready to just close the accounts and exit. Back then, she took the chance to use the same set the documents required by Bank A to open another set of accounts in Bank C, just in case Bank A did not work out. She did not want to go through the process again and therefore prepared to leave. Ms Emily shows us that, even though she did not agree with the bank's requirements, it is still the bank's own discretion to impose them. She would have been left with the decision to either ask the bank to make an exception, to accept it, or to leave the bank. She repeatedly indicated that *'it is the bank's own policy'* (Ms Emily, the interview), indicating her helplessness when facing rather different standards among different banks, arguably caused by the use of language in the regulations (Chapter 2, Section 2.4).

1.4.4.7.4 Mr Collins (not real name)

The fourth case, Mr Collins, is a senior counsel (barrister-at-law) in HK, and his expertise was in criminal cases. He filed a writ in court but later dropped it, as the private bank settled the matter immediately. Mr Collins could have told our other interviewees whether going to the court was worth the effort. Mr. Collins was a renowned barrister in HK. He was regarded as one of the most prominent criminal barristers in HK. In the summer of 2016, I was admitted to Mr Collins's chamber to handle a high court case together with his junior counsel as a summer pupil. It was an extremely engaging two months where we spent the first five weeks at the chambers preparing for the case and then later two weeks at the high court. I sat behind the barristers at the high court (instead of their appointed solicitor) to provide all necessary support for the case. Besides the excitement at this close angle inside the court, this was also when I started to question the function of the court – questions which started to emerge and arguably started my research journey in this book.

When I started to know more about Mr Collins, I found out that he filed a court case back in 2013 against his private bank. I invited him for an interview, and he addressed all my questions through email. He provided very comprehensive responses to the questions that he chose to respond to, and for some questions, he did not provide a response, which also proved insightful in many ways given his expertise. In his responses, it appeared that no transformation was needed when he started a 'dispute' and filed a court case, which appears to be the most efficient to make the bank respond. He described his impression of arbitration as follows:

> No, I have never been involved with arbitration. I did not choose arbitration because I needed to the public know what this bank had done.
>
> *(Mr Collins, interview)*

1.4.4.8 Limitations of case studies and mitigation thereof

There are three general limitations in this study. First is the small number of participants, which might make generalisations challenging (Hamel et al., 1993, p. 36). This is mitigated by conducting content analysis and online surveys to support the phenomenon discussed in the interviews. Interviewees responded to issues that have been surveyed previously or contained in a document. Second, only one of the interviewees was interviewed in person while two were interviewed using video conferencing software. One of the interviewees selectively responded via email to the questions I prepared.

These methods may influence the depth of interaction with the interviewees and affect post-interview follow-ups. This was mitigated by the fact that I have personal links with all interviewees and have the ability to follow up immediately. This was further advantageous during the conversations, as it facilitated open dialogue. Lastly, the findings of this research should be qualified by noting that each case is specific to the experiences of each interviewee. Although their own distinct features and experiences added further dynamics and representation to the analysis, this further justifies the need to conduct a mixed methods approach.

1.4.5 Analysing through the theoretical framework of 'naming, blaming, and claiming' under three thematic issues

In 'The Emergence and Transformation of Disputes: Naming, Blaming, Claiming', Flestiner et al. (1980) proposed the study of transformation processes from the formation of injurious experiences to dispute in litigation (Felstiner et al., 1980, p. 636). As a short recap, there are three stages before disputes are formed. The first stage is the naming that occurs when an unperceived injurious experience, or UnPIE, is perceived or recognised as an injurious experience, or PIE, or viewed as 'violations of norms and as remediable' (Felstiner et al., 1980, p. 635). The transformation of this stage is likely to be affected by an individual's 'class, education, work situation, social network, etc' (Felstiner et al., 1980, p. 633). The second stage is blaming, which involves the transformation of a perceived injurious experience into a grievance where 'a person attributes an injury to the fault of another individual or social entity' (Felstiner et al., 1980, p. 635). The third stage is claiming, which occurs when disputants ask for remedy from someone responsible. Should the claim be rejected, a dispute arises.

The transformation is characterised as 'subjective, unstable, reactive, complicated, and incomplete' (Felstiner et al., 1980, pp. 637–639). As illustrated in Table 1.1 and Section 1.2.2, each of these three dispute transformation stages under 'naming, blaming, and claiming' is associated with the factors that could both be the subject (what is being transformed) and agent (what does the transformation). The factors impact the attributional processes through a range of behaviour otherwise unconstrained in an alternate platform, such as the court, and institutional patterns will restrict social structural variables and personality traits when disputes are being handled. It is unclear whether the factors, attributional process, and attrition behaviour are systematically connected.

Whilst this framework is widely adopted in different types of disputes as described per Section 1.2.2.3, private banking disputes are not one of them. This study sought to understand the characteristics of HK private banking clients under the 'naming, blaming, and claiming' framework through qualitative analysis, which supplements the limitations of quantitative analyses. This study relates three stages of private banking businesses during their interactions with clients (to be described in the next section) to the factors identified in individuals' attributional processes, such as the number of people exposed to potential harm and the availability of relief from alternative sources (Felstiner et al., 1980, pp. 637–649), experience in past conflicts (Bruce, 1988), and expected positive outcomes through legal action (Lind et al., 2000).

In relation to the overarching research, the interview questions unveiled clients' thinking processes under a structured framework to find out whether a dispute can be formed in the first place, and if so, whether arbitration would be the right platform to be followed by the reason of its under-utilisation. Clients were invited to share their own disputing experiences and reflect upon those events based on four common business stages (Chapter 2, Section 2.2.2), namely the account opening stage, clients' declaration of product knowledge and risk appetites, communication between bankers and individual clients, and availability of a dispute resolution mechanism.

Linking these four stages comes creates three thematic issues. The first is related to the contract. This refers to whether clients understood their rights and obligations when they signed the one-sided contract, which aims to elaborate transformation factors of 'parties', 'attributions', and 'scope'. The second, the dispute resolution process, refers to whether clients have any preference for the dispute resolution process, which aims to elaborate transformation factors such as 'choice of mechanisms', 'objective sought', and 'ideology', which refers to the sense of entitlement to certain experiences and to be free from others. The third is the communication channels between clients and banks, and between clients and regulators when clients could not resolve their issues internally with the bank, translating to the transformation factors of the 'reference group' and 'representatives and official'. These three thematic issues of contract, dispute resolution process, and communication channel have been identified in our literature review (Section 1.2), content analysis (Chapters 2 and 3), online survey (Chapter 4), and have been validated by business practices. It provides partial answers to the research questions, and now the qualitative analysis will be used in order to explain the observations made in prior chapters of this book.

1.4.5.1 Unequal contractual relationship

The signed documents between a bank and a client set the fundamental legal basis of their relationship. It affects whether arbitration could be an option in the first place, which in Hong Kong, as we have seen in this chapter, is not usual, due to the implementation of the *Control of Exemption Clause Ordinance*. Even if it is allowed or both parties are voluntarily willing to opt for arbitration, the context of the contract would have presumably affected clients' perception of their own bargaining power in a dispute resolution process, in terms of whether their grievance is within the scope of the legal relationship between the bank and client, making it meaningless to start a dispute in the first place, not to speak of resolving one.

In Annex I, sample questions 4 to 7 mainly address this. One example of how the questions have been influenced by this thematic issue is question 4, 'Do you usually read all the terms and conditions of the account opening documents?', where the interviewees were expected to elaborate upon their answers. In this question, clients were prone to reflect on their interactions with the banks, leading to the fact that the contracts might or might not govern the business relationship in the first place, which would be fundamentally influential. Should the contract between the parties be the fundamental foundation to engage in arbitration, a lack of a meaningful contractual relationship may already explain why arbitration is not a viable option, addressing sub-question 1. It naturally leads to the next question: if it is not the contract, what governs the relationship? Does the client pay sufficient attention to what they have signed? Are clients happy with this situation and the potential impact in the event of some unpleasant experience? This leads to subsequent questions to address their feelings and reactions that relate to their perceptions in arbitration through contractual obligations.

1.4.5.2 Process, suitability, and perception of the dispute resolution process

As we will see in Chapter 2 and Chapter 3, in a regulated industry like banking there are layers of laws, regulations, and rules that tightly govern the business conduct of banks and bankers. In the area of dispute resolution, the process is pretty much driven by the banks themselves. The bank appears to act like a judge in the process, whilst the regulator in many incidents only acts as a facilitator; see for example my own grievance experience described in Chapter 3, Section 3.5.3, which also illustrates how the bank could have already acted as an arbitrator when clients have submitted their complaints to the bank directly. Nevertheless, the process itself is not transparent as complainants basically have nothing to do but wait for the results. It also indicates the hands-off approach for banks to self-regulate and govern. It has been indicated in the survey results that arbitration has not been popular among private banking clients. Further analysis in the FDRC has indicated that, even among banking disputes, the formation of a dispute has not been popular, as evidenced by the high enquiries rate and very low eligible rate (Table 3.1, Chapter 3), and the fact that private banking disputes have been ruled out from the FDRC. Questions 8 to 15 (Annex I) explore clients' preferences, addressing sub-question 4.3 of whether the under-utilisation of arbitration could be explained by clients' perceptions of the process.

1.4.5.3 Communication

The communication between clients and banks has not been tightly governed by the regulators. Whilst the regulators play a very important role to ensure the banking system is intact through the issuance of regulatory guidance and supervision, the requirements on how banks communicate with clients remain relatively shallow. Whilst regulators ensure the integrity of the system and market activities, the interaction between banks and clients may not receive much regulatory attention. Whether regulatory dialogues between banks and regulators have incorporated the best interests of clients could be in question and hence should be explored through face-to-face interviews, for example, with Questions 16 to 18 of Annex I which were incorporated to understand whether clients were aware of all possible available challenges offered by the HKMA in an event of a private banking dispute. Associated with this is the conduct of bankers, who are the agents of the bank and who are the first point of contact between clients and banks, featured with a very close personal relationship (Chapter 2, Section 2.2.3). Whether the regulator has sufficient governance, supervision, and monitoring is to be explored and analysed in subsequent chapters. Although there were no set questions for the role of bankers in the face-to-face interviews, as we will see the responses related to bankers were extensive.

1.4.6 Research limitations and mitigation thereof

1.4.6.1 Clients are unfamiliar with the arbitration process

Our focus on clients' perceptions is restricted by the fact that clients are unfamiliar with the arbitration process. There has been a lack of access and media coverage to observe the process, and private banking clients would have considered whether arbitration is suitable without understanding what arbitration is about and without observing the actual process or seeing how other cases are arbitrated. Clients only come with their own perceptions and describe what works and what might not. This is mitigated by the fact that clients might have experienced an arbitration process although not under the name of arbitration.

1.4.6.2 Small sample size due to issues of access

It is difficult to locate private banking clients, and it is even more difficult to get them to talk on the record, for they generally do not want to share their status as a private banking client. This research has been limited to the views and experiences of my own network of private banking clients and their referrals. The sample size of the survey was a relatively small number of 32 respondents and might not draw very strong statistical inferences. Similar challenges have been experienced with the interviews, where clients were not willing to put what they said on record due to worries of breaching confidentiality agreements. Nevertheless, this study can be reflective of the exact scenario where there has been a very small number of cases. For example, according to the 2009–2010 Annual Report of the Consumer Council, there were 2,380 complaints against financial services in 2008, which dropped to only 490 and 481 in 2019 and 2020 respectively (Consumer Council, 2021).

1.4.6.3 Representation restricted to private banking clients in Hong Kong

Apart from the sample size issues, this research only targets private banking clients in Hong Kong. This study did not reach out to other lay members in the private banking business, for example, the private bankers who face clients directly, senior management of the banks who oversee the overall business, the regulators who set up and execute the rules and regulations, and other gatekeepers within and outside banks such as the compliance office of the bank, members of the trade union, etc. The insights from the empirical studies might not be representative of the entire population in the industry and hence might only offer initial generalised insights from the view of private banking clients only. This is mitigated by the fact that the interviewees also carry dual roles, such as lawyer and banker. This research only focuses on the Hong Kong experience, which may also affect global representation; this is arguably a minor issue because the implications from Hong Kong would be applicable across the globe as over 300 authorised institutions (AIs) operate in Hong Kong. It can serve as a good proxy to the global trend, coupled with my own experiences in the field handling clients and potential disputes.

1.5 Organisation of the book

This book is structured into six chapters. Chapter 1 provides the overall background to this project, outlining the research gap, questions, and methodology of the book. Chapter 2 provides a comparative analysis of the business landscape and regulatory framework of the private banking industry in Hong Kong and selected jurisdictions. Chapter 3 evaluates the merits and limitations of arbitration as a channel to resolve private banking disputes. Chapter 4 describes clients' knowledge or perceived knowledge of the laws and regulations of private banking versus their actual experiences with private banks. Chapter 5 describes the three stages that distort dispute transformation. Chapter 6 reflects the theoretical implications of the studies, identifies the contribution of this book to the scholarship, identifies research limitations, and offers recommendations for further research. The concluding remarks advocate for regulatory support to clients experiencing this self-corrective mechanism when a grievance is formed.

CHAPTER 2

Private banking in Hong Kong

2.1 Introduction: Private banking as a segment of the financial conglomerate

This chapter elaborates on the importance of private banking in Hong Kong and outlines how a sound legal and regulatory framework maintains Hong Kong's status as an international financial centre. This chapter sets out the background scope of the thesis, the business landscape of private banking in Hong Kong, its key feature, uniqueness, and the legal and regulatory framework. It offers two analyses: the first is to analyse how the bank–client relationship in the private bank setting is regulated. The second is to analyse the formation of such a relationship by examining the account opening form. The analysis on the legal basis of the private bank–client relationship lays the foundation for quantitative and qualitative analysis using the NBC framework. It facilitates the design of the survey and face-to-face interviews to assess whether the clients are aware of the gap between what is written in the contract and what is required under bank regulation and to assess whether it affects clients' choice of dispute resolution mechanism.

This chapter contributes to the research questions in the following aspects. It provides the background and scope of the research by describing the legal foundation of a bank–client relationship. It offers a contextual analysis that contributes to the survey and interview questions for use in empirical studies. It also supports the hypothesis that the issue of a one-sided contract might be negatively perceived by clients when it comes to bargaining with the banks directly. The one-sided contract, featured by the varied approach to the use of language, enforcement standards, and sharing of information among different banks, could create a perception that the client is a weaker party in a contractual relationship and hence also during a dispute resolution process. The chapter concludes with theoretical implications from the findings at stage 3.

DOI: 10.4324/9781003407591-2

2.2 The private banking business

2.2.1 The definition of a private bank and its significance in Hong Kong

The legal definition of a bank is somewhat tautological. For example, the Bills of Exchange Act 1882 defines it as 'a body of persons whether incorporated or not who carry on the business of banking' (Bills of Exchange Act, 1882, section 2), and the common law offers three cardinal principles (Ellinger et al., 2011):

(1) It can change from time to time (*Woods v Martins Bank Ltd, 1959*), and it is nowadays multifunctional, engaged in a wide range of activities beyond the traditional core activities of deposit-taking and lending. These activities are carried out by different subsidiary companies or teams within the same banking group. Private banking can be regarded as one of the activities carried out by a bank serving the banking needs of wealthy individuals.

(2) 'Banking business in one place is not necessarily so considered elsewhere'. For example, current accounts operable by cheques are often not required in Irish and Australian cases, but this is not the case in the UK. Private banks are no different; and

(3) Whether an institution's reputation is considered important. Reputation is equally important to a private bank, and it must sustain its own reputation instead of riding on the reputation of the wider banking group.

In the landmark case of *United Dominions Trust Ltd v Kirkwood* (1966 2 QB 431), Lord Denning described the main facets of banking business as threefold: accepting money, collecting and honouring cheques, and keeping a current account to maintain its debit and credit entries. Nevertheless, the term 'bank' is becoming less important. For example, there is a lack of uniformity of the term 'bank' in English statutes (Ellinger et al., 2011, p. 92), and the *Financial Services and Markets Act 2000* did not provide any regulations as to which institutions could call themselves a bank.[1] Nevertheless, in Hong Kong, the definition of 'bank' offered in the Banking Ordinance (BO) defines a bank as a company which holds a valid banking licence (Banking Ordinance, Cap 155). This means that any institution that operates a business of banking would be regulated.

The relationship between bank and client is defined by the *activities* between them, and this defines the legal relationship between them. Both customers and banks have a duty in the bank–client relationship. For example, in *London Joint Stock Bank Ltd v Macmillan (1918)*, Atkin LJ said: 'the customer on his part undertakes to exercise reasonable care in executing his written orders so as not to mislead the bank or facilitate forgery' (1921, 3 KB

1 Used to be defined under section 67 Banking Act 1987.

110 at 127). In *Greenwood v Martins Bank Ltd (1933)*, the activities were that the bank offers cheque services, and hence banks and customers are in a debtor–customer relationship. The customer, who is a creditor of the bank, therefore has an obligation to ensure that an instruction (i.e., the cheque) to the bank (debtor) to repay a loan (i.e., bank's deposits) to a third party is genuine. Conversely, in *Woods v Martins Bank Ltd. (1959*, 1 QB 55*)*, where the bank acts as a trustee and offers investment advice to customers, the bank becomes an adviser to the customer, and therefore the bank has a fiduciary duty to advise customers with reasonable skills and care.

Similarly, there is no definition of a bank customer (for example, in the Bills of Exchange Act 1882 or Cheques Act 1957). It is, nevertheless, sometimes important to determine when a person becomes a customer of a bank, as a bank only conducts banking business or provides banking services to its customers (Weerasooria & Wallace, 1994, ch. 12). This is often determined under case law. For example, in *Woods v Martins Bank Ltd*, the court determined a person becomes a customer when a bank agrees to open the account in question (1959, 1 QB 55). However, often this is a less straightforward task. For example in *Marfani & Co. Ltd. v Midland Bank Ltd*, a rogue who opened an account in the name of 'Eliaszade' was held to be the customer, as the alter-ego 'Eliaszade' would not have the legal intention to open an account. Once a customer–banker relationship is defined, there are certain scopes of duties and fiduciary duties in specific situations arising out of the relationship (1968, 2 Lloyd's Rep. 373).

Legal relationship aside, any corporation hoping to operate a banking business or a business of taking deposits must obtain a licence issued by the HKMA according to the type of deposit-taking business they wish to be engaged in (Hong Kong Monetary Authority, 2021). These corporations are called authorised institutions (AIs). AIs will need registration if they carry on a business of conducting certain types of SFC-regulated activities (Securities and Futures Commission, 2019).

Hence it would be useful to provide a short overview of what a bank actually is in a legal context before we discuss the business nature of a private bank. Private banks operating in Hong Kong are subject to the same requirements as any other banks. There is no separate licence for a private bank. Private banking can be defined broadly as financial and related services provided to wealthy clients (United States General Accounting Office, 1999). Private banks often refer to themselves as wealth managers that help 'clients preserve wealth and achieve their financial objectives' (UBS, 2021). They provide a range of services from investment advice to execution, as well as managing assets under full discretion, often called discretionary services or designated services. This means that with an agreed boundary such as specific investment goals, banks can execute investment transactions under a pre-agreed scope and duty, instead of seeking clients' investment for every transaction. For example, clients can restrict their bank from investing in stocks listed on the London Stock Exchange or fixed-income products that incorporate derivative features. Private banks often offer an open-architecture platform, with some only accessible to their client group, so that their clients have access to investment opportunities literally everywhere. In general, they provide access to products listed on a formal exchange such as the Hong Kong Stock Exchange. They can also act as intermediaries to other fund managers who invest a portfolio of assets from listed markets or non-listed markets. They can also directly invest from the issuers or owners of financial assets for their clients (referred to as 'over-the-counter' trading). A private bank is often one of the business units operating within a financial conglomerate.

From a business perspective, a private bank offers more personal and customised services than its retail-banking counterparts. According to the Federal Reserve, the hallmark of private banking is the 'personal delivery of financial products and services to affluent clients' (United States General Accounting Office, 1997). In Hong Kong, section 1, schedule 14 of the BO defines private banking as institutions serving high net worth (HNW) clients. Private banking clients are 'professional investors' defined under section 5 of the Securities and Futures (Professional Investor) Rule, meaning they have HK$8 m or more in their private bank accounts (section 5 of the Securities and Futures (Professional Investor) Rule (CAP571D)). In fact, private banks generally require more than HK$8 million of 'assets under management' (AUM) to justify the cost of servicing them. This only includes liquid assets that can be turned into cash or cash equivalents within one week, such as stocks, bonds, and funds. An example of an illiquid asset is a residential property. Different banks have different thresholds of AUM to onboard a client. For example, JPMorgan Private Bank required a minimum liquid asset size of US$15 m per each onboard client, US$5 m for Bank A, US$3 m for Bank B, and US$2 m for Bank C at the time the author was a private banker.

2.2.2 Identifying the four business stages in private banking

For the purpose of this analysis, the business cycle of a private bank is divided into four stages based on information provided in the account opening forms, respective guidelines, and my own practical experience in private banking business operations:

(a) Account opening: where a bank will follow rigorous onboarding requirements to assess whether clients are eligible to be private banking clients. Once a client is on board, a private banking account is opened.
(b) Risk profiling: clients' declaration of product and investment knowledge, and risk appetite. This is essential to assess the client's risk profile and investment knowledge before offering advice on investment strategies and investment products.

(c) Communication between banks and clients: where clients are provided with a channel to communicate with the banks; and
(d) Dispute resolution: whether the bank has provided a channel to resolve clients' complaints.

(a) Account opening: where banks request basic client information in order to facilitate the opening of an account. A private bank must ensure that the clients are legitimate private banking clients, which means the source of wealth (SOW) and the channel of the funds injected into the banking system are legal, which should be in accordance with HKMA guidelines, such as the Guideline on Anti-Money Laundering and Counter-Financing of Terrorism (for authorised institutions) issued by the HKMA ('the Guideline') (Hong Kong Monetary Authority, 2018).
(b) Clients' declaration of product & investment knowledge and risk appetite knowledge: private banks must make a 'portfolio-based' assessment of their clients' product knowledge and risk appetites as part of the suitability requirement within para. 5.2 of the SFC Code of Conduct for Persons Licensed by or Registered with the Securities and Futures Commissions (Hong Kong Monetary Authority, 2012a). Otherwise, private banks cannot not offer advice or recommendations to their clients on investment products. This assessment is usually conducted alongside the account opening stage.
(c) Day-to-day communication between bankers and individual clients: once the account is opened, banks will inform their clients where they can access their account, how to inject assets, where to view their portfolio, and who to call or send an email to when they have enquiries or would like to conduct a trade. Some banks will formally issue a letter to clients, and this letter will also inform the clients of their risk appetite, as well as inform them of the scope of the investment services. It also governs the way banks and bankers communicate and advise clients on various investment products.
(d) Dispute resolution stage: it is a regulatory requirement to ensure that banks assist their customers to make any complaint against the bank. This stage will not take place if there is no dispute.

The information contained in the account opening forms from the three banks examined in this study has been analysed and compared under the four business stages in private banking. The information includes the information filled in by the onboarding clients, the declaration made by the onboarding clients, and the terms and conditions written by the private banks. The four categories have been created after studying the law and regulations governing banks and private banks. These analyses and comparisons are depicted in Table 2.1 and Table 2.2. Table 2.1 illustrates the regulatory requirement under

Table 2.1 Key regulations for private banks associated with the four business stages

Criteria	*Rules and regulations*
Account opening	Treat Customers Fairly Charter for Private Wealth Management Industry Section III: Code on Investment-Linked Assurance Schemes Guideline on Anti-Money Laundering and Counter-Financing of Terrorism Private Wealth Management Association – Code of Ethics and Conduct Fund Manager Code of Conduct The DTC Association – Code of Banking Practice Anti-Money Laundering and Counter-Terrorist Financing Ordinance (Cap. 615)
Clients' product and investment knowledge and risk appetite	Treat Customers Fairly Charter for Private Wealth Management Industry Section III: Code on Investment-Linked Assurance Schemes Code on Pooled Retirement Funds SFC Code on MPF Products
Communication	Advertising Guidelines Applicable to Collective Investment Schemes Authorized under the Product Codes Treat Customers Fairly Charter for Private Wealth Management Industry Section III: Code on Investment-Linked Assurance Schemes Private Wealth Management Association – Code of Ethics and Conduct Fund Manager Code of Conduct Misrepresentation Ordinance (Cap. 284)
Dispute resolution	Treat Customers Fairly Charter for Private Wealth Management Industry HKMA Supervisory Policy Manual IC-4 Complaint Handling Procedures Private Wealth Management Association – Code of Ethics and Conduct Fund Manager Code of Conduct The DTC Association – Code of Banking Practice
Others	Private Wealth Management Association – Code of Ethics and Conduct Unconscionable Contracts Ordinance (Cap. 458) Securities and Futures Ordinance (Cap. 571) Control Exemption Clauses Ordinance (Cap. 71) HKMA supervisory manual policy (CG-3 Code of Conduct) Section II: Code on Unit Trusts and Mutual Funds ('UT Code')

Note: The above is not an exhaustive list of the laws and regulations governing the industry. There are more that would relate to the above business stages and other issues associated with the banks. A more elaborate list is shown in Annex IIII.

Table 2.2 Overview of the account opening forms under the four business stages

Category	*Title of the account opening form:* *Area of consent, declaration, confirmation, or acknowledgement*
Account opening	Deposit Protection Scheme Indemnity Instructions Laws and regulations Personal data Received all documents and fully understand and agree Tax Terms and conditions
Clients' product and investment knowledge and risk appetite knowledge	Product knowledge Professional investor/product knowledge Terms and conditions Risk level Risk disclosure
Communication channel between bank and client	Indemnity Instructions Internet banking Laws and regulations Literacy Personal data Professional investor/product knowledge Tax Terms and conditions Property rights
Dispute resolution	N/A

Source: Account opening form of Bank A, Bank B, and Bank C obtained in November 2019.

each business stage. Table 2.2 lists the respective documents needed in the business stage with their respective rules and regulations. Table 2.2 matches the business stages with respective documents in the account opening forms. The following observations can be noted.

First, there is no single set of rules regulating a particular business stage. Table 2.1 shows that there are at least seven pieces of regulations governing the account opening process: four on governing product knowledge, six on communication, and five on dispute resolution channels. Some documents also cover all four stages, for example, the Treat Customers Fairly Charter. This suggests that the rules and regulations replicate similar clauses and provisions: some are more banking-focused (e.g., Treat Customers Fairly

Charter, the Guideline), some are more product-focused (e.g., Code on Pooled Retirement Funds, Code on Pooled Retirement Fund, SFC Code on MPF Products), and some are more role-focused (e.g., Fund Manager Code of Conduct, The DTC Association – Code of Banking Practice). Given the wide spectrum of services available within private banking, it is subject to numerous regulations governing a very specific area of business within which banks might get involved with. It should also be noted that there are no single guidelines which only specifically refer to one of these stages. Instead, each guideline describes similar rules, except IC4 of the HKMA SPM which specifically handles the complaint-handling procedures.

Second, notably, there was no dispute resolution clause provided in the account opening form, nor was there any description of any complaint-handling process. Similarly, in the account opening form, there was no communication information for clients to refer to. If a client has enquiries, there is no phone number or email address for them to use. It is only once the account is opened that the bank will send an email to the clients detailing their risk profile, together with the name of the banker who will serve the account. There is no official number to contact the bank. This is different from a retail bank form, in which a customer hotline will be provided to the clients.

Finally, there are no references to rules and regulations in the account opening forms, except for tax-related statements for clients to declare their tax jurisdiction and the handling of personal data. Most of the terms and conditions stated in the account opening forms describe the service scope of the bank and various disclaimers. They also require clients to provide the information necessary to open an account and offer investment services under the respective regulatory requirements. The regulatory requirements are not provided to the clients, meaning that the legal basis for requesting the information has not been explained in the account opening forms. Moreover, clients' rights and banks' responsibilities are not detailed in these documents. These regulations might shape the general characteristics of private banking clients, which will be discussed in the next section.

2.2.3 The general characteristic of private banking clients

Some general characteristics of private banking clients can be identified as follows: they are very wealthy individual clients who expect to receive prestigious services from their banks. They are 'professional investors', as defined in section 5 of the Securities and Futures (Professional Investor) Rules (Cap 571D), meaning that each of their bank accounts has more than HK$8 million in liquid assets. In fact, the asset size of a private bank is usually more than HK$8 million because private banks usually set a business threshold on the minimum liquid assets for each bank account. Based on author's experience in Hong Kong, the threshold can range from US$2 million (e.g., Bank

C) to US$15 m (e.g., JPMorgan). Some private banks further categorise their clients as 'ultra-high net worth individuals' if their accounts have more than US$15 m or 'high net worth individuals' (HNWI) if otherwise (e.g., Bank C). These clients usually have business relationships with other segments of the banks as well. For example, if a private banking client is a business owner, his/her company might have a bank account with the corporate segment of the bank whilst s/he is also a client of the private bank segment of the same organisation. It is also acknowledged that private bankers usually have a close personal relationship with their clients and the 'all-inclusive' money management services provided (Hong Kong Monetary Authority, 2009). The investment amount is usually large. Also, they are financially capable of commencing and are not necessarily a weaker party in terms of their financial scale.

The legal relationships between private banks and their clients are established through contracts (Hudson, 2013, Ch 5 and 30). The inequality of arms between private banking clients and their banks in the contract formation process puts clients at a legal disadvantage in any dispute resolution process (Nader, 1980). Clients enter into the contract by signing the account opening forms prepared solely by the private bank. Clients rarely read the terms, not to speak of negotiating the terms. However, this might not necessarily jeopardise clients' interests, as has been argued by the informed minority argument where under the world of imperfect information, non-reading buyers benefit from an informed minority whose willingness to pay for a product is sufficiently sensitive to the quality of the standard terms; hence, this competitive-market logic can be used to resist regulation and advocates rules to join the 'informed minority'. Yet, in reality, there is little empirical evidence to support this (Bakos et al., 2014a). Clients either accept the contract in full or do not accept it at all. The private banks have the procedural power to include information and expert knowledge in the account opening forms, which is otherwise not obvious to private banking clients, tipping the scale of power in favour of private banks (Waldman, 2011).

As a result, whether clients would give meaningful consent to the terms and conditions (including arbitration clause if incorporated) in the account opening forms is questionable. Reynolds (2014) showed evidence of diminished consent to arbitration through the use of boilerplate and adhesion contracts. In Hong Kong, arbitration clauses are not allowed to be incorporated in the account opening documents due to section 15 (1) of the Control of Exemption Clause Ordinance which has refrained customer contracts from incorporating an arbitration agreement in order not to restrict access to the court. Further legal complications, such as the issue of unconscionability and good faith, may arise when enforcing the arbitration clause (Nehf, 2017). In the US, there are four consent-related defences in the Federal Arbitration Act (1994) covering the formation, scope, validity, and public policy in order not to enforce an arbitration clause.[2] All these would make (mandatory) arbitration unavailable for clients, regardless of the availability and suitability of the platform (Sternlight, 2004).

2.2.4 Importance of private banking in Hong Kong

In his speech in 2012, Mr Norman Chan, the Chief Executive of HKMA at the time, described 'Hong Kong as a Private Banking Hub' (Hong Kong Monetary Authority, 2012b). The HKMA has set the tone to capture the affluent population in 'China and rest of Asia', in the hope that they will choose Hong Kong to manage their wealth. From the HKMA's point of view, the robust legal framework, independent judiciary, and low tax rate remain strong attributes that make Hong Kong well-placed for this, coupled with being a leading initial public offering (IPO) centre and positioned as the most important gateway for capital flows into and out of China. All these factors create a good environment for private banking businesses to blossom.

Therefore, it is of paramount concern that the private banking industry is well regulated. The following three points have been highlighted: (1) it is essential to clarify the definition of private banking clients to facilitate a robust 'know your client' process to onboard the client; (2) private banks shall manage risk on a portfolio basis, instead of a transaction basis, as part of the holistic risk management process; and (3) talents in the industry must be both technically and ethnically competent. These features echo the regulatory framework that is user-friendly and yet sufficiently robust to offer investor protection, which is aligned with the description of a 'disclosure-based regime, supported by suitability assessment by intermediaries at the point of sale' (Hong Kong Monetary Authority, 2012a, para. 8). However, a dispute resolution mechanism is not mentioned.

2.3 The regulatory framework of private banking in Hong Kong and selected jurisdictions

2.3.1 Bank–customer relationship

The bank–client relationship is a contractual one. A contract creates the legal basis to adopt an ADR platform. The bank–customer relationship discussed

2 The four consent related defences under section 2 of the Federal Arbitration Act (1994): (a) there was no agreement in writing to arbitrate anything (the formation question); (b) the dispute involved or the remedy awarded was not within the scope of the written agreement to arbitrate (the scope question); (c) the written agreement to arbitrate was induced by fraud or duress, was entered by mistake, or was unconscionable (the validity defence), and (d) although the dispute is otherwise arbitrable, it was not suitable or appropriate for arbitration (the public policy exception).

here focuses mainly on the issue of consent and power balance. These two issues affect the choice of dispute resolution platform.

2.3.1.1 Bank contract and the issue of consent

> Banking law mediates the relationship between banks and customers. Historically, it provided parameters within which bank transactions took place and provided a fairness across those transactions. But the existing legal framework has been eroded by the increasing complexity of the banking relationship, more detailed contractual agreements, and the development of new banking products.
>
> *(House Committee of Parliament of Australia, 1991)*

Banking law is a collection and extract of certain principles and rules from the general body of the law related to the business of banking, including but not limited to contract law, the law of torts, the law of property, the law of guarantees, the law of bailment, the law of principal and agent, the law relating to agency, partnerships, companies and trusts, the law relating to the carriage of goods by sea and to marine insurance, the law of bankruptcy, insurance law, and the law relating to the sales of good (Weerasooria & Wallace, 1994, pp. 75–76). Banks are also regulated by regulators who have power vested in law. Regulators issue guidelines, policy manuals, and codes of conduct to supervise and allow banks to self-regulate in order to respond to changes in customer expectations, service levels, and disclosure and transparency standards. This aligns with international practice to foster customer confidence and loyalty (Hong Kong Monetary Authority, 2008) and to govern the launch of new products (Hong Kong Monetary Authority, 2017).

The contract is crucial as the legal basis of a bank–customer relationship. The contract formation process in banking features one-sided drafting, and the contracts are very unlikely to be read by clients. Clients have very limited power, and very often have no desire, to amend the content of the contracts prepared by the bank – at best they could opt to not sign some contracts with the expectation that some services would be unavailable to them. The existing literature examining contracts helps us to understand the legal foundation between disputants in a dispute. To approach this, the theory of contract is relied on to identify important processes in contract formation which might not exist in private banking businesses. It is essential to consider the role of power balance in this contract formation process. Through a contextual analysis of account opening documents, it is possible to identify important directions and questions for empirical studies.

The definition of a contract is not often straightforward. It could mean the series of operative acts of the parties expressing their assent with a physical document executed by the parties through establishing the legal relations resulting from the operative acts of the parties. A contract is an enforceable promise supported by consideration requiring an offer and an acceptance.

As the banking industry has developed, the customer–banker relationship has further developed from its traditional stance. Hudson (2013) examined this relationship by stating that the normal relationship is governed 'entirely' by the law of contract unless specific circumstances have arisen to justify the inference of a fiduciary relationship. Banks owe duties, such as the duty of confidentiality as stated in *Tournier v National Provincial and Union Bank of England (*1924 1 K.B. 461. 472–473, per Bankes LJ), with the exception of (a) compulsion by law; (b) duty to the public to disclose; (c) interest of the bank require disclosure; and (d) consent of the consumer. Next is negligence to impose liability, applicable to the banking law once economic loss is recognised under tort, as seen in the leading case *of Hedley Byrne & Co Ltd v Heller & Partners Ltd (*1964, AC 465; 1963, 3 WLR 101; 1963, 2 ALL er 575*),* but it was noted that there is no implied contractual term that a banker owes a duty to customers. For example, in *Williams & Glyn's Bank Ltd. v Barnes (*1981, Com LR 205), the court ruled that there is no implied contractual term to advise his customer on the adverse consequences of borrowing money; on the other hand, bankers may be held liable if an untrue statement is negligently made should there be no exclusion clause protecting him. Last is trustee-beneficiary, but this is a rare approach.

The law of contract has an economic perspective embedded with an objective to maximise the net benefits of exchange that is binding with legal commitment and, hence, creditable. It also provides normal or default terms for an incomplete agreement, especially when only a verbal agreement exists. The doctrine of unconscionability, generally defined as any terms that shock the conscience of the court which would render the entire contract unenforceable, also plays a role in the following two aspects: firstly, procedural unconscionability arising during the process of contract formation, and secondly, substantive unconscionability due to unfair terms. The former deals with the situation involved in fraud, duress, undue influence, incompetence, or other factors that prone a party to enter into a contract. It is usually mitigated by a 'cooling off' period to give the consumer a chance to rescind it. Secondly, substantive unconscionability is often more controversial as to how it is defined, instead of it being a judgment call from the court to determine what is fair to consumers. Besides contract law, customers are further protected by the regulators. Davies (1998) reasoned that regulation protected and benefited customers by relieving them from over-complex contracts. The difficulty in obtaining reliable information about the quality of complex financial products is described below:

> First consumers suffer from bounded rationality. This means that their ability to deal with information is limited. Secondly, consumers may differ greatly in the extent to which they can deal with information. Therefore, it will be difficult for firms to supply information which will benefit large numbers of consumers. Thirdly, there will often be an incentive upon banks not to supply accurate

> information to consumers. The rational banks will only supply information where this puts the bank in a favourable light and where the information can be supplied cost-effectively. Some valuable information will therefore be withheld.
> *(Campbell & Cartwright, 2017, p. 27)*

In arbitration, studies in contract formation have focused on the validity of arbitration clauses incorporated into a contract. In banking and finance transactions, arbitration clauses are often found, if incorporated, on loan agreements between banks and corporation clients or derivatives agreements between two financial institutions. Parties can negotiate the agreement before full commitment in these cases. For consumer contracts, given there is no meaningful consent from the consumer, the validity of arbitration clauses is often difficult to confirm, and hence in Hong Kong banks are not allowed to incorporate an arbitration clause into their account opening form (the contract between clients and banks) under s.15 of the Control of Exemption Clause Ordinance that refrains consumer contracts from incorporating an arbitration agreement in order to not restrict access to the court.

The issue of meaningful consent deserves further scrutiny. Bakos et al. (2014a) conducted an empirical study to answer one central question: 'Does anyone read the fine print?'. Their hypothesis was that in a competitive market, a minority of term-conscious buyers would be sufficient to discipline sellers, as they would check the terms and voice out any unreasonable ones. Yet, the empirical studies do not sustain this conclusion, and this hypothesis is not conclusive. Slawson (1971) studied fairness and consent of standard form contracts where the court might face challenges when contract makers imposed their own 'law'. He recommended that the imposition of standard terms is essential after considering the principles of coercion, consent, economic benefits in a competitive market, and unconscionability, with two conditions, namely, '[restoring] the principle that a contract includes on those terms which both parties can reasonably be expected to understand', and '[recognising] that contracts of adhesion gain no legitimacy from the supposed consent of the party for whom they are *adhesive*, since manifestations which are known to be the product of adhesion do not express consent' (Slawson, 1971, p. 566). Schwartz (1973) explored the possibility of judicial interventions on standardised contracts, as it invokes the issue of unequal bargaining power. He argued that the usual two approaches to defining unequal bargaining power are not ideal for the court but instead 'whether particular clause yields contrary to judicial goal and if so, will buyer consent insulate the clause from attack' (Schwartz, 1973, p. 369). He specifically pointed out that this understanding prevents the court from making the following three errors: (a) producing results inconsistent with the court's conception of public policy; (b) striking down clauses solely because of the seller's market power; and (c) ensuring buyers' expectations may result in them only knowing the clause but being unable to change it (Schwartz, 1973, pp. 392–393). Becher

(2008) also elaborated upon how unequal bargaining power will impact the well-recognised common law doctrine of the duty to read the contract, which is not reflected in actual practice because of legal language, jargon, and confusing terms in the small print. As a result, the receiving party will have to rely on the legal system to provide relief from an unreasonable provision, yet the court might want to keep any interventions to a minimum. However, it may amplify the problem of imposing 'obligational asymmetric information' in a contractual relationship, which leads to market failure and other negative effects such as choosing the wrong product, accepting poor bargains, and ignoring the legal relationships between sellers.

2.3.1.2 The impact of consent on power balance

The impact of consent on power balance in a business relationship is an important part of a dispute resolution process. To appraise this process through face-to-face interviews, it could be useful to connect the concept of the two here, based on what we know from the existing literature.

The first issue is the lack of a unified legal relationship. The relationship is largely based on the nature of transactions between banks and clients (e.g., *Foley v Hill 1848, Woods v Martins Bank Ltd, 1959*). Therefore, there are many contracts between a bank and its clients, and the account opening form is only one, which happens to be the first contract between banks and customers. This means that once the relationship is established, a further contractual relationship will be needed for different transactions such as lending, investment transactions, advisory, and trust. Once a second contract is signed, the clients will be influenced by the fact that they have already established the relationship and clients might feel restricted to not agree with the additional terms, given the difficulty and long process to open an account in the first place. If clients have already had numerous private bank accounts, their restriction may be less imminent, but it would reflect clients' financial constraints as to whether they would be able to open many private bank accounts of a significant size. This hypothesis is later incorporated into our survey (Chapter 4) to identify any possible impact on their bargaining power between 'small' private banking clients and 'big' private banking clients.

The second issue is that clients are unlikely to read the one-sided contract (Bakos et al., 2014b). This means that clients are unlikely to be aware of the terms and conditions associated with the contract. Without an awareness of their obligations when engaged with the bank, any dispute escalated by the client's side might or might not arise out of a breach of contract. The source of any dispute might be caused by other causes, and any disputes outside the contractual scope might be difficult to put forward in a court or through arbitration. Mayer (1987) defines relating as 'the capacity to influence behaviour of others', where clients would not be able to impose any influence on the bank if they are disputing things that were not agreed upon by the bank in the first place. To substantiate this hypothesis, our empirical study will need to confirm whether clients have knowledge and awareness of the obligations of banks and clients.

The third issue is that clients have little chance to negotiate or amend the terms and conditions (Barr, 2014). Clients often simply agree (and sign) to everything they are presented with. If this hypothesis is substantiated, it would further weaken the clients' position, as there is no longer a 'level playing field' because clients might have given up any rights once they signed the contract, and clients will find it difficult to disagree with any subsequent contract, as mentioned above (see Chapter 1, Section 1.2.1.2).

The above scenarios put private banking clients in a weak position in both the business relationship and during any dispute resolution process. These weak positions are difficult to rectify because contract formation is difficult to regulate: regulators have to regulate and supervise a bank's behaviour on behalf of different stakeholders in the industry (Davies, 1998). As Section 2.3.2 of this chapter will reveal, regulators' primary concern is to protect the stability and integrity of the banking and financial system. The protection of customers may only be an ancillary objective as one of the contributing factors to the overall stability of the wider financial system. Banks would have taken a heavier role to safeguard clients' interests under this regulatory focus.

In Hong Kong, there is one legal restriction imposed to restrict the use of arbitration clauses in consumer contracts. The Control and Exemption Clause Ordinance has restricted the incorporation of mandatory arbitration clauses for consumer contracts because it may be regarded as unconscionable and mala fide (Nehf, 2017). On the other hand, customers might be reluctant to incorporate arbitration agreements as consent is questionable (Nolan-Haley, 2018). In Hong Kong, regulators have layers of guidance to handle customer complaints, and it is essential in order to ensure the banks take a customer's complaint seriously and react promptly, as we shall see in Chapter 3.

Therefore, the existence of ambiguous and unequal contractual relations is often believed to be carried through into dispute resolution (Nader, 1980). Banking contracts could be described as being ambiguous and unequal due to the many contracts that often follow the first contract, with potentially high exit costs for clients to bargain for more equal relations. More importantly, practically it is difficult for clients to read the contract before engaging with a bank's services. This would put private banking clients in a very unfavourable position to engage in any dispute resolution process, but this hypothesis has to be examined empirically and is conducted in Chapters 5 and 6.

These studies provide food for thought to derive important questions to ask in stages 2 and 3 of the empirical study, based on our theoretical understanding of power and contracts, to examine whether these observations exist between private banks and individual clients. These studies also offer rationales for the questions to be asked in exploring how private banking clients regard their legal relationship with the banks, the role played by contracts, and how these contractual relationships influence their perception of power balances between banks and clients.

2.3.2 Law, regulation, and code of conduct

2.3.2.1 The law, regulation, and code of conduct

In Hong Kong, creating a suitable environment to maintain the country as an international finance centre is mandated in the Hong Kong Basic Law. Article 109 of the Hong Kong Basic Law states that the HKSAR 'shall provide an appropriate economic and legal environment for the maintenance of the status of Hong Kong as an international finance centre'. To secure this, there are many relevant sections in Hong Kong Ordinances to govern banks.[3] The two key regulators of banks are the HKMA on AIs under the power given by the BO and the SFC on market activities. It is helpful to outline the regulatory framework governing the HK financial industry before examining the legal dynamics between banks and customers. Although the purpose of BO is 'to provide a measure of protection to depositors' (Banking Ordinance, Preface) and to 'promote and encourage proper standards of conduct' (Banking Ordinance: Section 7(2)(c)), the HKMA has also acknowledged that BO is not well suited to dealing with consumer matters (Hong Kong Monetary Authority, 2001, para. 11).

HKMA has the main functions of maintaining currency stability within the framework of the Linked Exchange Rate System; promoting the stability and integrity of the financial system including the banking system; helping to maintain Hong Kong's status as an international financial centre, including the maintenance and development of Hong Kong's financial infrastructure; and managing the Exchange Fund (Hong Kong Monetary Authority, 2021). The SFC has principal responsibility for 2.5 maintaining and promoting the fairness, efficiency, competitiveness, transparency, and orderliness of the securities and futures industry (Securities and Futures Commission, 2020). HKMA and SFC often adopt a 'coordinated approach' to supervise banks and licensed corporations. For example, on 10 September 2019, the SFC reprimanded and fined HSBC $2.1 m for breaching telephone recording requirements when the case was referred to the SFC following an investigation by the HKMA as part of the 'joint enforcement collaboration between the SFC and the HKMA' (Securities and Futures Commission, 2010). HKMA

3 (i) S. 2 and 3 of Misrepresentation Ordinance (CAP 284); (ii) s. 7, 8, and 15 of the Control Exemption Clauses Ordinance (CAP 458); (iii) s. 3 and 6 of Unconscionable Contracts Ordinance (CAP 458); (iv) s. 107 and 108 of Securities and Futures Ordinance (CAP 571); (v) s. 40 and 40A of Companies (Winding Up and Miscellaneous Provisions) Ordinance (CAP 32); and (vi) Banking Ordinance (CAP 155).

and SFC issue supervisory manual policies, guidelines, circulars, and rules in which banks must observe a set of regulations.

Nevertheless, customer protection may not be an explicit function of these bodies. A 2011 HKMA report comparing the protection of banking consumers in various jurisdictions states that, unlike the UK Office of Fair Trading and Competition Commissions and Australian Competition and Consumer Commission and Australian Securities and Investment Commission in Australia, there is no specific agency in HK to protect bank consumers (Hong Kong Monetary Authority, 2001). The HKMA lacks an explicit mandate to protect banking consumers, unlike in the UK where the Office for Fair Trading is responsible for enforcing legislation in relation to consumer protection and promoting competition in general. It has statutory duties under the Fair Trading Act to encourage traders to provide high standards of customer service and to ensure that complaints are tackled quickly and fairly. Together with the Competition Commission, they are responsible for prohibiting anti-competitive practices as well as practices arising from the abuse of dominant positions. Also, in Australia, the Australian Competition and Consumer Commission is the national agency responsible for protecting consumer interests and safeguarding competition. Under the Trade Practices Act 1974 and the Price Surveillance Act 1983, the Commission seeks to promote competition and efficiency in markets, fosters adherence to fair trading, promotes competitive pricing, and restrains price raises in a market where competition is less than effective. Within the financial sector, the Australian Securities and Investment Commission is the agency charged with the responsibility for consumer protection' (Hong Kong Monetary Authority, 2001, paras. 4 and 5).

Financial regulation carries the purpose of transparency and accountability. The common universal objectives are to maintain market confidence, public awareness, consumer protection, reduce financial crimes, create financial stability, control the money system, and maintain the competitiveness of the financial markets. Campbell and Cartwright (2017) explained the rationale for regulation from an economic perspective to address the issues of systemic risk and information asymmetry. Systemic risk is an externality in which market failure would impose additional costs on the banks attempting to fix losses or to implement extra measures to address the market failure. This thesis does not examine the regulation from a structural perspective, as there are already studies examining the different options of financial regulatory structures, such as single regulators in countries such as the UK, Korea, Germany, and multiple authorities in countries such as France and Hong Kong (Amer & Lin, 2003). There are also extensive studies on cross-border issues, for example, whether there exists a regulatory convergence between offshore and onshore markets which impacts bank operations in a jurisdiction given stricter cross-border and domestic regulation, double-taxation agreements and tax information exchange agreements. As an example, the Foreign Account Tax Compliance Act (FACTA) was set up to deter tax evasion in offshore accounts and aims to increase transparency through double-taxation agreements and tax information exchange agreements between counterparties (McKinsey & Company, 2013).

Regulators also set codes of conduct for banks and bankers to regulate business behaviour. This affects contract formation through the incorporation of clients' legal rights and obligations of different parties. Those codes apply a mixed use of rules and principles, which could lead to confusion in the interpretation of what proper conduct consists of, as the binding and non-binding nature of those roles may request further clarification (Braithwaite, 2002). These rules are not always set by the regulators alone but more often are the result of ongoing dialogues and communication between different banks and regulators. The regulators make an assessment to determine whether a bank has adopted a 'best practice' or 'market practice' which could be aligned with a 'judgment call'. This provides the regulators with the flexibility to regulate when there have been changes in circumstances. A breach of these regulations may result in penalties such as fines or suspension of banking licences. Private banking would be subject to the same set of rules. The major codes of conduct are the HKMA SPM CG-3 Code of Conduct (Hong Kong Monetary Authority, 2021) and The Code of Conduct for Persons Licensed by or Registered with the Securities and Futures Commissions issued by the SFC (Securities and Futures Commission, 2020). The Code of Banking Practice issued by the Hong Kong Association of Banks also recommends a set of banking practices related to the relationship between institutions and customers (The Hong Kong Association of Banks, 2021, part 2, ch 1).

It should be noted that these rules are not set by clients, although they could be a result of following clients' complaints. A comparative study between the requirements of bank regulations and the content of bank contracts (through an examination of account opening forms) would allow us to reveal the substance of the legal relationship between banks and individual clients by examining what has been laid down within the framework.

2.3.2.2 Key features of private banking regulation in Hong Kong

Private banks, despite following all the same regulations that a licensed bank does, have a particular focus on some other regulations that are examined in this section.

Private banks can only onboard 'professional investors'. Also, private banks must conduct the 'know your client' (KYC) requirements, of which the SOW of the potential client must be thoroughly assessed before onboarding. KYC is conducted through a customer due diligence (CDD) process under the requirements of the Anti-Money Laundering and Counter-Terrorist Financing Ordinance (Cap. 615) (AMLO) and the Guideline.

The client suitability requirement also requires the bank to ensure the client risk profile has been thoroughly assessed on a portfolio-based approach. The assessment includes, but is not limited to, assessing clients' ability, willingness, and tolerance to take on risk associated with investment, their objective of investment, as well as their relevant knowledge and experience. These matters are explicitly highlighted in private banking, and it is the purpose of the thesis to see how these requirements are incorporated into the account opening form. This would particularly affect how market participants (banks, bankers, and private banking clients) conduct their business under the regulatory requirement of professional investors and suitability, and how these requirements are incorporated into the contracts between banks and clients. The impact of the regulatory framework in contract formation, interpretation, and the efficiency and effectiveness of incorporating these regulations into a contract could be worthy of a separate discussion, for example, to examine whether a more comprehensive code of conduct for private banking should be introduced (KPMG and PWMA, 2018).

On top of the above requirements, private bankers need to observe the Code of Ethics and Conduct issued by the Private Wealth Management Association (PWMA, 2021), and the Treat Customers Fairly Charter for Private Wealth Management Industry issued by the HKMA (Hong Kong Monetary Authority, 2017). The difference between the retail version of the Treat Customer Fairly Charter and the private banking version is minimal, where the only difference is Principle 5. In both versions, both retail and private banks should promote financial literacy with joint efforts from government, regulatory bodies, and stakeholders, but only the retail banks are required to 'provide reasonable access to basic banking services to members of the public, paying special attention to the needs of vulnerable groups', indicating the exclusiveness of private bank services. The private banking version also contains more examples to elaborate upon each principle, which is largely in line with the SPM issued by HKMA, the codes of conduct issued by SFC, and the Code of Ethics and Conduct issued by PWMA. In general, private bankers follow similar requirements such as complying with laws and regulations, diligence and professionalism, honesty, fairness and conflicts of interest, confidentiality, and competence (PWMA, 2021).

These guidelines also request that institutions ensure that banks should provide a reasonable channel for clients to make complaints and for banks to investigate them (PWMA, 2021). Private banks should also provide a channel for customers to seek redress, which includes switching between private bank accounts (Hong Kong Monetary Authority, 2017). These laws and regulations shape how solid the regulatory landscape is for the banking industry (private banking included) in Hong Kong. The emphasis on the bank to have a complaint-handling mechanism indicates that the banks operating in Hong

Kong are required to have dedicated internal resources to handle customers' grievances before they turn into disputes.

2.3.2.3 An overview of private banking regulation in selected jurisdictions

The framework of private banking regulation in Hong Kong is similar to that of the other selected jurisdictions. It is illustrated in a comparative analysis as shown in Table 2.3 where Singapore, the United States, France, and China are selected because the arbitration centres originated in those jurisdictions are analysed (Chapter 3, Section 3.4). Two further jurisdictions, namely Switzerland and the United Kingdom, are also included for their popularity in the private banking and wealth management industries. The analysis mainly highlights the regulatory landscape of private banking in those jurisdictions at the following four levels: definition of private banking and specific regulations for private banks; client segmentation; regulation on contract provision; and channel for dispute resolution. Table 2.3 and Table 2.4 show three general patterns.

First, private banks are usually a segment of a financial institution and usually carry no specific legal identity. Not all jurisdictions have a legal definition of private banks but instead govern private banks based on the onboarding requirements and the activities of the institutions. Among the selected jurisdictions, only Hong Kong and China have provided a legal definition of private banking. In Hong Kong, section 1 of Schedule 14 in the BO defines private banking as institutions providing services for the HNW, which is not defined in the BO (Section 2.2.1). In China, the Notice of Interim Measures for the Administration of Commercial Banks' Personal Financial Management Services describes private banking as comprehensive entrusted investment services to manage clients' wealth on their behalf. The definitions offered in Hong Kong and China are based on client categorisation and the specific onboarding requirement mainly on AML and tax reporting, as well as the service provided which is usually investments, wealth management, and other services which are not available for retail bank clients. Subsequently, there are no specific regulations, regulators, or licensing requirements just for specific private banks (Table 2.4). Most regulations that apply to financial institutions would apply also to the private bank but are slightly different due to the client's categorisation and the investment activities. There are some examples of private banking-specific regulation: in Hong Kong, chapter 12 of the Guideline relates to specific onboarding requirements for private banking and the Treat the Customer Fairly for Private Wealth Management issued by the Private Wealth Management Association governs the bank conduct for private banking clients. In Singapore, there is the Private Banking Code of Conduct issued by the Association of Banks of Singapore; other private banking-specific guidelines issued by the Monetary Authority of Singapore

Table 2.3 Comparison of private banking regulation in selected jurisdictions

Item	*Hong Kong*	*Singapore*	*China*	*Switzerland*	*France*	*UK*	*US*
Regulators specific for the private bank?	No	No	No	No	No	No	No
Legal definition of private banks	Yes	No	Yes	No	No	No	No
Specific guidelines for private banks	No	Yes	No	No	No	No	No
Client categorisation	Professional investor	Accredited investors	HNW individual	HNW individual	Professional client	HNW individual	Sophisticated investors
Asset size/net worth threshold	HK$8 m	S$2 m	CNY6m	CHF2 m	No specific threshold	GBP3 m (or annual net income is GBP300 k or above)	US$1 m
Specific regulation on contract provision for private banks	No	No	No	No	No	No	No
Specific regulations on dispute resolution for private banks	No	No	No	No	No	No	No
Online channel to complain about banks to a regulatory body	Yes	Yes	No (phone only)	Yes	Yes	No	Yes

Source: Legal and regulatory documents and lexology.com (accessed 25 May 2022), see full list in Annex III.

Table 2.4 Key laws and regulations relating to private banking in selected jurisdictions

Hong Kong	Banking Ordinance, Securities and Futures Ordinance, SFC Code of Conduct for Persons Licensed by or Register with the Securities and Futures Commission, Code of Banking Practice. **Private banking-specific:** Treat Customer Fair Treaty for Private Wealth Management; Chapter 12 of the Guideline
Singapore	Securities and Futures Act, Chapter 289 of Singapore, Financial Advisers Act, Chapter 110 of Singapore, Banking Act, the Monetary Authority of Singapore Act, Chapter 186 of Singapore. **Private banking-specific:** Private Banking Code of Conduct issued by the Association of Banks in Singapore, and other private banking-specific guidelines issued by the Monetary Authority of Singapore in 2020, the Guidance on Private Banking Control issued in June 2014, and the Private Banking Sales and Advisory Practice – Observations and Supervisory Expectations from Thematic Inspection
China	The Law of the PRC on Supervision over the Banking Industry; the Interim Administrative Measures for Commercial Banks to Provide Overseas Financial Management Services; the Interim Measures for the Administration of Commercial Banks' Personal Financial Management Services; the Measures for Pilot Assets Management for Specific Clients by Fund Management Companies; the Measures on the Administration and Due Diligence Procedures for Non-Residents' Financial Accounts Information Relating to Tax Matter; the Measure for Punishment of Illegal Financial Acts; the Guiding Opinions on Regulating Asset Management Business of Financial Institutions; the Notice of the China Banking Regulatory Commission on Promulgation of the Administrative Measures on Trust Registration; and other laws
Switzerland	The Federal Banking Act of 1934; The Federal Stock Exchanges and Securities Trading Act of 1995; The Federal Collective Investment Schemes Act of 2006; The Federal Act on the Swiss Financial Market Supervisory Authority; The Federal Act on Combating Money Laundering and Terrorist Financing in the Financial Sector of 1997The Financial Institutions Act; the Financial Services Act
France	Monetary Financial Code; EU Directive No. 2014/65 (MiFID 2), and other European Union Law
UK	The Financial Services and Markets Act 2000 (FSMA); FSMA 2000 (Regulated Activities) Order 2001; Financial Conduct Authority's Handbook of Rules and Guidance; Prudential Regulation Authority's Rulebook (PRA Rulebook); other European Union law
US	The Federal Reserve Act; the Federal Deposit Insurance Act; the National Bank Act; the Bank Holding Company Act of 1956; the Bank Secrecy Act of 1970; the Securities Exchange Act of 1934; the Investment Advisers Act of 1940; the Employee Retirement Income Security Act of 1974; US Code of Federal Regulations (Title, 12, 17, 29, 31)

Source: lexology.com (accessed 25 May 2022), see full list in Annex III.

in 2020, which is the Guidance on Private Banking Control issued in June 2014; and the Private Banking Sales and Advisory Practice – Observations and Supervisory Expectations from Thematic Inspection, issued in February 2020. Issuing private banking-specific regulation, nevertheless, seem to be an exception, not the norm.

Second, client categorisation is clearly defined. Similar to the professional investor categorisation in Hong Kong, other jurisdictions also introduce client segmentation. For example, in Switzerland, in the Financial Institutions Act and the Financial Service Act issued in January 2020, there are three main segments: private clients, professional clients, and institutional clients, where a HNW individual is considered a professional client if they have a net wealth of CHF2 million. Under the EU Directive No. 2014/65 (i.e., MiFiDII) implemented in June 2016, France has three types of clients: non-professional clients, professional clients, and eligible counterparties, which are categorised based on a client's experience, knowledge, expertise, and investment nature and size. In Singapore, the private banking clients are accredited investors but are subject to the opt-in regime which came into effect on 8 April 2019, under the Securities and Futures Act, Chapter 289 of Singapore. The UK has an opt-up option for HNW individuals to obtain a professional client status under the requirement stated in Chapter 3 of the Financial Conduct Authority's Handbook of Rules and Guidance on investment portfolio size (EUR500k) and work experience in the financial industry (one year). Note that this regulation has been implemented relatively recently, and the categorisation serves the purpose of identifying specific requirements about making additional enquiries during client onboarding, assessment of appropriateness and suitability of products, and requiring additional disclosure obligations when dealing with private banking clients. The threshold for private banks in terms of investment size is set at various levels based on the client's net worth, except in the UK where the net annual income is also considered.

Third, as in Hong Kong, there is no specific law or regulation specifically for private banks. Different statutes and regulations for banking generally apply to private banking. None of the selected jurisdictions has specific regulations relating to contract provisions and dispute resolution for private banks. With regards to the contract provisions, it is recognised that there are many different contracts for different business activities but the most important ones are the following three types that relate to investment activities: a discretionary contract is where banks would make investments on the client's behalf without seeking the client's prior approval on each investment transaction after clients have delegated the authority to the bank to invest in a specific pattern; an advisory contract is where the client is in charge of making his or her own investment decision under the benefits of bank's advice; and an execution-only contract is where the bank has no obligation to provide any investment advice, and the client can make his or her own investment decision. These contracts are drafted based on general principles of the contract and associated law and based on business needs. With regards to the dispute resolution channel, it is embedded within the overall banking supervision. Similarly, the bank complaint-handling procedure follows the one that governs the bank, which is also in line with the global practice (Section 3.2.3, Chapter 3), and it should be noted that although all regulators (except in the UK) have channels for clients to make a complaint about banks, the regulators do not have jurisdictions to intervene with the bank decisions (Annex III).

To investigate the regulatory issues at a more granular level, one can refer to the Swiss Banking Association (Swiss Banking Association, 2018), which has conducted a regulatory competitiveness assessment for private banking. It benchmarks 10 factors among 12 jurisdictions, as summarised in Table 2.5. It is observed that out of the ten factors selected, Hong Kong has been on a weaker range on Automatic Exchange of Financial Account Information, and on AML/KYC/Politically Exposed Persons. Hong Kong is in the stronger range of Data Protection whilst the others are in the middle range. Particularly relevant to this thesis is the factor of 'client protection in light of the rule of law', which evaluates the stability of the legal framework that includes dispute resolution, customer services, handling of transparency, suitability and appropriateness, or client segmentation. For this factor, Hong Kong has been placed in the middle range (pp. 16–17, Swiss Banking Association, 2018). This report suggests that Hong Kong could be falling behind in offering client protection, which may be due to a lack of mandate for customer protection (Section 2.3.2.1).

The regulatory framework of private banking in Hong Kong is largely in line with that of the selected jurisdictions but with two exceptions that relate to the onboarding requirements regulated by guidelines at the institutional level and the transactional level. These requirements are usually addressed during the onboarding process by the account opening forms, and hence this thesis further investigates the clients' onboarding requirements among different banks to study whether these guidelines may result in a more consistent approach among different private banks.

2.4 The content of the account opening forms

With the legal and regulatory background outlined above, it appears that the language adopted in these codes is relatively broad. For example, the Treat Customers Fairly Charter for Private Wealth Management Industry is less than three pages long, although the length is further extended by the examples applied. The content is also quite similar to the general code of conduct issued by the HKMA (CG-3 Code of Conduct). Language such as 'honest, fair, integrity, care, exemplify, best interest, due care' are more principles than specific practical guidance. It still leaves it up to the bank to decide

Table 2.5 Regulatory competitiveness benchmarking: The Hong Kong standing

Factor	*Not compliant range (Level playing field)*	*International standard*	*Over-compliant (Swiss Finish)*
Automatic exchange of financial account information	USA, **Hong Kong**	Switzerland, UK, Singapore/China	
AML/KYC/ politically exposed persons	**Hong Kong**, China	USA, Singapore, UK, Switzerland	
Capital and liquidity requirements		**Hong Kong,** China, UK, Singapore, USA	Switzerland
Corporate governance	China	USA, **Hong Kong,** UK, Switzerland	Singapore
Factor	*Low (disadvantage)*	*Middle*	*High (advantages)*
Client protection in light of the rule of law	China	USA, **Hong Kong**, UK	Singapore, Switzerland
Digitisation	China	**Hong Kong,** Singapore	USA, UK, Switzerland
Labour market	China	UK, **Hong Kong**	USA, Singapore/ Switzerland
Taxation		UK, China, USA, Switzerland, Singapore, **Hong Kong,**	
Market access	China, USA, Switzerland	Singapore, **Hong Kong,** UK	
Data protection	China	Switzerland, UK, Singapore	**Hong Kong,** USA

The sequence of the name represents the ranking proposed by the report. For example, under 'Taxation', although all jurisdictions are in the 'middle' range, the order of competitiveness is UK, China, USA, Switzerland, Singapore, and Hong Kong, meaning that Hong Kong is the most competitive. (For example, Singapore/Switzerland under 'Labour market' means they are of equal standing.) France is not included in the study and hence is not reported.

Source: The Swiss Banking Association (2018).

how to exercise these principles. This leads to the need to research how these principles are applied. In this research, the first point of contact is the account opening forms, hence the need for a contextual analysis of the account opening forms of selected private banks.

The results of stage 1 content analysis are presented in this section by comparing the content of the account opening form and the relevant regulations as shown in Table 2.1 and Table 2.2. It is observed that there is no standardised approach to the drafting of the account opening forms. Different practices are adopted by different private banks. The account opening forms of three private banks (namely: Bank A, Bank B, and Bank C) are selected, among others, and their contents are compared by referring to *the Guideline*. The comparison shows that banks request clients to provide more information than required in terms of scope and granularity. This may be the result of the wide and ambiguous language used in writing the terms and conditions in the contract, with the banks interpreting it on their own accord. Also, the selected account opening forms do not seek information on the SOW, which is often requested separately by bankers. This leads to extortive documentation requirements, difficulties in assessing the SOW with corroboration, complex structures, a lack of definitions in a risk-based approach, and a lack of standardised policies, all leading to a prolonged client onboarding process (KMPG, 2014). Also, the lack of standards among the different practices of banks in their written documentation indicates a potential missing link and confusion for clients to understand their rights in their banking relationships. Subsequently, most of the content in the account opening form is to request clients to, for example, confirm, acknowledge, agree, and undertake various terms and conditions, which appears to shift the compliance responsibilities entirely to the clients. It is less likely to have a specific or standardised approach because the HKMA does not lay down these requirements with hard rules, instead only issuing generic directions and principles.

2.4.1 Anti-money laundering, counter-financing of terrorism and 'know your client' in the private bank

In other to comply with the stringent client onboarding requirements stated under Anti-Money Laundering and Counter-Terrorism Financing Ordinance (Cap 615), Drug Trafficking (Recovery of Proceeds) Ordinance (Cap 405), Organized and Serious Crime Ordinance SCO (Cap 455), United Nations (Anti-Terrorism Measures) Ordinance (Cap. 575), and the Guideline by the HKMA (2018), private banks require clients to provide detailed sources of their wealth with corroboration on top of filling in the account opening form.

A robust KYC protocol is put in place to acquire a thorough knowledge of a client's identity, source of funds, and the purpose of account opening. For example, bankers will ask questions to justify the legitimacy of the SOW to be transacted in the private bank; a thorough knowledge of the purpose and future activities of the accounts should be acquired by the banks. Banks also need to collect information from clients regarding KYC and address clients' suitability for making financial investments.

The three steps of money laundering are placement, layering, and integration. Placement is where funds are deposited into the financial system. Layering is where the funds are separated from their original source by conducting different layers of transactions through the bank accounts. Integration involves conducting more transactions in order to make these funds look legitimate. The proper AML procedures in a bank help to reconstruct an audit trail for prosecution (United States General Accounting Office, 1997). It could be achieved by the adoption of prudent and effective procedures during the client onboarding stage but inevitably at the consequence of prolonging the time required for account opening (Law, 2019, p. 3).

Fulfilling these requirements is a long process. A study conducted by the Private Wealth Management Association and KPMG (the PWMA report 2018) showed that the average onboarding time steadily increased from 30 days in 2016 to 40 days in 2018. In 2018, only 76% of bankers (compared with 93% in 2016) could complete onboarding within 60 days (KPMG and PWMA, 2018). Unlike retail banking, where the account can be opened immediately with all necessary information provided, the onboarding process in private banking is still largely dependent on many factors and considerations not written in the contract. Bankers need to have the resources to identify, obtain, and analyse additional information in order to assess the SOW. Since there is no single approach to incorporate every regulatory requirement into a single form, the duration of the process depends on the experience and expertise of the bank and bankers and is complicated by the changing compliance environment on AML/CFT initiatives driven by the ongoing need to improve AML compliance. It has already imposed a risk of disruption to legitimate business lines (Johnston & Carrington, 2006). Moyano and Ross (2017) estimated that it could cost up to US$500 m per year per bank to conduct the conventional KYC due diligence process. Complying with these rules could adversely affect the bank's profitability.

2.4.2 Globally applied rules on AML/CFT/KYC

To further elaborate on the complexity involved, there are more globally applicable rules and regulations to comply with on top of the SPM, codes, or guidelines issued by HK regulators alone. The interpretation of these rules, the risk appetite of the bank, and management decisions to set the standards to comply with these rules hugely impact the internal requirements to onboard a client. There are more rules and regulations in this area alone, and the rules are growing through the emergence of more and more cases.

This section reviews the AML/KYC-related rules, namely the USA PATRIOT Act, (FATF) Recommendation, and the Wolfsberg Principles, and highlights key literature in the AML/KYC process. This is followed by commentary arising from journal articles and the HSBC Swiss case. It aims to lay the legal and regulatory background for subsequent analysis and identify common concerns shared in the international standards. These rules are detailed in the following paragraphs.

Uniting and Strengthening America by Providing Appropriate Tools Required to Intercept and Obstruct Terrorism (USA PATRIOT) Act of 2001: The USA PATRIOT Act imposes the minimum requirements to identify a client before accepting a client as a bank customer through a client identification programme. A risk-based procedure is adopted to help a bank form a reasonable belief that it knows the identities of each of its customers, be it a foreign or domestic bank client at the retail or private bank side. The procedures involve identifying the ultimate beneficial owners of the accounts, flagging situations when the bank cannot verify the customers, and stating circumstances where an account cannot be opened. It must specify to what extent a customer can use an account whilst the bank is trying to verify the identity of customers. The bank should close an account if it fails to verify a customer's identity (USA PATRIOT Act, section 326).

Wolfsberg Anti-Money Laundering Principles for Private Banking (The Wolfsberg Principles): Before the USA PATRIOT Act was enacted, 11 private banks established the Wolfsberg Principles.[4] There are 11 primary voluntary and non-binding AML principles for private banks, including client acceptances, additional due diligence, and measures in addressing special situations, updating clients' files, writing policies on identification, monitoring, and the retention requirements of all AML-related documents (Wolfsberg Principles, 2012, pp. 2–7).

The FATF Recommendations on money laundering: FATF is an intergovernmental body to develop and promote AML policies (United States General Accounting Office, 1999). The FATF Recommendations were first published in 1996 and later reviewed in 2003. Financial institutions should obtain and verify customer information to identify the beneficial owner of the account and to facilitate later monitoring and ongoing due diligence. There are 40 recommendations involving customer due diligence (CDD) and record keeping. The most relevant one is Recommendation 5, which

4 ABN AMRO Bank; Banco Santander Central Hispano, SA; Bank of Tokyo-Mitsubishi, Ltd.; Barclays Bank; JPMorgan Chase; Citibank; Credit Suisse Group; Deutsche Bank AG; Goldman Sachs; HSBC; Societe Generale; UBS AG.

reads, 'Financial institutions should be prohibited from keeping anonymous accounts or accounts in obviously fictitious names ... [and should] undertake CDD measures, including identifying and verifying the identity of their customers' (Recommendations, FATF, 2012, p. 14).

HSBC Swiss case in 2015: HSBC was exposed to be associated with more than 2,000 diamond dealers, with alleged participation in blood diamonds amounting to US$135 m through accounts which are also suspected of dealing illegal arms (Chittum, 2018). HSBC did not trigger any warning signs for these transactions within any of its compliance or reporting systems. This case provided important insights into how AML measures could be implemented. The case was settled with a fine without any admission of liability, except for promises to improve AML measures, including whistleblowing and other official reporting channels built within the AML compliance system to identify AML irregularities (Naheem, 2015). Another highlight of the case was that HSBC Swiss tried to sue the whistle-blower. This case has led to extensive literature studying the implications for future internal reporting and whistleblowing approaches to support AML compliance. AML compliance needs to be embedded into a proactive corporate social responsibility approach rather than relying solely on regulation. This means that laws and regulations would not be the only answer to all AML measures and that the onboarding process is only the beginning. It should also include the detection and reporting of any suspicious activities, such as why Bank A could onboard these accounts in the first place (Law, 2019).

Regulator's Circulars: These often involve releasing the results of investigations as to whether banks have fulfilled the AML requirements and issued notices of any breaches. For example, in 2015, the State Bank of India was involved in a case of internal control failures relating to AML/CFT systems that contravened section 3(1), s. 5(1), section 19(1), and section 19(3) of Schedule 2 to the AMLO (Hong Kong Monetary Authority, 2015). These circulars further guide the banks on how to set and implement their policies (Law, 2019).

This illustrates that filling in the account opening form alone does not seem to provide all the information needed to onboard a client, nor does it provide all the necessary information to clients in relation to how the legal relationship between the bank and client is established. The rules disseminated by the regulators are not specific but often rely on ongoing interpretations by regulators and banks in different jurisdictions. This suggests that there is no one-size-fits-all rule to onboard a client. Banks are subject to rules and regulations that are meant to be drafted using broad language, which is often subject to interpretation and circumstances before one can determine whether a bank has complied or not. It is not difficult to infer that a client would find it very difficult to understand their rights, as well as the bank's obligations towards them.

2.4.3 Lack of specific guidelines for the drafting of the account opening form

To illustrate the above observation in the context of complexity and difficulty to find standardised sources of regulatory guidelines, it is useful to scrutinise the key regulations for client onboarding in the private banking industry in Hong Kong: namely section 7 of the *AMLO* and HKMA circulars issued under the power vested in section 7(3) of the BO.

To comply with section 7 of the *AMLO* and section 7(3) of the BO, which sets out general background about AML, CFT, and practical guidelines to assist AIs including registered institutions to comply with the statutory requirements, HKMA issued the Guideline covering a wide range of AML and CFT issues and providing guidance on how banks should operate in compliance with those requirements. It covers requirements such as a risk-based approach, systems, CDD, monitoring, recording keeping, staff training, and wire transfers. There is no specific section discussing client onboarding in private banking. They are scattered throughout different sections; mainly in Chapter 2: Risk-Based Approach; Chapter 4: Customer Due Diligence; and Chapter 12: Private Banking (Law, 2019).

Chapter 2 states that money laundering and terrorist financing risks should be identified, assessed, and understood by an institution at customers' individual and jurisdictional levels. Sections 2.3–2.9 lay out the requirements and considerations on documentation, senior management engagement, record keeping, and reporting to HKMA (Section 2.3), factors (Section 2.4), and scope (Sections 2.5–2.7). In terms of customer risk assessments, it states 'the amount and type of information obtained, and the extent to which this information is verified, should be increased where the ML/TF risks associated with the business relationship are higher' (the Guideline, section 2.12); 'the risk assessment conducted will also assist the AI to differentiate between the risks of individual customers and business relationships, as well as apply appropriate and proportionate CDD and risk mitigating measures' (the Guideline, section 2.12); AI should 'adopt a balanced and common-sense approach' to assess ML/TF risk; and decide 'the extent of CDD measures and ongoing monitoring is appropriate based on that customer's ML/TF risks' (the Guideline, footnote 4). The rest of the sub-section lays down requirements on record keeping, documentation, and ongoing monitoring (Sections 2.12–2.15) (Law, 2019, p. 11).

Chapter 4 describes in detail how AI would identify and verify customers and beneficial owners (Section 4.1.3) with reliable and independent sources such as government bodies, HKMA, and other relevant authorities (section 4.3.1) and obtain 'information on the purpose and intended nature of the business relationship established with the AI' (section 4.3.1 (b), the Guideline). It also sets out the minimal information to verify the identity of the natural or legal person, and connected parties are also defined (section 4.3) in CDD measures, which are categorised as Simplified Due Diligence (SDD) (section 4.8) and Enhanced Due Diligence (EDD) (section 4.9) (Law, 2019, pp. 11–12).

There are special requirements for private banking. Chapter 12 starts by stating that a 'private banking relationship can represent an increased risk of ML/TF' (section 12.1, the Guideline), and special provisions are made for private banking (section 12.2). Chapter 12.3 states that additional customer profile information, on top of section 4.9 of the Guideline, should include verification or corroboration (section 12.5), adverse news screening (section 12.6), additional measures to understand complex corporate structures (section 12.7), association with ongoing monitoring (Section 12.9–12.11), as well as dedicated relationship management coupled with proper reporting and review (section 12.12) (Law, 2019, p. 12).

SDD measures can be applied only if low ML/TF risk is assessed with adequate analysis. Examples of the low-risk factors are provided under section 4.8.10 of the Guideline, including clients which are government entities, listed corporate entities subject to disclosure requirements, FI as defined in the *AMLO*, and collective investment schemes. This includes countries being regarded as at risk of lower levels of corruption or other criminal activity, as identified by creditable sources. Possible SDD measures are to 'accept other documents, data or information', facilitate 'reducing the frequency of updates of customer ID', and 'not collecting specific information… but inferring the purpose and intended nature from the type of transactions or business relationship established'. Under the SDD approach, there is no need to 'identify or verify the beneficial owners of that entity' (section 4.8.10, the Guideline) (Law, 2019, p. 12).

EDD applies to business relationships or transactions that are high risk or specifically noted by the HKMA. Senior management approval is mandatory to onboard these clients required to onboard these clients, as they have potentially higher risks in terms of the identity of the person such as politically exposed persons domestically or internationally, products, services, transactions, delivery channels, and country-related concerns. Possible EDD measures to obtain additional information are regarding customers' information, the intended nature of the business relationship, the source of funds or SOW of the customers, and the reasons for intended or performed transactions (section 4.9.6, the Guideline) (Law, 2019, pp. 12–13).

Specific requirements for private banking: A close relationship between relationship managers and their customers represents an increased risk. There are specific provisions for private banking customers in its customer acceptance, CDD procedures, and in its ongoing monitoring programme. Additional customer profiles are also required, which include but are not limited to business background, SOW, source of funds, family background, anticipated account activity, and references. Senior management approval is required. Appropriate EDD measures should be applied if an account is assessed as high risk. Reasonable steps on a risk-based approach to verify or corroborate information and perform adverse news screening should be undertaken. 'Meeting the customer is also an important part of the CDD process' (section 12.8, the Guideline). RMs must provide a report of their activities, and such shall be revised by supervisors (Law, 2019, p. 13).

FAQs issued by HKMA in response to incidents: HKMA regularly updates its FAQs, which have been consolidated into the FAQs of the Hong Kong Association of Banks (The Hong Kong Association of Banks, 2021). For example, HKMA issued a letter entitled 'Frequently Asked Questions on Customer Due Diligence' to clarify and explain the legal and regulatory requirements in relation to CDD (Hong Kong Monetary Authority, 2017, p. 1). It clarifies that AI does not need to establish SOW for every customer, elaborating that 'for most customers (i.e., non-high-risk customers), certain information obtained as to understand the purpose and intended nature of the business relationship... occupation or employment... the HKMA has conducted training and issued guidance which may be referred to understand our expectation' (Hong Kong Monetary Authority, 2017, pp. 3–4) (Law, 2019, pp. 13–14).

Given that the content of the account opening forms is guided by principles instead of specific instructions, different banks have different ways of complying with these principles. This creates a source of power imbalance because it is very difficult for clients to challenge banks for non-compliance when there are many possible ways to interpret the relevant requirements. Different banks have different ways of complying with the rules and regulations.

2.4.4 Does the account opening form collect sufficient information to fulfil KYC requirements?

The regulatory Guideline does not specify KYC information: Chapter 4 of the Guideline is 36 pages long and serves to provide detailed direction to guide bank staff to review an onboarding client. It is observed that the drafting of these guidelines is generic. Banks will need to provide more guidelines through their internal policy. The content of these policies will vary among banks, as it depends on the resources dedicated to detail the requirements. Different banks might have different requirements based on their own previous experiences, which are not shared with other banks. The policies also provide the key factors to determine what is high risk and what additional measures should be imposed when onboarding a high risk customer. Nevertheless, none of these procedures, as observed, required more than a full name and HKID number from the account opening form. The length of the internal policy and frequency of training that will drive different standards among different banks runs to about 30 pages. Based on the author's own experience, the length of these internal policies could vary between 30 pages and 150 pages. Some are step-by-step manuals, but some simply repeat the regulatory Guideline. The contrast between the length of the internal guidelines between different banks might indicate the reliance on the professional judgment of bank staff versus compliance with procedures. These differences in length are also observed in the account opening forms.

The length of the account opening forms is different: After analysing the account opening forms from three private banks (Bank A, Bank B, and Bank C), which are publicly available upon request from the private bankers, I counted the number of forms, pages, fields, and clauses, and summarised them in Table 2.6 (Law, 2019, p. 15), and Tables 2.7 a, b, and c (Law, 2019, pp. 21–23). When counting, it is assumed that the client applies for a single-name individual account with one power of attorney. To avoid repetition, the same information required multiple times in the same set of documents is counted as one time, and fields that are multiple-choice (e.g., the title of the customer: Mr, Mrs, Ms) are also counted as one. Signature fields are separately counted. Fields that are 'bank only' are excluded. For the number of clauses, only the first level of the provision is counted, and sub-sections have been ignored because some documents use paragraphs to separate different clauses.

Table 2.6 shows the number of forms, respective pages, clauses, fields to fill in, and signatures required from the client. Different banks have different lengths of account opening forms. Bank A has 12 forms with 10 signatures required but only consists of 83 pages and 149 clauses. Bank B has 12 forms and requires only 7 signatures; it contains 157 pages and 192 clauses. Bank C only requests five sets of forms and five sets of signatures with a total of 42 pages and 75 clauses. Bank C appears to be the most efficient in terms of onboarding clients. A closer look at the number of fields to fill in also reveals that (in Tables 2.7 a, b, and c): Bank C requires 123 pieces of information, which is significantly lower than that of Bank B (192 pieces) and

Table 2.6 The overall information requirements in terms of quantity

Bank	*No. of forms*	*No. of pages*	*No. of clauses*	*No. of fields to fill in*	*No. of signatures required*
Bank A	12	83	149	210	10
Bank B	12	157	333	192	7
Bank C	5	42	75	123	5

Source: Account opening forms of Bank A, Bank B, and Bank C (Law, 2019, p. 15).

Table 2.7a Forms to submit to open a private bank account in Bank A

Bank A	*Form*	*Function of the forms (Note 4)*	*No. of pages*	*No. of terms*	*No. of fields*	*No. of signatures*	*Chinese version available?*
1	**Bank A: W-8BEN (External Form)**Bank B: W-8BEN (External Form)Bank C: embedded in Onboarding Form	To declare whether you are a US citizen or other US persons	1	5	13	1	No
2	**Bank A: Product Suitability & Risk Disclosure Checklist** Bank B: Product Booklets Acknowledgement Bank C: embedded in Onboarding Form	To acknowledge and confirm to the bank receipts of product booklets and CDs	3	3	13	1	No
3	**Bank A: Individual Tax Residency Self-Certification Form** [Bank B: embedded in Account Application: Self-Certification (HK) Bank C: embedded in Onboarding Form]	To help protect the integrity of tax systems, banks are required to determine where a client is a tax resident outside the jurisdiction where the account is held	3	3	10	1	Yes
4	**Bank A: Tax Transparency Certification** [Bank B/Bank C: N/A]	To certify tax transparency	5	2	23	1	No
5	**Bank A: Email indemnity application form**Bank B: NA Bank C: NA	To authorise the bank to accept electronic instructions from clients prepared to undertake such risks and that they have satisfied themselves in all respects with regard to such authorisation	4	8	4	1	No

(*Continued*)

Table 2.7a Continued

Bank A	*Form*	*Function of the forms (Note 4)*	*No. of pages*	*No. of terms*	*No. of fields*	*No. of signatures*	*Chinese version available?*
6	**Bank A: Disclosure of Monetary and Non-Monetary Benefits and Other sales related information**	To disclose the nature of monetary and non-monetary benefits banks received	2	10	0	0	Yes
7	**Bank A: Request for Access to Bank B Private Banking Knowledge & Research Centre**	To request the bank to provide materials from the 'Knowledge & Research Centre'	6	20	5	1	No
8	**Bank A: Derivative Knowledge disclosure statement**	To assess the client's knowledge of derivatives and to characterise the client by reference to such knowledge	2	0	8	1	Yes
9	**Bank A: Completion of derivative training**	To complete training and declare understanding of such derivatives	1	0	5	1	Chinese Version Only
10	**Bank A: Private Bank 1 FEE Schedule**	To list the fee charge	7	8	0	Yes	Yes
11	**Bank A: Client Investment Profiler**[Bank B: Investment Objective Settings/Bank C: Embedded in Onboarding Form]	To understand the client's investment profile	15	9	54	Yes	Yes
12	**Bank A: Account opening booklet**	To provide personal details and acknowledge various matters	34	81	75	2	No
		Total	83	149	210	10	

Source: Bank A account opening forms (Law, 2019, p. 22).

Table 2.7b Forms to submit to open a private bank account in Bank B

Bank B	*Form*	*Function of the forms*	*No. of pages*	*No. of terms*	*No. of fields*	*No. of signatures*	*Chinese version available?*
1	**Bank B:** W-8BEN (external Form)	To declare whether you are a US citizen or other US persons	1	5	13	1	No
2	**Bank B:** Product booklets acknowledgement	To acknowledge and confirm to the bank receipts of product booklets and CDs	2	12	14	1	Yes
3	**Bank B:** Investment objective settings	To understand the client's investment profile	15	8	86	2	Yes
4	**Bank B:** Account application	To provide personal details and acknowledge various matters	34	42	73	1	Yes
5	**Bank B:** Bank 1 master agreement	General Terms and Conditions (Bank B)	17	40	0	0	Yes
		Investment Services Terms (Bank B)	5	15	0	0	Yes
		E-Cheques Terms (Bank B)	2	4	0	0	Yes
		Self-Directed Investment Terms and Conditions (Bank B)	1	2	0	0	Yes
		China Connect Terms and Risk Disclosures(Shanghai and Shenzhen Stock Connect) (Bank B)	11	38	0	0	Yes
		Risk Disclosure Statement	11	55	0	0	Yes
6	**Bank B:** ISDA 2002 master agreement	ISDA 2002 Master Agreement	25	14	3	1	No
		Schedule to the 2002 ISDA Master Agreement	13	63	3	1	No
		Generic Risk Disclosure Statement on OTC Derivatives	2	7	0	0	No

(Continued)

Table 2.7b Continued

Bank B	*Form*	*Function of the forms*	*No. of pages*	*No. of terms*	*No. of fields*	*No. of signatures*	*Chinese version available?*
7	**Bank B:** Tax requirements notice	To set out terms relating to tax withholding, reporting, and associated requirements	6	6	0	0	Yes
8	**Bank B:** Explanatory note on professional investor	To explain 'professional investor' under s. 1 of Part 1 of Schedule 1 to the SFO, and to facilitate the signing of Part E of account application	1	4	0	0	Yes
9	**Bank B:** Data Policy Notice	Sets out the data policies of the bank that form part of the account terms and conditions and/or the agreement or arrangements that a data subject enters into with the company	4	17	0	0	Yes
10	**Bank B:** Regulation relating to investors residing in the European Economic Area (EEA) (the ERIIPs Regulation)	to explain the ERIIPS regulations for EEA residents	1	1	0	0	Yes
11	**Bank B:** Private Bank 1 Fee Schedule	To list the fee charges	4	0	0	0	Yes
12	**Bank B:** HK Deposit Protection Board Leaflet	To inform potential clients on the deposit protection scheme of HK	2	0	0	0	Yes
		Total	157	333	192	7	

Source: Bank B account opening forms (Law, 2019, p. 21).

Table 2.7c Forms to submit to open a private bank account in Bank C

Bank C	*Form*	*Function of the forms (Note 4)*	*No. of pages*	*No. of terms*	*No. of fields*	*No. of signatures*	*Chinese version available?*
1	**Bank C:** Onboarding formBank B: account application and master agreement Bank A: account opening booklet	Welcoming page and table of contents	3	0	0	0	Yes
		Personal details	5	11	27	0	Yes
		Bank C digital banking declaration	6	12	27	0	Yes
		Correspondence instructions	3	0	8	0	Yes
		Investor profile	6	14	36	0	Yes
		Declarations	2	0	3	0	Yes
		Additional services	2	2	3	0	Yes
		Agreement	3	10	0	0	Yes
		Signature(s)	3	0	4	1	Yes
2	**Bank C:** General derivative knowledge questionnaire	To help the bank understand client experience and knowledge of derivatives	1	0	4	1	No
3	**Bank C:** Client declaration and instruction form	To request and authorise the bank to provide information on products	2	3	5	1	No
4	**Bank C:** Client request and authorisation form for fixed income new issues	To request and authorise the bank to provide information on new issues of debenture offered by corporate borrower	1	5	3	1	No
5	**Bank C:** Securities P pooled L lending A agreement	To agree that the bank may borrow the securities held currently or in future of any account in client's account	5	18	3	1	No
		Total	42	75	123	5	

Source: Bank C account opening forms (Law, 2019, p. 23).

Bank A (210 pieces). Tables 2.7 a, b, and c show that other than the client identifiers such as name, address, and date of birth, the extra information requested by Bank A and Bank B comes from account applications (Bank A: 75 fields; Bank B: 73 fields; Bank C: 27 fields) and investment objective setting (Bank A: 54 fields; Bank B: 86 fields; Bank C: 36 fields). There is a different way to handle external forms: for example, whilst the W-Ben form (for clients to declare US citizenship status) is a separate form downloadable from the internet that contains 13 fields and needs one signature, Bank C has this embedded in the account opening form without the need to fill in additional information. Similarly, the data policy notice and Hong Kong Deposit Protection Board leaflet are separately provided by Bank B, but Bank A and Bank C have them embedded in one clause in their account opening forms. Most notably, Bank B issues a separate booklet for the master agreement (139 clauses, Tables 2.7 a, b, and c), whilst Bank A (58 clauses) and Bank C (10 clauses) have it embedded in their account opening form. Tables 2.7 a, b, and c depict the specific requirements, which show that most, if not all, documents focus on requesting clients' information, putting down the terms and conditions, and detailing the scope of banking services offered. They do not state the bank's legal obligations or clients' rights, except for providing the leaflet of the Deposit Protection Scheme (see also Law, 2019, pp. 15–16).

The differences in length imply that the account opening form may not function as a contract practically, nor does it serve to fulfil the AML requirements. Specifically, there are three observations (Law, 2019, p. 16): (i) clients are subject to different terms and conditions when they engage with different private banks; (ii) the bank has discretion on how the CDD is conducted, and it might not be totally reflected in the account opening forms themselves; and (iii) the account opening document does not inquire about the SOW (except for Bank B that asks for current occupation, which is part of the information usually asked under CDD requirements). Important information such as past occupation and salary are not incorporated in the form. The account opening forms also do not request clients to provide any proof of the SOW. Naturally, clients will be required to provide more information later when the bankers cannot identify the information themselves. In fact, the PWMA report from 2018 shows a lack of a (much-wanted) private banking-oriented guidance because 'circulars do not adequately take into account the unique characteristics of PWM industry' (PWMA report, 2021, p. 24).

2.4.5 The account opening form does not function as a contract between banks and clients

2.4.5.1 The use of language

Parties often solidify a business relationship by signing a written contract, yet a contract cannot govern all essential obligations. Émile Durkheim (2014) explained that some critical obligations cannot be written such as the manifestation of free will, consent between parties, the need for division of labour, and maintenance of social order. He elaborated:

> But it is not only outside of contractual relations, it is in the play of these relations themselves that social action makes itself felt. For everything in the contract is not contractual. The only engagements which deserve this name are those which have been desired by the individuals and which have no other origin except in this manifestation of free will. Inversely, every obligation which has not been mutually consented to has nothing contractual about it. But wherever a contract exists, it is submitted to regulatory forces that is imposed by society and not by individuals: it is a force that becomes ever more weighty and complex (pp. 158). ... Undoubtedly, when men unite in a contract, it is because, through the division of labor, either simple or complex, they need each other. But in order for them to co-operate harmoniously, it is not enough that they enter into a relationship, nor even that they feel the state of mutual dependence in which they find themselves. It is still necessary that the conditions of this co-operation be fixed for the duration of their relations (pp. 160).
>
> *(Durkheim, 2014)*

The account opening form reflects the lack of certainty to cover all essential obligations from the banks. It mainly provides the scope of the banking services available, the rights of the bank, and the responsibilities of clients, but very often it does not include the responsibilities of the bank as well as clients' rights under the law. Relating this observation to Durkheim's quote, banks and clients are connected possibly due to their need and mutual dependence to cooperate within a fixed duration of their relations, indicated by the existence of an account in the private bank. This account is only a beginning, and there are more services and contractual relationships to be built, and their relationship, subject to regulations which are arguably based on Durkheim's quote, is not the work of individuals but rather the work of society.

Given that there are expectations to have more cooperation (and hence contracts) between banks and clients, the first contract of opening an account could already restrict parties from cooperating freely and efficiently. This restriction appears to be resolved by adopting a mixed use of both vague and precise provisions in contract design. Schwartz and Watson (2004) compared commercial contracts with judicial opinions and observed that the prospects of litigation influence the use of vague or precise terms in the drafting of substantive and procedural provisions. When the parties agree to vague substantive provisions, they delegate more resources to the 'back-end' to enforce those vague terms. These processes are often regarded as 'selecting the proxies'. Proxies mean operative facts. This is relevant to establishing compliance with precise and vague contract terms. A precise term narrowly confines the content of the operative facts. A vague term (or standard) defines a broader space within which a court can select the evidentiary proxy that best establishes compliance with the terms (Scott & Triantis, 2005, p. 818).

When parties devote resources to agree on precise terms or rules, they invest in the 'front end' to negotiate the contract in detail. Litigation can be very expensive, so resources allocated between the front-end and back-end should be carefully assessed. That is equivalent to assessing the burden of proof in court and the expected mechanism of enforcement during a business transaction. Schwartz and Waston (2004) observed that the commercial practice prefers using vague terms for more flexibility in conducting business. This is contrary to contract theory in economics, which prefers precise terms because of the less realistic assumption of costless and error-free enforcement of verifiable terms in contract theory. Schwartz and Watson (2004) adopted this assumption in their model of the trade-off between front-end investment in complex rules and back-end investment in renegotiating simple rules after uncertainty is resolved.

As we have seen, the regulatory requirements focus on identifying customers. It is an ongoing process of due diligence and monitoring of the account that involves record keeping of any changes in their identities and transactions. Notably, these rules do not explicitly request banks to obtain customers' sources of wealth, and these requirements also focus on both the customer (beneficial owner) and account level. It offers general principles of what must be collected but, in my own view, little is described as to how these rules assist the prevention of AML. Johnston and Carrington (2006) summarised the challenges faced by banks to implement AML measures, aside from the increased resources needed. They included active CDD and account monitoring, reporting of suspicious transactions, outsourcing of key functions in the KYC processes, and robust arrangement with cross-border arrangements. They further illustrated the complexity of ensuring all these measures are implemented as there were no standard practices, as each client scenario could be different. Shehu (2010) further illustrated that the implementation of FATF is constrained by a lack of resources and skilled personnel, especially in countries with weaknesses in legal institutions, a dominance of the informal sector and a cash-based economy. This creates an arbitrary opportunity to choose an easier country and institutions to handle proceeds from crime. KYC processes have been too complicated for some countries, and hence a loophole could exist, and the AML could become meaningless when criminals choose a jurisdiction with laxer requirements to launder their proceeds. Ruce (2011) observed that these basic requirements originate from both legislation and self-imposed policies by the private banks, where the latter consider their own requirements, such as whether to accept a photocopy of the documents or accept office addresses as corresponding addresses. This affects how these procedures are executed by private banks, indicating the non-existence of a unified standard specific enough for all banks to comply with (see also, Law, 2019, p. 8).

The drafting of a bank's account opening form adopts broad and vague terms when drafting the provisions. It reflects the style of the regulatory guidelines which adopt wordings such as 'appropriate and proportionate CDD', a 'balanced and common-sense approach' (section 2.12 of the Guideline), 'reliable and independent' sources (section 4.3.1 of the Guideline), and 'special provisions' (section 12.2 of the Guideline), which are examples of the broad language to be standardised among the banks. The language used to specify standards is mainly 'reasonable, specific, adequate, high, low, purposive approach' without defining the meaning of these standards in detail. These lead to diverse handling of the content to be put in the account opening forms, reflecting individual ways to interpret and fulfil these guidelines. With the broad language being adopted, as well as when HKMA issues circulars with a relative lack of details of how it was not complied with, at least in the public domain, it is difficult for the public to understand the detail sufficiently. The notices only list which clauses have been breached but not how they have been breached or where the deficiencies lie. It is not easy to find precedent in a regulator's notice. The only standard specific enough would be from the court, and yet this is only relevant to the facts associated with a specific case.

KYC is a complicated process in the client onboarding process. Account opening forms do not contain most of the usual KYC questions. For example, the forms do not require clients to submit 'corroboration' or 'proof' of SOW. Yet, bankers must be able to describe the SOW, with corroboration, to onboard a private banking client. It makes the onboarding requirement more dependent on individual bankers' judgment, and a standard checklist has limited effect, given that each client would have a different story of how they earned their first bucket of gold. It also affects how bankers collect the information. Some public figures might have appeared in the news where their SOW is publicly available or accessible. For others, we may need to make an assumption to calculate the individual's net worth. For example, if a client is an owner of a company, the net worth could be assessed by calculating the percentage of shares of the company s/he owns, of which the value is easier to identify from the stock exchange market if the company is a listed company, but this is not the case for a private company where a valuation would need to be estimated from a less objective source. There is no specific definition for what a reliable source consists of in section 4.3.1. of the Guideline.

2.4.5.2 Enforcement of contract

Different banks have different ways to enforce their contracts. It can be extremely costly for clients to enforce the terms and conditions stated in the account opening form and track which terms have been breached in the event of a dispute. Given the bank can draft its own one-sided terms, the bank can choose its own procedures in private arbitration which are not revealed to clients (Noyes, 2006, pp. 638–645) or by imposing specific rules or general standards in resolving disputes privately (Scott & Triantis, 2005, p. 822). However, a court may preclude the modified rule or render the ex-ante contract unenforceable (Noyes, 2006). Feldman and Lifshitz (2011) conducted an experimental survey of a representative panel of the Israeli population on employment practice and analysed people's behaviour in how they made decisions or how they perceived others making decisions. They factored in elements such as the intention of pattern, the profitability of enforcement, fairness of legal arrangement, jurisprudential argument, legal setting, risk, and demographics. It turns out that legal *uncertainty* could be desirable and rewarding from parties' and social perspectives. A veil of ignorance in contract design can mask parties' awareness and knowledge of the ex-post legal consequences in exchange for more flexibility in conducting business. It encourages parties to act without legal incentives. Because this veil of ignorance is restricted to specific contract types involving law that drives (a) decisions in court; (b) certain motives in a course of action; and (c) certain course of action, it has not discarded the function of the law but further justifies why vague terms are often used (Scott & Triantis, 2005).

The court might acknowledge the parties' desire to act freely outside of the contract as well. Gilson et al. (2010) looked at the braid contract, meaning a contract incorporating both formal and informal contracts. The formal contract is enforced by judicial intervention whilst the latter relies on the threat of lost reputation and expected future dealings or a taste for reciprocity. Whilst the literature treats the two strategies as separate phenomena, a rich experimental literature considers whether the introduction of formal contracting and state enforcement 'crowds out' or degrades the operation of informal contracting. Formal contracts act as a system of incentives inducing parties to perform substantive actions. Yet, it is presumed a pre-existing level of trust exists to effectively enforce the contract informally. It is executed through information-sharing mechanisms on the progress of parties' joint activities. In examining court judgments of braid contracts featuring instances of (a) technological innovation, (b) commercial ventures, and (c) corporate acquisitions where the uncertainty centres on the importance of the search for new partners, the court imposes low-powered sanctions to protect formal contractual provisions without creating potential liability that will crowd out informal contracting. Gilson argued that formal contracts should play a lower role to complement informal mechanisms to foster collaboration in unforeseen uncertainties. However, contrary to the court's attitude, parties often expand legal sanctions and undermine informal arrangements due to contemporary duties to negotiate in good faith.

Lessons learnt from specific cases would be a useful way to identify good practices. But they are not often informative. The HSBC Swiss case only indicates what is an inadequate process without defining what would be adequate. The HSBC Swiss case involves helping diamond dealers, but this does not mean that banks could not transact with any other diamond dealer. If banks opt to deal with a diamond dealer, what kind of onboarding standard should be applied? What kind of documents must one obtain for onboarding? These are important lessons learnt that the banking community should agree to, but even if agreed, it is difficult to assess whether the bank has the resources to thoroughly assess their clients, as indicated in Shehu (2010). The matter is often wider than the onboarding process alone (Law, 2019).

The relationship between the bank, client, and regulator can be understood through contractual behaviour. There are two angles of the relationship: one exists between a bank and a client through the signing of an account opening form. Another exists between a bank and regulators through licensing. How the contract between regulators and banks informally affects the contract between a bank and its clients is still to be explored. It is therefore inevitable that the rules would keep changing to fulfil the requirement of the broad guidance provided by the regulator. And therefore, despite various guidelines issued by the regulators, it is very difficult to have an objective application procedure across all banks.

2.4.5.3 Sharing of information

Only a little information related to the KYC process (name, passport number, address proof, tax declaration) is required in the account opening forms. The bank needs more information to onboard a client. Regulatory guidelines on information requirements are not specified due to the vague and generic language adopted. As we have seen, the account opening form does not facilitate the KYC process (Section 2.4.5). The information contained in the contract between clients and banks is not applicable to other banks, and the information required in the account opening form does not help the KYC process in terms of understanding the SOW.

Despite this, in the absence of a concrete rule, technology might be the answer. Moyano and Ross (2017) advocated a new system based on distributed ledger technology to reduce the costs of core KYC verification processes, as well as improve customer experiences; and customers could share such verification with all private banks to improve efficiency. This is like the Transunion in Hong Kong, where banks voluntarily submit the positive and negative credit data of their customers to a centralised platform for banking enquiries (Transunion, 2021). Banks could obtain the credit quality of the potential debtor through a system in which data is provided by all member banks. Similarly, the banks could also upload the KYC information to a common platform for other banks to retrieve. Given the potential, the concern on free-riding problem that other banks might use the data without offering their own data might hinder the bank from submitting useful information to benefit other banks, the sharing mechanism might be funded and made mandatory by the regulator, and with a service pledge performance at least banks would have a standardised turnaround time. The need to continuously monitor the customers after onboarding would also derive long-term benefits for member banks. It will not replace the bank's own assessment because the banks will still have their own assessment such as risk appetite and risk capacity, and ongoing monitoring. Digital solutions with coordinated government and industry approaches are also within the expectation of market participants, as per the Hong Kong PWMA report of 2018 advocating for an industry code of conduct. Nevertheless, these have not yet been put in place, and different banks continue to apply their own procedures (Law, 2019).

2.5 Formation of power in bank–client relationship under dispute

2.5.1 Source of bargaining power from private bank clients: Fear of floodgates

Besides the legal threat, Mr Young's case suggests that the bargaining power clients have can be used to impose the fear of a floodgate – namely an invisible reference group described in the NBC model:

> The bank wants to let all parties cool down, close the door and try to settle, but the bank has to show initiative to settle. If settlement does not work, then it will become public. At the time, the bank was very scared as well because once it is public, other customers who also signed this type of contract would know that the bank had lost. Other people would follow. There would be a chain reaction.
>
> *(Mr Young, the FX accumulator event see section 5.2.2.1, Chapter 5)*

This description fits in well with the *reference group* factor where the interactions with audiences or sponsors are different, especially when it comes to a difference between individual disputes and collective ones (Felstiner et al., 1980, p. 644). According to Mr Young, it drives the bank into two different behaviours. Either it facilitates a private settlement as soon as possible as per the risky shares event or to fight as in the FX accumulator event. In the risky shares event, Mr Young recalled that he had been chasing a response for a long time but did not get any meaningful conversation until he threatened to take legal action:

> [after the complaint] I have been chasing him monthly, he finally came back to me. But it was probably because they saw my name and their name on the newspaper. I told them that if I do not get any explanation from them, I will take legal actions as well as I believed I was the first one in HK to take legal actions against the bank.
>
> I was chasing them for about two months. After threatening them about taking legal action, I had a conference call with the manager and discussed about it, and they started looking into the recording of the conversation of the previous manager. Another month later, I rang again and started chasing them. I think they realised that is also their fault as well, but they did not word it this way.

> They worded as if, 'Yes, we have listened to the conversation and our senior management decided to compensate you for this transaction'. I have to sign some documents for the compensation plus they also introduced me to some other pretty profitable bonds at that time to trade with big discount and I was able to make my money back from the differences as well. They paid me back 80% of the trade and they recommended me to buy a very good bond that was trading at 50% and I was able to make extra money back.
>
> *(Mr Young, the FX accumulator event)*

To Mr Young, it was apparent that bringing the attention of the issue to a wider network imposed a potential threat to the reputation of the bank. The bank also asked Mr Young to sign a non-disclosure agreement upon resolution. In Mr Young's view, this means the bank wanted to quieten things down. For the FX accumulator event, the situation was very different. The bank representative fought extremely hard when meeting with Mr Young:

> They were not there to settle. They were there to tell you what you did wrong and you are liable for everything that you did, and you are liable for everything you signed. The banker involved in that incident no longer worked in the bank anymore, the one talked to me solely relied on what I had signed and just did not yield at all. I told them I did not read Chinese at all and I simply trusted the banker. Not to speak of the very small print and the many pages involved. It turned out that the most important part of the contract was written in the Chinese part.
>
> At that time, the bank was very scared as well because once it goes public, other customers that also sign this type of contract know that the bank has lost, and it has to pay for the differences. People will follow. There will be a chain reaction. Lots of customers will follow and sue the bank.
>
> *(Mr Young, the FX accumulator event)*

According to Mr Young, although he was on his own in this dispute, the external effect on his 'remedy-seeking behaviour' could create an invisible threat to the bank as the bank was likely to conduct the same practice with other clients as well. If other clients started to be aware of this claim, an individual dispute could become a collective one. The success of one case can encourage other clients in a similar situation to raise potential lawsuits. Hence, an individual complaint could create pressure on the bank to settle the matter privately or raise it to the public court to defend its position. This kills the transformation or simply escalates the incident into a formal dispute without any transformation.

Mr Young's further elaborated on how an invisible *reference group* would force the bank to settle. It is the 'fear of floodgate' – how both the clients and the bank would *react* – whilst the former would threaten the bank by bringing more alliance that the bank obviously wanted to avoid.[5] Mr Young stayed in a passive role and *reacted* to how the bank and banker handled his

5 Although banks would sometimes prefer to fight in the court to avoid a judgment against them.

grievance when he escalated the matter. He expected the bank and the banker to guide him under a proper *mechanism* and he regarded the bank itself as the *dispute institution.* Mr Young also demonstrated an *ideology* herein; instead of legislating morality, the only purpose for him to proceed was to get his money back. It is such that he can continue to engage with the bank but would no longer trust the banker. These *complicated* and somehow conflicting thoughts aligned with Mr Peterson's action, who in the end still avoid the formation of a dispute despite a strong grievance.

After all, the clients would still need to use the private bank, as it is unlikely that the private bank needs the client. The regulators are likely to respect the bank's decision (Chapter 3, Section 3.5.4). The only way to form power is to create a possible floodgate situation with other clients through publicity.

2.5.2 The influence of third parties in a bank–customer relationship: bankers and regulator

The influence of a lawyer has been presumed because disputants usually think of engaging a lawyer. It is unclear whether lawyers and non-lawyers would make different considerations and hence offer different advice in choosing a dispute resolution platform. It is often perceived that a lawyer's value is often valued by the disputants due to their professional roles, their conduct, their natural position as repeated players in the legal platform, and their better understanding of the legal process (Sternlight, 2002). This can be contrasted with non-lawyers who are perceived to be unsophisticated in legal concepts and unfamiliar with the legal process, and hence to them, the prior knowledge of accepted conventions or expected outcomes might not be considered. This may not necessarily apply to private banking clients because they do have the resources and access to legal recourse given their extraordinary wealth. Many are entrepreneurs and have their own in-house lawyers for their businesses (Dezalay & Garth, 1996). In this thesis, lawyers appear to create a real impact on the relationship between banks and clients.

In the usual private banking setting, the power play consists of three parties: the regulator, banks, and private banking clients. The regulators set up the rules for banks to comply with, supervise their operations, and conduct necessary investigations to ensure banks comply with regulations. Banks are accountable to regulators, as a failure to comply with their rules will result in a penalty which in turn damages their much-needed reputation. Private banking clients are customers who engage with the bank; for example, they deposit money with the bank, transact through their channels, borrow money, and obtain investment advice. They are the users of the service governed by the regulators. Banks are the intermediaries who need to fulfil the regulatory requirements set by the regulators and also their clients' requests. Banks must provide services within the regulatory framework. Among these three parties, they are represented by bankers who are the first line of defence in both attracting new businesses and complying with the regulatory requirements. The behaviour of bankers is extremely vital. This leads to the need to re-examine the conceptions between a professional and a layperson because a decision made by someone using their own resources might be different from using a company's resources. The decision made when a banker supervises his/her direct reports might be different than when the same banker is advising his/her own clients.

This echoes the judgment in *Woods v Martins Bank Ltd [1959]*, in which Salmon J observed that the definition of bank presents a limit on what a banker gives advice on in relation to financial matters, which constitutes a banking business. In *Woods v Martins Bank Ltd [1959]*, Salmon J described: 'a banker's business cannot be laid down as a matter of law. The nature of such a business must in each case be a matter of fact'. The purpose of that judgment was to allow for more flexibility in defining a banking business such that it will not be restricted by the name of the organisation. Yet, it might not have considered the dynamics added when bankers are involved. Bankers might not act according to the contract but the ambiguity of its duties, which are not stated in the contract, could create further complications in laying blame, hence leading to dispute formation (Chapter 5, Section 5.5).

2.5.3 Take it, leave it, or shame it?

Banks might prefer the complainant to simply close the account to avoid a bigger crisis. If clients accept the explanation or compensation proposed by the bank, it may lead to injustice as the bank may not need to face their wrongdoing. Clients might want to leave the bank to have a fresh start. Matters might be better off being left unresolved. In my own experience related to a complaint made to the bank, once I ceased being a client the bank did not seem to be obliged to address my concerns anymore until I made another complaint through the HKMA (Chapter 3, Section 3.5.3). In an actual dispute situation between clients and banks, clients would want to leave the bank to regard it as a threat. But if the threat is realised, then the bank would no longer be fearful of losing the client, as it has now become a reality. The bank could just move on and find new clients. This could be better understood through the concept of power balance between banks and clients.

The power imbalance between private banks and private banking clients in establishing the legal relationship should be understood as what choice clients have: accept the bank's explanation and carry on the relationship, continue with the negotiation, sue the bank, or close the account. This reality is usually incorporated into any mediation process, but it appears that none of these options impacts the bank as a whole. After all, it is just one client among many clients. Despite many advantages mentioned, this form of informal justice could be 'ineffectual and incapable of compensating for the ineffective bargaining position of the individual' (Singer, 1979). It renders mediation for consumer disputes inappropriate (Nader, 1980). It would also lead to 'second class justice' (Menkel-Meadow, 1999). The asymmetries would lead to inbuilt power inequalities and ultimately make consumers dissatisfied (Ali, 2013). The focus in private banking is different. Private banking clients cannot be regarded as being on the weaker side in terms of legal access, and their transaction size and potential claims could mean that financially it may be meaningful to start a legal claim, but in terms of their available options should the negotiation fail, they are likely to be on the weaker side because clients will then realise they can only take it or leave it because of the unfavourable position brought to them by the one-sided contract.

Whilst a power imbalance also comes from perception (Waldman, 2011), clients might impose pressure on the bank by leaving the bank. It appears to be the best way to shame the bank to vote on the foot, but as we will see in Section 3.5.3 in Chapter 3, the bank will unlikely be harmed by your vote of no confidence but instead may be benefited by your exit because the bank's duty would also end upon your departure. Yet this route could be further distorted by the involvement of private bankers who might take a personal stake in this relationship. They might make more effort than the actual intent of the bank. Therefore, the dynamic in this issue is often fact-based and difficult to generalise. Clients gain bargaining power through the threat of exiting the relationship, but it is unlikely to impact the bank as a whole if they really exit. More likely it impacts the bankers who need the relationship more than that of the bank, which makes the bankers more influential in the dispute transformation process.

2.5.4 Before the disputing process

Different classes might have different factors impacting their ability to gain an equal footing in a dispute resolution process, and they are difficult to summarise or generate. In different types of disputes, such as employment (Estlund, 2017) and divorce (Ellis, 2022), and considering different groups of people in areas such as gender, nature of work, race, gender identity, geography, and occupational position, there appears to be no stable way to define a variable, and there are different patterns and reasons for not engaging (Silbey, 2005, p. 351). For example, lower-paid workers may fear retaliation (Fritz-Mauer, 2022). Engel (2016) suggests the eight patterns that describe the social, political, and cultural environment which are embedded in the legal sense (Engel, 2016, pp. 70, 90). They are due to three major reasons. The first relates to negative experiences (Engel, 2016, pp. 73–75). The second relates to the limited role of regulation in only prevention but not compensation (pp. 188, 190). The third relates to the emotional experience of being a victim and even self-blame (Silbey, 2005, p. 351). Hence, the dispute resolution institutions being mandated to handle particular types of disputes may not help the disputants at all because it is only the institution that has the expertise and experience, not the disputants. In the case studies, the bank has a definite advantage in a dispute resolution process because they can control the process which does not have to be disclosed to the clients.

The example of the class of the wealthy, represented by the private banking clients, sometimes appears to share the same pattern as the other classes, although it is difficult to generalise and compare. Firstly, they have the financial means to pursue a claim and thus have a real option to submit a claim, but instead they may lump those potential claims, and it happens before any dispute has occurred as if they had predicted it would happen. The clients seem to have predicted disputes likely to arise because clients are not prepared to be bound by the contract in all events. Clients appear to impose another set of rules where they are prepared to engage their private bankers who will execute the transactions for them. Two sets of rules are formed: an informal rule which is dictated by clients' preference and executed by the private bankers, and the formal rule which is required by regulators. In fact, people still engage with the law but just the informal law, which slightly extends the usual legal consciousness debate where people do not engage with the law due to all the limitations associated (Silbey, 2005, p. 353).

Secondly, there is the scope that expands from tortious claims to contractual claims. Lumping happens before any perceived or unperceived injurious experience has occurred. It appears to confirm the notion that an attempt to gain power through law would make one feel powerless (Silbey, 2005, p. 352), and it appears to be particularly true in a one-sided contract like private banking because the more the clients rely on the law (i.e., contracts), the more they find the law unable to help them. This emotional experience is further worsened by the fact that there is nothing clients can do to fit their own needs, but they must use the banking services offered to them. It also creates a perception that banks could never be on the wrong side of the law and regulations, and therefore making a complaint to the bank is unreasonable, as it is simply the bank's own discretion, as evidenced by Ms Emily (Section 5.4.1, Chapter 5). In this case, banks do not have advantages because they are the repeated players (Galanter, 1974) but rather the advantage to make their own law, especially when the regulation available to the public is mainly drafted based on principles (Section 2.3.2.1, Chapter 2), and it is difficult for clients to identify their wrong without engaging external help.

Whilst the bank might have repeated player advantages as they are presumed to deal with numerous complaints and have the experience, the real issue seems to be the ineffectiveness of the law (e.g., Sarat, 1985), caused by both substantive and procedural issues. The lack of a formal legal relationship that clients truly intend to be bound by is the core of the substantive defects. The lack of transparency is the core of the procedural defects, as clients have no rules to read when engaged in a dispute resolution process with the bank. There is no other way to experience and understand the law by ordinary people – wealthy or not. It makes any legal action rather high risk, and therefore clients give up. Mr Young is an example, and he gave up because of the fatigue involved with the internal process, and hence an external one is a definite no for him (see also Section 5.2.2, Chapter 5).

It turns out that the wealthier one is, the more likely he is to give up or to endure their unsatisfaction (to lump) if the dispute is just about money, for this is exactly what they do not lack.

2.6 Conclusion: Lack of specific laws and regulations for private banking

Private banks are a business segment of a bank that only serve a small group of professional investors defined under section 5 of the Securities and Futures (Professional Investor) Rule, where clients have more than HK$8 million or more in their bank accounts. The importance of private banks in Hong Kong has been well recognised by the HKMA, and hence specific regulatory requirements to govern private banks have been imposed. Whilst the regulatory framework for private banking is largely identical to that of normal banks, the relationship between private banks and their clients has been featured by a more strengthened 'know your client' requirement for client onboarding, underpinning portfolio risk management and imposing a specific code of conduct for private bankers.

This chapter revisited how this legal relationship is defined, formed, and executed through contract formation between a bank and its clients, and observed how different banks have fulfilled the regulatory requirements through the different fields required in their account opening forms. It contains a comparative analysis of the law and regulatory framework on private banking in selected jurisdictions and a contextual analysis of the account opening forms of three international private banks operating in Hong Kong to illustrate the phenomenon that the legal relationship between private banking clients and private banks does not rely solely on the one-sided contracts signed between them. It explains how differences in the context of account opening forms, unclear enforcement efforts of contractual clauses, and different information provided imply a weak legal contractual foundation to facilitate ADR mechanisms and provide the background to sub-research question 1 by laying down possible sources of power imbalances. It concludes by describing the factors that form power for the private banking client–private bank relationship, the role of third parties (particularly the private banker), and the 'take it or leave it' attitude by both clients and banks.

Notably, the content in the account opening form is only a small part of a more complete picture. A contextual analysis of the account opening forms and other regulatory guidelines shows that whilst there is sufficient information provided to private banking clients to establish a legal relationship, it appears that they do not meet the entire client onboarding requirements. Rather, the account opening form serves as a notification to clients of what the bank will offer and a request made to clients to acknowledge and understand the scope of banking services. The language adopted in the account opening form is rather broad. It implies that the banks are more willing to spend resources at the 'back-end' to enforce the contract by issuing more contracts on specific services. The codes of conduct and guidelines issued by regulators have not been incorporated in the one-sided contracts drafted by the bank. All this has created room for different banks to apply different procedures even if they are subject to the same laws and regulations. This creates legal uncertainty in the relationship between private banks and their clients, and facilitates the regulation of business transactions and the resolution of disputes.

All these might have imposed hurdles for clients to name their grievances. Clients might find it hard to file a complaint against the bank due to the lack of precedent or comparable references to support their claims. A power imbalance has been created since formation of a one-sided contract. There is no consistent interpretation of proper practice commonly accepted and made available to clients. Whilst legal uncertainty seems to offer parties flexibility, it may come at the expense of weakening clients' bargaining power, which does not seem to facilitate the use of arbitration to resolve disputes. The factors affecting clients' perceptions of their power are negatively impacted by (a) scattered sources of law and regulations governing the bank; (b) the account opening form, which does not fully cover all of the legal relationships between the bank and the client; and (c) different bank practices on the same set of laws and regulations. These features do not seem to offer a proper legal foundation for arbitration, which could explain why arbitration is underutilised (research question 3). The preference of the regulatory system for the internal resolution of disputes appears to further create a negative perception of the use of arbitration. This will be further explored in Chapter 3.

CHAPTER 3

Arbitration and dispute resolution for banks in Hong Kong

3.1 Introduction: Internationalisation of the dispute-resolution process

Clients can file a complaint with the HKMA if their disputes are not resolved with the banks directly. Upon receiving the complaint, the HKMA will follow up on each case by requiring the bank concerned to handle the complaint properly and provide a reply to the complainant without interfering in the bank's commercial decisions. The HKMA will not intervene or adjudicate upon the disputes, nor order the bank to pay compensation. The information received by the HKMA in the complaint-handling process may uncover supervisory or disciplinary issues which require follow-up action, including opening an investigation and considering supervisory and disciplinary actions (Hong Kong Monetary Authority, 2021). The HKMA has requested that banks to establish their own internal processes to handle customer complaints (Chapter 2, Section 2.3.2). It is therefore essential to explore whether these institutional and regulatory approaches have replaced other informal out-of-court processes. These informal processes include negotiation, mediation, and arbitration.

Chapter 3 examines the main regulations governing the dispute-resolution mechanisms for banks in Hong Kong as stipulated in the Code of Banking Practice, the HKMA Supervisory Manual (IC-4 – Handling Complaint Procedure) and the HKMA online complaints channel. These regulations are compared to the following arbitration rules of different arbitration centres: the FDRC which provides the Financial Dispute Resolution Scheme (FDRS) Mediation and Arbitration Rules under the FDRC, and arbitral rules adopted by the FIDReC, the CIETAC, P.R.I.M.E., and HKIAC. These institutions are selected as they claimed to have arbitration procedures catered specifically for financial disputes. A specific focus has been placed on FDRC given the scope of this thesis' focuses on Hong Kong. The comparison is made for two purposes: to study any similarities and differences, and to identify potential survey and interview questions for the empirical studies.

Chapter 3 explores the notion that should existing regulatory frameworks be able to handle private banking disputes, a dispute-resolution mechanism

DOI: 10.4324/9781003407591-3

outside the banking industry would not be necessary. It addresses mainly the sub-research questions relating to utilisation: arbitration might not be utilised because it has already been incorporated into the bank's internal complaint-handling procedures, hence the under-utilisation of banking disputes. The under-utilisation of arbitration in private banking disputes might be due to the fact that the FDRC does not include private banking disputes by setting a low maximum claimable amount.

3.2 ADR mechanism for banks in Hong Kong

3.2.1 ADR for banking and finance in a global context

It is vital to first acknowledge the relevant global standards and principles that guide financial regulators in Hong Kong when setting regulations, including the resolution of consumer financial disputes.

First are the Equator Principles. This is a financial industry benchmark for determining, assessing, and managing social and environmental risk in project financing (Equator Principles, 2021). It requires a grievance mechanism to be established under Principle 6, which allows the borrower to receive and facilitate the resolution of concerns and grievances.

Second are the UN Guidelines for Consumer Protection, which address the right to redress; the right to information; the right to consumer education; and the right to representation. Member states should implement consumer protection laws, standards, guidelines, and practices at the national level (United Nations, 2016). Businesses should also

> make available complaints-handling mechanisms that provide consumers with expeditious, fair, transparent, inexpensive, accessible, speedy and effective dispute resolution without unnecessary cost or burden. Businesses should consider subscribing to domestic and international standards pertaining to internal complaints handling, ADR services and customer satisfaction codes.
>
> *(United Nations, 2016, part IV 11(f))*

Third, the Basel Accords handle consumer financial disputes through the prevention of market failure by requiring transparency in terms of risk disclosure and providing adequate capital reserves on the part of banking institutions which are essential to prevent another financial crisis and hence another series of disputes (Bank for International Settlements, 2019, pp. 1232–1517). Supervisory triggers must be made for repeated disputes, for example, if a bank has experienced more than two margin call disputes, then the bank must make a record (e.g., pp. 502–503, 526–527, 533).

Fourth, a similar effort to prevent financial disputes can also be found in the UN Millennium Development Goals, with one of the goals to 'develop further an open, rule-based, predictable, non-discriminatory trading and financial system' (The Millennium Development Goals and Beyond, 2015).

This responds to the rising inequality between institutions and individuals that leads to an unstable financial system that is vulnerable to external economic shocks, hence prone to disputes.

Additionally, some key fundamental principles of natural justice such as impartiality, fairness, transparency, and consistency guide the design, development, and regulation of dispute-resolution mechanisms globally, including in Hong Kong (Ali, 2013).

The Lehman crisis in 2009 revealed that the public adjudication system has a major weakness in its ability to cope with high numbers of complainants, as observed by Arner et al. (2010). However, clients making complaints to regulators or other intermediaries may face their own problems. First, the different fact-finding processes between an adversarial system and an inquisitorial process will result in information imbalance. Second, there is a lack of transparency, speediness, and predictability, often resulting in inconsistent judgments and hence varied rates of compensation. Making complaints to a bank directly may not work either: there exists a disparity between the settlements offered by intermediaries and by banks. In the Lehman settlements, bank customers only received 60 to 70% of the amount they had invested, whilst customers of intermediaries received their full settlement. Therefore, introducing a class action process to facilitate collective efforts against a bank directly or through regulators might not be a solution. ADR should be considered, even though the private banking industry as its client group is most capable of commencing litigation in court.

3.2.2 Guidance from regulators on handling customer complaints

3.2.2.1 Code of banking practice

The Code of Banking Practice, issued jointly by The Hong Kong Association of Banks and the DTC Association, is an industry association endorsed by the HKMA (Hong Kong Association of Banks, 2021). AIs, their subsidiaries, and affiliated institutions dealing with and providing services to their customers are to observe these codes on a voluntary basis. Despite its voluntary nature, the HKMA expects institutions to comply with these practices and monitors and supervises them in accordance with the Code (The Hong Kong Association of Banks, 2021).

There are eight general principles laid down in the Code of Banking Practice, with some related to the handling of customer complaints. Under the general principles of 'Equitable and Fair Treatment of Customers' customers must be treated 'equitably, honestly and fairly at all stages of their relationship' (The Hong Kong Association of Banks, 2021, para. 2.1), whilst general principles of 'Disclosure and Transparency' state that 'appropriate information should be provided at all stages of the relationship with the customers' (The Hong Kong Association of Banks, 2021, para. 2.2). The 'stages' mentioned in these two principles include complaint-handling stages. Explicitly under the general principles 'Complaints-Handling and Redress', institutions and their authorised agents should

> provide customers with reasonable channels to submit claims, make complaints, and seek redress that are accessible, fair, accountable, timely, and efficient. Such channels should not impose unreasonable costs, delays or burdens on customers [to submit claims, make complaints and seek redress].
>
> *(The Hong Kong Association of Banks, 2021, para. 2.7)*

There are seven chapters under the Code of Banking Practice, covering accounts and loans, card services, payment services, recovery of loans and advances, electronic banking services, and stored value cards (or devices). In the 'Relationship between Institutions and Customers', section 13 of the Code of Banking Practice, there is mention of how to handle customer complaints, with four principles quoted below:

> Handling Customer Complaints
>
> 13.1. Institutions should establish procedures for handling customer complaints in a fair and speedy manner. The complaint procedures should take into account the following criteria –
>
> (a) transparency – the applicable procedures should be documented;
> (b) accessibility – the procedures should be easily invoked by customers; and
> (c) effectiveness – the procedures should provide for the speedy resolution of disputes in a fair and equitable manner.
>
> 13.2. Details of how to invoke complaint procedures should be made available to customers and other interested parties such as personal referees and guarantors so that they know what steps to take if they wish to make a complaint. Institutions are encouraged to make available details of how to invoke complaint procedures in tape recording or in Braille for the visually-impaired.
>
> 13.3. Institutions should ensure that all their staff who deal directly with customers are made aware of the complaint procedures and are able to help customers by giving correct information about these procedures.
>
> 13.4. Institutions should send an acknowledgment to the complainant within 7 days upon receiving a written complaint (where the complaint cannot be resolved within 7 days) and a written response to the complaint within a reasonable period, normally not exceeding 30 days. Correspondence with the complainant should be sent in Chinese or English in accordance with the language of the complaint.
>
> *(The Hong Kong Association of Banks, 2021, paras. 13.1–13.4)*

The Code of Banking Practice has the following features which might impact a customer's perception of whether they should rely on the bank's internal processes to resolve disputes.

First, there is no requirement for banks to disclose what the banks shall do once the complaint procedure is invoked. The three criteria of the complaint procedures, namely transparency, accessibility, and effectiveness, appear to only encourage the bank to actively attend to any complaint received and resolve it promptly. Section 13.2 and 13.3 further elaborate that it is important for banks to assist customers to make a complaint to the banks. However, there is no requirement for the banks to disclose how they will process the complaints, what kind of documents they will investigate, who they will interview, what kind of information customers should provide, who will look into the complaints, etc. This can be contrasted to the arbitral rules (to be further evaluated in Section 3.5.1), where detailed procedures and requirements such as submission requirements, selection of an arbitrator, and availability of appeal are listed. In the Code of Banking Practice, there are no such procedures that need to be disclosed to a customer who makes a complaint.

Second, besides ensuring accessibility to the complaint channel stipulated in sections 13.2 and 13.3, the focus appears to be on the turnaround time. Under 13.4, it is stated that banks must acknowledge receipt of a complaint within seven days of receiving a written complaint, and complaints must be responded to in a reasonable timeframe, usually within 30 days. If read in conjunction with the prior three sections (13.1, 13.2, and 13.3), the focus of the Code of Banking Practice on complaint-handling seems to rest on banks accepting complaints and responding to clients. Only 13.1 (c) requests the bank to provide speedy resolution of disputes in a fair and equitable manner. But there is no requirement as to how complaints should handle the complaints procedurally, and such procedure is not disclosed to customers either. There is no description of how the substance of the complaints should be handled. To validate this observation, the researcher incorporated his first-hand experience of escalating a complaint on bank charges, arguably violating Principle 5 of The Treat Customer Fairly Charter. For the purposes of this section, it is clear that the bank is likely to keep responding to clients' complaints as long as they write back saying they are not satisfied with the response. It is unclear when a complainant is able to submit a complaint directly to the HKMA.

Third, there is no mention of any appeal mechanism for customers if they are not satisfied with the outcome of the complaint. There is no indication as to whether a complaint is handled up to standard. Unlike some arbitral rules which state whether there are provisions stipulating whether an appeal mechanism is available, the bank customers could persist with the same complaints if they are not satisfied with the complaints.

To give an example to help visualise the above through an actual observation experienced by the researcher, I made a complaint about a bank service to the HKMA. The complaint related to the excessive time required to complete a simple transaction involving moving a sum of money from a current account to a fixed deposit account under the same account holder. This should have been a five-minute operation, but it took bank staff 45 minutes to execute. I questioned whether the staff involved in the transaction had received proper training and therefore were 'fit and proper' to conduct banking services, as they had arguably not complied with the HKMA SPM (Competence and Ethical Behaviour), such as section 1.5 where AIs should ensure the 'competence... of their staff' (Hong Kong Monetary Authority, 2017). Once the complaint was submitted to the HKMA, HKMA wrote back and requested that I allow the bank to resolve the situation by themselves first. The exact wording they applied was

> After a preliminary review of the relevant information, we considered it appropriate for the Bank to handle your complaint first in order to give it the chance to resolve your complaint at an early stage
>
> *(email communication with HKMA, 23 June 2021)*

It appears to be rather emotional as the HKMA implore me to 'give it the chance' to resolve my complaint with the bank directly, yet it indicates HKMA's strong preference to encourage customers to directly handle their complaints with the bank, and the bank will always cater to their customer enquiries but lack of guidance as to when they can stop responding or whether customers should accept the response from the bank. My first-hand experience in making a complaint directly with the bank has created a hassle. This would also be the case when the issues are complicated and cannot be resolved by offering monetary compensation to the clients.

3.2.2.2 Internal complaint-handling procedures within banks

Section 7 of the BO states that the HKMA has the function to take all reasonable steps to ensure banks are operated in a responsible, honest, and business-like manner, to promote and encourage proper standards of conduct, and to suppress illegal, dishonourable or improper practices (*Banking Ordinance*). Paragraph 10 of the Seventh Schedule of the BO requires banks to have adequate accounting systems and systems of control, whilst paragraph 12 requires banks to conduct their business with integrity, competence and in a manner that is not detrimental to the interests of depositors and potential depositors.

The HKMA has issued SPM – Complaint-Handling Procedures (IC-4) to provide guidance on specific procedures to handle complaints in relation to personal and small business customers specifically (Hong Kong Monetary Authority, 2002). IC-4 has been issued to fulfil the requirement under section 7 of the BO, to ensure that effective arrangements to handle customer complaints reflect whether the AIs have satisfied the requirements of paras 10 and 13 of the Seventh Schedule. Similar to the Code of Banking Practice, IC-4 focuses on procedures and provides key elements that should be in the overall complaint management systems. It is observed that five out of the seven general principles of an effective complaint management system are focused on procedural matters. These elements including comprehensiveness in the coverage, transparency, making it accessible and easy to invoke, making it fair and impartial as possible between both parties, ensuring it is consistent with the approach to the provision of redress, flexible, simple, efficient with appropriate and measurable minimum performance standards, and the ability to provide appropriate feedback to the regulator (i.e., the HKMA). The provisions focus on the turnaround time (section 3), record keeping (section 4) cooperation with the HKMA and other complaint-handling organisations, as well as the need to respond promptly and offer assistance (section 5).

Arguably, two of the principles are more procedural in nature, requiring the bank to ensure fairness and impartiality between customers/complainants and AIs, including their staff. It also requests that banks provide appropriate feedback, meaning that the response should be reasonable. The most relevant guidance which might contribute to the procedural fairness of a complaint might come from section 2.5 of the IC-4, which states that the bank must involve an employee who was not directly involved in the original matter to investigate, and persons subject to the complaints or responding to the complaints would not have the authority to settle. Complaints must have a channel to the personal attention of senior management of the bank, and responses to the complaint should offer appropriate redress (Hong Kong Monetary Authority, 2002). It is also specifically stated that redress may not always involve a financial element (e.g., an apology) but if it does, interest should be considered. Also, section 4.2 requests AIs to keep records for inspection and reporting.

The issues associated with the Code of Banking Practice described in Section 3.2.2.1 of this chapter continue to exist. There is no requirement for disclosure of how the banks handle the complaints, instead focus has been placed on turnaround time and accessibility to the complaint channels, with little detail on the recourse mechanism should the dispute-handling process fail. HKMA appears to be relatively hands-off in the exact details of how these procedures should be implemented. In one HKMA circular back in July 2002, not long after IC-4 was issued, it was made clear that banks should always try to resolve their disputes through their own internal procedures before referring to the HKMA. It appears that the HKMA will not intervene in the bank's decision-making process, even when it comes to complaints that may breach the regulatory requirements.

The HKMA seems to position itself at the back-end by supervising inspections and requesting banks to cooperate fully. But it is unclear as to what the HKMA will do to ensure all complaints have been handled appropriately, at least in the documents publicly available to the public. The rule-maker will regularly inspect a bank's full cooperation (e.g., the bank must reply to

HKMA's investigation within 30 days), but without the standards being made publicly accessible to the public, it appears insufficient to only lay down the key elements and what the HKMA expects to see under the system created by the bank alone.

Lastly, and perhaps more notably, there are no instructions on how to handle complaints relating to a bank. Technically, not every employee in the bank will be in a position to address those questions because under section 2.5.1 of IC-4, everyone will be directly involved because it may concern the general operations of the bank, and no one will have the authority to investigate or to settle on behalf of the bank when it is the subject matter of the complaint. The complaint-handling procedures assume that every complaint made to the bank might be event-driven and must be connected to a particular department or person, hence it is possible to find an independent party within the bank who is able to objectively investigate the matter. This assumption might not be entirely accurate, and it seems to be a loophole inherent within the rules. For example, if a bank has decided to close a branch and the affected stakeholders launch a complaint, it is very likely that the issues involve a general societal concern rather than a bank compliance issue.

3.2.2.3 HKMA complaint channel

HKMA can identify potential breaches of regulatory requirements through complaints in the following two manners: first through an inspection of the record kept by the bank; and second through clients making a complaint through the HKMA complaint channel. Banks are required to put in place appropriate and effective mechanisms and procedures to handle customer complaints about their banking products or services, making sure that individual cases are followed up in a fair and expeditious manner. If a customer considers that a bank has not handled his/her case properly, s/he can make a complaint to the bank concerned or to the HKMA against the bank concerned (Hong Kong Monetary Authority, 2002, section 5.2.2).

With the HKMA being vested with a duty to ensure that all banks have proper procedures to handle customers' complaints, bank customers could seek assistance from the HKMA. The process is as follows: clients can file a complaint to the HKMA against the bank should clients experience trouble in resolving their disputes. Then, HKMA can require the banks to handle the complaint properly. If the HKMA believes that the complaint raises issues of supervisory concern that may breach the Code of Banking Practice or other relevant codes, then it may launch an open investigation and the bank could face potential supervisory and disciplinary actions. The HKMA commits a performance pledge of acknowledging receipts of a complaint within five working days, a preliminary response in ten working days and a reply to related enquiries in fifteen working days. However, the HKMA cannot interfere with a bank's commercial decision, adjudicate or intervene in a dispute between a bank and its customers or order a bank to pay compensation. The HKMA will follow up on each complaint case, and require the bank concerned to handle the complaint properly and provide a reply to the complainant. The information received by the HKMA in handling a complaint may assist in identifying issues of supervisory or disciplinary concern that require follow-up action, including opening an investigation and considering supervisory and disciplinary actions. Similar requirements are also found in the Code of Banking Practice which requests that banks have transparent, accessible, and effective complaint procedures, meaning that banks must acknowledge a complaint within seven days of receiving a written complaint and a written response to the complaint must be done within 30 days (Hong Kong Association of Banks, 2021, section 13 and 13.4).

The HKMA seems to intervene less than what is vested in the BO. For example, the BO states in section 7(b) that the HKMA should take all reasonable steps to ensure the business is operated in a responsible, honest, and business-like manner, however, the complaint procedure issued by the HKMA states that it cannot interfere with a bank's commercial decision. It is unclear how the HKMA could take meaningful and reasonable steps if it does not have the authority to interfere. There are other issues concerning this complaint procedure. For example, the HKMA failed to handle the high number of complaints that rose during the Lehman crisis (Arner et al., 2012). It lacks the commercial incentive for clients to spend time and resources just to provide evidence for the HKMA to pursue regulatory sanctions instead of ordering compensation to clients (Ali & Kwok, 2010). Hence the perceptions of private banking clients around the HKMA complaint procedure are relevant and will be examined, addressing the questions inspired by literature such as whether clients perceive that filing a complaint with the HKMA will create a more 'level-playing field' between banks and clients. (Galanter, 1974). Will the HKMA play a mediator role for the parties in this complaint process? (Mayer, 1987). These issues require an exploration of how private banking clients perceive such processes when the HKMA has no power to order compensation (Hong Kong Monetary Authority, 2002). The interview questions that were drafted to address the above three questions are listed in Annex I.

3.2.3 Synthesis of existing complaint-handling system

The three guidelines appear to perform the same function of ensuring banks resolve their disputes in their own ways. This means that banks can do whatever they find proper to resolve a conflict and do not need to explain to the clients how their complaints will be resolved. This arguably creates uncertainty for the complainants.

The regulatory preference for clients to resolve disputes internally is clear. Other than the Basel Requirements (Section 3.2.1, Chapter 3), the World Bank Technical Note clearly indicates that dispute resolution with the bank should be an ecosystem consisting of both internal and external elements. The World Bank Technical Note, namely the Complaints-Handling within Financial Service Providers: Principles, Practices, and Regulatory Approaches (World Bank, 2019), offers a definition of a complaint and respective requirements for internal dispute resolution (p. 2). However, from the response of the 112 jurisdictions, different jurisdictions impose different requirements. Particularly, only half of the respondents indicate the complaints data will be reported to the government agency and will provide customers with the details of a relevant alternative dispute-resolution mechanism (p. 3), and these two requirements are not explicit in HK. In Hong Kong, the reporting is initiated by HKMA (section 4.2.2, Hong Kong Monetary Authority, 2002); in the UK, there is no mentioning of reporting under the DISP 1.3 Complaints-handling rules issued by the Financial Conduct Authority; whilst in China, it is a requirement under Article 9 of the Financial Advisers (Complaints-Handling and Resolution) Regulations 2021 and Article 26 of the Order No. 5 [2020] of the People's Bank of China (Implementation Measures of the People's Bank of China for Financial Consumer Protection). For those regulators who operate a website for clients to lodge their complaints, they will direct complainants to do so only if they cannot resolve the disputes with the bank (Section 2.3, Chapter 2).

Despite a clear mandate to first internally resolve a dispute, the bank is not duty-bound to disclose how it resolves disputes. Common disclosures are usually confined to the turnaround time, implementation of independent procedures, and record keeping. Therefore, different banks will have different disclosure practices. For example, the review of the annual report of Bank A, Bank B, and Bank C at the group level shows that different banks have different standards of disclosure. Bank A revealed more data on the number of complaints received at each business segment including wealth and personal banking, and explained the nature of the complaints and described the procedure of how it resolves those complaints (pp. 70, 370, Bank A, 2021). Bank C only reports high-level information relating to the nature of the complaints received in the Group annual report the nature of the complaints received (pp. 333–335, Bank C, 2021a). The Group of Bank B makes no mention other than the assertion that it is one of their targets to reduce the number of customers at their call centre in the 2021 report (p. 30, Bank B, 2021). The regulators do not have consistent disclosure requirements on bank complaints: for example, HKMA will report the number of complaints received and handled but the Monetary Authority of Singapore will not. It is posited that the lack of control in the complaint-handling process and disclosure requirements might be a global norm and therefore clients have no idea what procedures they must undertake.

The uncertainty arises from a lack of control in the complaint-handling process, and this appears to link back to the existing literature that explains the disadvantages associated with ADR. For example, clients lack the *information and expert knowledge* (Waldman, 2011) to participate in the complaint-handling process, and clients do not have the power to influence through their *behaviour, motions*, or through the *course of the event* (Mayer, 1987) except for when they submit their complaints. The next step is already the judgment. The only influencing power is the fact that banks are obliged to respond to clients' complaints. If clients are not satisfied with the reply, the bank must continue to respond. However, neither the bank nor the HKMA is able to change existing laws and regulations. Therefore, if banks could really act in accordance with the rules and regulations, which are written in board languages, then there is little the clients can do. This clearly forms a power imbalance that *negatively influences the settlements* created in private informal dispute-resolution processes (Fiss, 1984). This informal process means that the '*weaker party has to choose between two unfavorable outcomes...* increases the power differentials, it should probably not be used' (Mayer, 1987). The two outcomes seem to be, on the one hand, to continue to proceed against the rules that clients might not know too well, or on the other hand, to accept the findings investigated by another department.

In the complaint-handling process, there are factors that impact the perception of powers. They include *resources, merits in the eyes of the law, moral conviction, personal traits*, and the *ability to inflict pain or irritation and perception.* But factors such as *access to resources and repeat experiences in the process* (Galanter, 1974) are not too relevant given the available resources that could have been spent. The only question is whether the clients want to devote resources to these aspects.

3.3 The under-utilisation of ADR in resolving banking disputes in Hong Kong

3.3.1 Lehman Brothers collapse and adoption of ADR in resolving finance disputes

The arbitration process is a private and confidential process normally conducted in accordance with an agreement between two parties, where disputants select their own arbitrator, who is usually an independent and impartial expert in the field relating to the dispute. S/he will act as a 'judge' to decide the dispute based on the merits of the case, whose decision is made in a final and binding arbitral award. The arbitration process is very similar to that of litigation, except that arbitration is a private process through an arbitrator mutually appointed by disputants, whilst litigation is a public legal process in which the parties resort to the relevant platform court (including the Market

Misconduct Tribunal) for the settlement of disputes, without a choice of who adjudicates (FDRC, 2021a).

The use of arbitration within the Hong Kong banking industry has not been widely adopted. This is despite the success of the Lehman Brothers-related Investment Product Disputes Mediation and Arbitration Scheme, sponsored by the HKMA, which triggered a vast number of consumer complaints and disputes in Hong Kong, many of which related to loss of money from investments in Lehman Brothers' products, in particular the infamous Minibonds where customers alleged that investments had been mis-sold by banks. Besides the Minibonds, other financial products such as accumulators and other complex structured products were also at the centre of disputes among the wealthier group of customers. HKMA received 21,770 complaints, with 246 being referred to the Securities and Futures Commission for further investigation. Being unable to handle this vast number of complaints, HKMA sponsored the Lehman Brothers-related Investment Product Disputes Mediation and Arbitration Scheme in October 2008 to handle settlement amounts ranging from HKD40,000 to over HKD5 million. The first mediation case was successfully concluded on 10 December 2008 and lasted for five hours, with an overall 88% success rate (Soo et al., 2010). It should be noted that there were no cases of arbitration in the Lehman Brothers-related Investment Product Disputes Mediation and Arbitration Scheme (Hong Kong Monetary Authority, 2008). The aftermath proposal for establishing an 'Ombudsman for Financial Services' put forward both by the HKMA and SFC in 2008 has not yet been adopted.

Instead, the FDRC was established in 2011 with an initial settlement threshold of HK$500k, later increased in 2016 to HK$1m, as opposed to the initial proposal of HK$3m (FDRC, 2021b). This literally, although not written, excludes all disputes arising from private banks, where the transaction threshold (i.e., investment size) is usually HK$1.6 million according to the researcher's experience. As an FDRC member, a bank must respond to a client's request for mediation, whilst banks have no right to request mediation. Nevertheless, clients do not seem to consider arbitration either: in the nine years between 2012 and 2020, the FDRC received 11,275 enquiries but had only 236 cases proceed to apply for the dispute-resolution process, with 184 applications being accepted consisting of 159 mediations, eight arbitration cases and the remaining cases were withdrawn (FDRC, 2021c). It is essential to look at the function of the FDRC to generate insights into why arbitration is not widely adopted.

3.3.2 The FDRC in Hong Kong

Following CJR (see Chapter 1, Section 1.1.1), Hong Kong's FDRC started to provide an alternative venue for the resolution of consumer financial disputes in June 2012. In October 2016, FDRC proposed amendments to the service scope of the FDRS. Among other proposed amendments (FDRC, 2017), the maximum claimable amount (MCA) only increased from HK$500,000 to HK$1 million, instead of the proposed HK$3 million. Based on the researchers' experience, this amount is usually too small and covers little, if any, private banking investment transactions as banks usually have a minimum investment size of HK$1.6 million (US$200k). This decision deserves scrutiny for the following reasons:

Firstly, it went against the growing trend of more high-MCA disputes. According to complaint enquiry data between 2012 and 2015, 270 monetary disputes were rejected by the FDRC due to them exceeding the maximum claimable amount, of which 85% a claim amounts ranged from HK$500,000 to HK$3,000,000. This indicated a growing demand for ADR, evidenced particularly by its high mediation success rate and user satisfaction rate, at 80% and 90% respectively in 2018 (FDRC, 2019, p. 24).

Secondly, although the increase in MCA echoed the higher financial limit for the civil jurisdiction and jurisdictional monetary limit for the district court and the small claims tribunal respectively, the threshold was still lower compared to comparably regulated overseas jurisdictions. For example, the FIDReC in Singapore had no claim limit for mediation, although the limit is set to SG$ 100,000 per claim for adjudication (FIDReC, 2005).

Among all the written submissions received during the public consultation process, the Hong Kong Association of Restricted License Banks and Deposit-taking Companies and The Hong Kong Association of Banks opposed the proposed increase in MCA. However, their rationales might not be justified. For example, they raised concerns about potential abuses of the mediation process due to low cost, and potential increased demand of the FDRC would increase operating costs which would ultimately be transferred to banks (FDRC, 2017, pp. 5–6), these concerns are not supported with facts or data in their response. They also claimed that more complex cases are covered by existing jurisdictions, which is not supported by evidence (FDRC, 2017, p. 26). Finally, it is submitted that most enquiries made to the FDRC were within the claimable threshold (FDRC, 2017, p. 36), which may not be substantiated as the non-eligible cases may not be considered.

Although it is asserted that the mediator or arbitrator panels are knowledgeable and capable of handling financial disputes of various complexities and amounts, stringent vetting procedures are in place to evaluate applications according to the intake criteria to combat abuse. In addition, measures to control and manage costs were imposed, with the FDRC following the threshold of the Insurance Claims Complaints Bureau (ICCB) in setting the amount to HK$1,000,000 in January 2016, whilst the proposed higher jurisdictional limits of the District Court is yet to be confirmed at that time. Out of the 270 complaint enquiries that exceed the current limit of HK$500,000, it is noticeable that cases with HK$1,000,000 claim amounts count for 50% of cases. Hence, the FDRC decided to adjust the maximum claimable amount to a measured amount of HK$1,000,000 instead of the proposed HK$3,000,000. It is also critical to state that the maximum compensation limited is HK$500k for the Investment Compensation Fund, which is raised from HK$150k, from 1 January 2020, this threshold would indicate that private banking clients are still unlikely to submit their investment-related claim (Investor Compensation Fund, 2022, Note 1).

3.3.3 The under-utilisation of FDRC services

3.3.3.1 Overall observations from 2012–2020 annual reports

This section organises figures gathered from the FDRC 2012–2020 annual reports and syntheses observations with the purpose of further consolidating the argument that it is difficult to form a case against a bank in an ADR process. This is associated with the difficulty in transforming an enquiry into a dispute, and the difficulty in moving from mediation to arbitration if mediation has not been successful. The data have been extracted from various paragraphs between 2012 and 2020. They are summarised in Table 3.1.

Table 3.1 summarises the data from the FDRC 2012–20120 annual reports with regard to the number of cases and their outcomes. Between these nine years, the FDRC received a total of 11,275 enquiries, of which 6,278 were related to complaints about financial products. They were either processed via mediation or arbitration with various outcomes or otherwise classified as 'ineligible disputes' during the initial stage. There are a number of observations that can be made.

First, there is a very low eligible rate for complaints about financial products. In 2012, only four out of 474 complaints (that is, less than 1%) were prima facie eligible. Although the figures have improved over years (to 18.3% in 2020), the eligible rate is still considered to be low (Row D in Table 3.1).

Secondly, there were an exceptionally low number of cases that were entered into the dispute-resolution process. Comparing the enquiries received versus the number of applications received (Row I in Table 3.1), an average of only about 2% of the enquiries/complaints were turned into applications for the dispute-resolution process. It should be noted that it is not clear whether these applications did process through the enquiries stage, but this could serve as a good proxy of the transformation rate, which has been extremely low. An exception is that once there was an application, the acceptance rate was unstable and ranged between 51% (2020) and 95% (2015) (Row J in Table 3.1). This could indicate a high gate-keeping process in accepting an application or, if the banks are responsible for the application, then it is likely

Table 3.1 Overview of FDRC utilisation, success rate and satisfaction rate (2012–2020)

Row	*Item*	*2012*	*2013*	*2014*	*2015*	*2016*	*2017*	*2018*	*2019*	*2020*	*Total*
A	Number of enquiries received – total	1,054	2,192	2,004	1,318	1,111	775	955	707	1,159	11,275
B	**of which:** complaints about financial products	474	1,182	1,117	833	664	446	573	403	586	6,278
C	Prima facie ineligible disputes under the intake criteria (under complaints about financial products)	470	1,082	1,012	755	587	352	487	333	479	5,557
D	Eligible rate % on complaints about financial products ((B- C) divided by B)	0.8%	8.5%	9.4%	9.4%	11.6%	21.1%	15.0%	17.4%	18.3%	11.5%
E	Number of applications for the dispute-resolution process (excluding cases brought forward)	16	31	35	21	39	24	15	20	35	236
F	**of which:** accepted	13	29	32	20	32	15	10	15	18	184
G	**of which:** rejected due to failure to fulfil intake criteria	2	1	1	1	5	4	3	4	5	26
H	**of which:** pending (vetting/withdrawn under vetting/resolved by case management)	1	1	2	0	2	5	2	1	12	26
I	Transformation rate % (E divided by A)	1.5%	1.4%	1.7%	1.6%	3.5%	3.1%	1.6%	2.8%	3.0%	2.1%
J	Application acceptance rate % (F divided by E)	81%	94%	91%	95%	82%	63%	67%	75%	51%	78%
K	Cases that proceeded with mediation	11	29	32	17	26	12	10	14	8	159
L	**of which:** settled and closed	7	18	29	14	18	9	4	10	7	116
M	Mediation success rate (L divided by K)	64%	62%	91%	82%	69%	75%	40%	71%	88%	73%

N	**of which:** NOT settled and closed	2	6	1	0	4	1	1	1	0	16
O	**of which:** in progress	0	4	0	0	0	0	5	2	1	12
P	**of which:** NOT settled and considering for arbitration	1	0	1	3	1	1	0	0	1	8
Q	**of which:** entered arbitration process from the case reported in current year	1	1	1	0	3	1	0	1	0	8
R	User satisfaction rates	N/A	87%	88%	88%	89%	89%	90%	91%	90%	NA
S	Fee from mediation service (HK$'000)	93	55	93	41	90	14	3	28	20	NA
T	Staff costs (HK$million)	6.9	9.2	9.6	7.8	7.2	6.1	5.6	5.2	5.4	NA

Source: FDRC Annual Report: 2012–2020.

that they would assess and ensure a high chance of acceptance, although there is no data to support this.[1]

Thirdly, there is a high success rate in mediation. Between 2012 and 2020, nearly all accepted cases were put through mediation (Row K in Table 3.1). There were 116 settled cases out of 159, representing a 73% success rate (Row M in Table 3.1) during the night-year period. The remaining were either still in progress, being considered, or were entered into the arbitration process. The success in mediation might have contributed to the observation that there was only a relatively small number of cases that required arbitration, with only eight cases between 2012–2020 (Row Q in Table 3.1). Nevertheless, it is unclear whether these arbitrated cases have been held or halted which was not reported in the annual report.

Fourth, it can be noted that users maintained a higher satisfaction rate with the services provided by the FDRC. It can also be observed that the satisfaction rate was high throughout the years 2013 and 2020, with a range of 87% in 2013 (note: this number was not available in 2012) to 90% in 2020 (Row R in Table 3.1).

3.3.3.2 Very low transformation rate

The transformation rate is defined by the number of enquiries versus the number of applications. At Row I in Table 3.1, the transformation rate is only at around 2%, meaning that out of 100 enquiries only on average two were transformed into disputes. This represents a very high drop-out rate for FDRC services, with many possible reasons. For example, the potential disputes might have been resolved internally between banks and clients, handled at other platforms such as through HKMA's assistance, or tabled at open-court litigation due to the client's preference or ineligibility of a case. This very low transformation rate might or might not be desirable, because it represents either the disputes being put off or being resolved.

The eligible rate focuses on measuring how many complaints about financial products are prima facie eligible disputes to be taken by the FDRC. It is calculated by the prima facie eligible disputes (Row B and Row C in Table 3.1) divided by the number of complaints about financial products (Row B in Table 3.1). The eligible rate was significantly higher than the transformation rate. For example, whilst the transformation rate was 2.8% in 2019,

---

1 FDRC annual reports disclose the number of cases that entered arbitration and arbitral awards rendered from the cases brought forward from previous years. According to the figures, there have been 18 cases entered into arbitration with 13 arbitral awards issued. However, since it is unclear how long have the cases been pending from within the FDRC, it is difficult to reconcile the numbers based on available data. For example, we cannot assume all the cases that are in progress (Row O in Table 9) have been entered into arbitration, as there have been 23 cases from previous years completed with mediation. Therefore the data has been disregarded as unclear based on the availability of the data.

the eligible rate for complaints about financial products was 17.4%, which is 14.6% higher.

The trend in the transformation and eligible rates can be explained by various reasons. For example, it may have been triggered by a decreasing number of enquiries over the year, from 1,054 enquiries in 2012 to a peak of 2,004 enquiries in 2014, and down to 1,159 cases in 2020; or the disputes being resolved after enquiries and before application. Regardless of the reasons, it is critical for the purpose of this thesis to acknowledge that the transformation from enquiries to disputes has been rather low. This indicates that there have been many potential disputes arising that have ultimately not been transformed into actual disputes. This echoes the proposition that there might have been few disputes appearing (see Chapter 1, Section 1.2.2 – overview). The missing gap is what lies between the enquiries (Row A in Table 3.1) and application (Row E in Table 3.1); and between complaints (Row B in Table 3.1) and eligibility (Row C in Table 3.1).

More data is offered in complaints about financial products. There were three main reasons for ineligibility: (a) the enquirer's knowledge of monetary loss exceeded the limitation period; (b) The disputes involved organisations which were not members of the FDRS, which include insurers, insurance brokers, independent financial advisers, money lenders, and most financial services providers providing platforms for trading precious metals (FDRC, 2021a, p. 23); and (c) The claims amount exceeded the maximum claimable amount (FDRC, 2019, p. 29). It should be particularly noted that these three major reasons have been in existence since 2012 and it is unclear which reason dominates. Noting that claim amounts exceeded the maximum claimable amount, this could indicate that there have been more excluded cases with higher transaction amounts, possibly that would include those from private banking disputes. Unfortunately, there is no further data to support this observation, but one cannot rule out the possibility that there might have been a significant number of private banking disputes excluded from the FDRC, making it difficult to assess the suitability of ADR in private banking disputes only from the figures of FDRC. The situation of FDRC provides a piece of evidence where mediation and arbitration might not be suitable for resolving private banking disputes and hence have not been included, and hence the low maximum claimable amount, which solidifies the hypothesis and drives the need to conduct empirical studies in subsequent chapters.

3.3.3.3 The effectiveness of mediation reduces the need for arbitration

Despite a low transformation rate, cases accepted into mediation enjoy a relatively high success rate of settlement. There were around 73%, on average, of cases settled and closed (Row M in Table 3.1). Except for 2018 when the success rate was only 40% (with the remaining cases still in progress at that time), the success rate of mediation resolving the disputes within the same year has been consistently high at a range between 62% and 91%.

Users have shown satisfaction with the services provided by the FDRC. The satisfaction rate ranged between 87% and 91%, reflected by the high success rate in mediation. In the annual reports, further data is provided (FDRC, 2019, p. 31). In 2019 alone, 92% of respondents indicated that they would recommend mediation services to others if they had similar disputes; and 90% of the users indicated they would use mediation again to settle disputes. These figures were consistently high over the years.

Notably the number of users might be too small to conclude whether mediation is suitable for financial disputes. It does reflect the high levels of effectiveness of mediation being able to resolve financial disputes, at least for those who have used mediation before. Such a high level of effectiveness might explain that arbitration may not be necessary, and hence the low usage of arbitration (Row P in Table 3.1).

3.3.3.4 Under-utilisation of FDRC?

This creates a dilemma: those who have used the services before found that the services were useful and helpful, but there were very few people using the service. The total annual income in 2019 and 2020 was HK$1 million and HK$459k respectively. The total expenditure in 2019 and 2020 was HK$11 million and HK$10 million, half of which were staff costs (Row T in Table 3.1). The number of cases accepted in 2019 and 2020 was only 15 and 18 respectively, bringing in revenue from mediation services of only HK$28k and HK$20k respectively. The total income from application fees for mediation services and in-house mediation service fees shows a clear decreasing trend (Row S in Table 3.1). The FDRC has never covered its cost. This justifies the notion that the FDRC has been under-utilised, leaving us to question whether it is ever essential for financial disputes to be resolved through ADR channels. This may not be the case, because the FIDReC in Singapore had much higher income through their daily operations. For example, in the 2019/20 financial year, the FIDReC recorded a surplus of S$253k with a levy fee of S$3.4 million, despite a loss of S$174k but with fees from the levy maintained at S$3.2 million (FIDReC, 2020).

As argued in Chapter 2, the laws and regulations governing the conduct of banks and bankers may not directly protect individual clients. Existing dispute-resolution channels might not offer the right process either. This can be explained by earlier literature that argued that individual complainants have no commercial incentive to spend time and resources in pursuit of regulatory sanctions (Ali & Kwok, 2010). In the European Union, regulators are unlikely to rely on individual complaints to safeguard the integrity of the banking industry. So far, there have been few comprehensive studies into how these regulations can help individual clients in Hong Kong, apart from the comparative study into the HKMA mentioned above (Hong Kong Monetary Authority, 2002). Other research has mainly focused on how regulations can better protect the integrity of the system through corporate governance frameworks, power for regulator-initiated investigations, and bank reporting.

The central question remains unanswered: whether regulation can offer protection to individual clients and replace the FDRC. At this point, it is notable that the FDRC does not allow legal representatives in arbitration and only provides for document-only hearings. These two special features are surveyed in a subsequent chapter (Chapter 4, 4.4.3). These two features might provide further barriers for clients to feel comfortable in adjudicating their matters privately.

Considering the above, whether and how ADR should be part of the private banking regulatory framework is under-researched. The only notable research for Hong Kong is the recommendation for the retail banking industry, for an 'In-House Multi-tier Dispute Resolution System' requiring direct input from the HKSAR Government, the HMKA, SFC, and retail banks (Ali & Kwok, 2010). The first tier involves experts' decisions led by the HKMA. The second tier involves mediation led by the FDRC and the third tier is arbitration arranged by the FDRC. It is suggested that a 'multi-tier dispute resolution clause' is to be inserted. Ali and Roza (2012) also compared the financial dispute-resolution models in the UK, Australia, Singapore, and the United States, and concluded that a dispute-resolution model should be an essential part of the regulatory framework, with both regulatory modes and non-regulatory modes. Regulatory modes could execute judicial functions to 'safeguard for disputants against the discretion of the third party' and non-regulatory modes could address the knowledge gap. They also pointed out that the FDRC is not a regulatory body with no role in the investigation and only deals with monetary aspects. Yet, it can be regarded as the de facto protector of consumer rights and therefore the FDRC can be enhanced to bridge the power and knowledge gap between consumers and financial providers; among the existing features of independence, impartiality, accessibility, speediness, cost-effectiveness, and confidentiality. The recommendations focused on mass retail banks, with a solution fit for private banks still unresolved. Nevertheless, their works justify the need for a financial dispute-resolution model for private banks.

The FDRC plays no role in private banking disputes and the question becomes 'why not?' This leads us to look instead at how banks and individual customers establish their relationships. One key factor is the contract between banks and customers: to the best of my knowledge, related research on international commercial arbitration addressing mandatory arbitration by law concerns only the situation where both parties negotiate the contract before commitment. In our case, the banking contract between the bank and individual clients is one-sided. This leads naturally to the next issue with regard to the nature of the relationship from the contract formation perspective.

3.3.4 A global perspective: the 2016 ICC report and usage of arbitration and complaint-handling in selected jurisdictions

3.3.4.1 The 2016 ICC report: Arbitration is not known to be a viable option among private banks

Notably, low utilisation of the FDRC might not mean that arbitration is not a viable option for general banking disputes. It may simply mean that the FDRC has restricted entry for general banking disputes, and no entry for private banking disputes. Nevertheless, it is argued that this is a global issue for arbitration, and it is not a popular dispute-resolution mechanism within the private banking sector, according to the 2016 ICC commission report.

> In some instances, the existence of arbitration was completely unknown to the interviewees.
>
> *(International Chamber of Commerce, 2018, p. 138)*

Those who know about arbitration hold great reserve. They are sceptical as to how arbitration could deal with the diverse meanings between literal interpretations of agreements and the actual practices in day-to-day business operations. Other deterrents are the 'cost, lack of speed and the absence of stare decisis (i.e. no system of establishing legal precedent). However, for asset management firms, arbitration presents some significant advantages including confidentiality, expertise, reasonable costs and speed, no appeal mechanism and worldwide enforcement (International Chamber of Commerce, 2018, p. 139). In that survey, it was also noted that private bankers generally deal with one or more individuals, the family estate, SMEs, or non-profit organisations, who typically have less expertise in financial investments. It is not entirely a 'business to business' relationship characterised by 'more or less equal powers and responsibilities' (International Chamber of Commerce, 2018, p. 137).

The survey results appear to show that the existing framework of arbitration may not cater to the unique features that exist within private banking in the following three aspects. First, individual clients are unlikely to give true or meaningful consent when they sign a contract with a bank because they have been given no chance to negotiate the terms (Barr, 2014). In the event of a dispute, customers might not be willing to enforce the arbitration clause, even if it is stated in the contract. Second, disputes of the same nature may involve different parties, as is the case in disputes between institutions. Third, the contract has been drafted by the banks and naturally the terms will be favourable to the banks. When it comes to a dispute, the bank is more likely to prefer court litigation because of the high chance of success and to set precedent to avoid similar challenges. Individual clients have few grounds to win in court and facing the banks privately might not be meaningful prima facie (Boeglin, 1998). The advantages associated with asset management firms seem to favour banks as well because the respondents seem to favour a 'no appeal' system, which is difficult to understand unless you recognise that the respondents have a very high chance of winning. This indicates the bank's desire to close the matter as soon as possible once it has been investigated and adjudicated. That leads to the conclusion that many legal counsels working in various banks do not know arbitration is an option for resolving private banking disputes (International Chamber of Commerce, 2018, p. 25).

This observation echoes existing empirical research. For example, there have been no new cases for the Leveraged Foreign Exchange Trading Arbitration Panel since it reported the number of new cases back in the 2006/07 financial year (Securities and Future Commission, 2021). Ali and Huang (2012) explained why financial dispute-resolution cases brought to the CIETAC are less preferred when compared to in-court litigation to resolve financial securities-related disputes in China. It involves a lack of demand (due to the small amounts associated with the disputes) and knowledge about arbitration; lack of consistent legalisation support to empower CIETAC to facilitate arbitration; a lack of arbitration clauses in financial services contracts; ongoing challenges to ensure the overall quality and integrity of arbitration; and cost concerns (Ali & Huang, 2012, pp. 77–100). These concerns were still valid in the 2016 ICC report and may continue to discourage people to participate in arbitration for financial disputes (Section 3.4.1).

3.3.4.2 Usage of arbitration and complaint-handling in selected jurisdictions

There is no specific complaint-handling institution or arbitration centre that specifically handles private banking disputes (Chapter 2, Section 2.3), this sub-section aims to offer an overview of the usage dispute-resolution mechanism, mainly the arbitration centre and complaint-handling system within the banking industry to unveil whether the situation of Hong Kong is an exception or the norm. Three factors are compared, namely: the number of complaints received in the eligible rate and the success rate of 2020 are stated. The figures in 2012 are also stated for comparative purposes. Table 3.2 illustrates the difference. The selected jurisdictions are identical to s. 4 and 5 to facilitate benchmark comparison with other analyses such as Table 3.2 and 3.3 although not all jurisdictions have the same set of publicly available data.

The first aspect relates to the availability and consistency of the data presented. The data presented is not consistent among different institutions and across different years within the same institutions. It makes benchmarking difficult. For example, only FDRC, FIDReC, and Financial Ombudsman Service

Table 3.2 Usage of key complaint-handling channel in selected jurisdictions

Jurisdiction/ Items	*Dispute-resolution channel*	*Number of enquiries received in 2020 (2012) (change in %**)*	*Number of new cases received in 2020 (2012) (change in %**)*	*Eligible Rate (case handled/enquiries received) in 2020 (2012) (change in %**)*	*Success Rate within one year in 2020 (2012) (change in %**)*	*Source*
Hong Kong	FDRC	1,159 (1,054) (+10%)	479 (470) (+2%)	18.3% (0.8%) (+17.5%)**	88% (64%) (+24 %)** (Mediation only)	Table 7
Hong Kong	HKMA	NA	2,524 (916) (+175%)	NA	NA	p. 97 (2020) p. 69 (2012)
Hong Kong	HKIAC	Only number of new cases is available: 43 (21) (+104%) (2019 v 2014) arbitration on bank/finance cases, not necessary complaint on HK banks)				p. 8 (2020) p. 5 (2014)
Singapore	MAS*	No publicly available data on the website				
Singapore	FIDReC	7,509 (3,220) (+133%) (2020 v 2015)	1,067 (903) (+18%)	14% (28%) (–14%)	93.56% (99.59%) (–6.03%)	p. 20 (2020) p. 29 (2015)
China	CBIRC*	No publicly available statistics from the official website of CBIRC				
China	CIETAC	NA	3,615 (113,660 (–97%) (2020 v. 2014)	NA	80%	2020 Work report p. 18 (2014)
Switzerland	SBO*	NA	2,175 (1,948) (+12%)	NA	98% (100%) (–2%)	pp. 66–77 (2020) pp. 12, 18 (2012)

France	P.R.I.M.E.	No publicly available data on the website				
UK	FOS*	454,259 (1,268,798) (–64%)	279,146 (264,375) (+5%)	61% (20%) (+41%)	90% (84%) (+6%)	p.12 (2020) pp. 1, 7 (2012)
US	AAA	No banking and financial specific data available in their annual report				

Source: Annual Report or website statistic of the respective organisation, see Annex III for the full list (page number and respective year in the annual report made in the bracket).

*MAS: Monetary Authority of Singapore; CBIRC: China Banking and Insurance Regulatory Commission; SBO: Swiss Banking Ombudsman; FOS: Financial Ombudsman Service. ** % = percent point.

Table 3.3 Key arbitral rules of finance dispute-centric arbitration centres

Arbitration rules	*FDRC*	*HKIAC*	*FIDReC*	*P.R.I.M.E.*	*CIETAC*
Name of the rule	Financial Dispute Resolution Scheme (FDRS) Mediation and Arbitration Rules	The 2018 HKIAC Administered Arbitration Rules	Terms of Reference	P.R.I.M.E. Finance Arbitration and Mediation Rules	CIETAC Financial Dispute Arbitration Rule
Number of pages related to arbitration	10 pages	70 pages	70 pages (not arbitration specific)	84 pages (Arbitration part)	5 pages (To be read along with the arbitration rules of 51 pages)
Types of dispute	HK$1,000,000 maximum claimable amount (not in the rule) **raised by the financial institution**	Disputes where parties agreed to be administered by arbitration (Article 1)	Maximum SG$100,000 per claim (section 4.3) from the consumer (section 2, point 6) No limit to mediation	Disputes arising between parties under a defined legal relationship	Between financial institutions, or between financial institutions and other natural or legal persons (Article 2)
Hearing	Document-only (s.3.8.3) with exception (section 3.9)	No special restriction	No special restriction	No special restriction (Article 28)	Mainly oral hearing unless parties agree otherwise (Article 20)
Initial pre-hearing conference	Not allowed (s.3.8.3 (b))	No special restriction	No special restriction	No special restriction	Allow (article 16)
Legal representative	Not allowed (3.8.3.I))	Allowed (Article 13.7)	No mention of restriction	No mention of restriction	No mention of restriction
Eligibility to arbitration	Must complete mediation (s.3.2.1)	If both parties agreed (Article 1)	If parties agree (section 4.4, point 26)	No mention	Financial transactions specifically defined (Article 2) between dispute

Appointment of arbitrator	Parties to agree (3.4.1), no mention of maximum number.	Parties to agree. (Article 6), maximum 3	Parties to agree on adjudicators, a maximum of three (section 4.4, point 22)	Parties to agree, (Articles 8–10), a maximum of 3	Parties to agree, (Article 6–7), with a maximum of 3 (Article 12)
Removal of arbitrator	Parties to request or FDRC discretion due to conflict (section 3.6)	Parties to request with HKIAC to determine (Article 12)	No mention	Parties to request (Article 14)	No mention
Arbitrator's jurisdiction	monetary awards; and other administrative requests (3.8.6)	Interim measures (Article 23), administrative request/ validity of arbitration agreement (Article 19) and issue award (Section V)	Make monetary award (section 5, point 27)	Interim measures (Article 26) and awards	Issue award (Chapter III)
Communication with arbitrator	Must be in writing through FDRC (3.10)	No special restriction	On without prejudice basis (annex 4)	Must be copied to all parties including P.R.I.M.E. (Article 16a)	No special mention
Confidentiality	Applied (3.11)	Applied (Article 45)	Applied (section 6, point 32)	Applied (Article 16)	No mention (general arbitration rule may apply, see Article 38 of CIETAC Arbitration Rule)
Appeal on point of law	Yes, with legal costs restricted to HK$25,000 (3.12)	Decision made by HKIAC not subject to appeal (2.2)	No mention	No mention	No mention
Source of reference	The website of the arbitral institution	The website of the arbitral institution	The website of the arbitral institution	The website of the arbitral institution	The website of the arbitral institution

Source: Arbitral rules of respective arbitration institutions downloaded from the respective websites on May 2022.

(FOS) display the number of enquiries received. The 2012 annual report is not available for HKIAC even if it was established in 1985. Annual reports are not available for CIETAC after 2018 instead, they have work reports. No data is publicly available for MAS, CBIRC, and P.R.I.M.E.; and the annual reports of AAA do not contain banking and financial dispute-related data. The data definition is also not clear, for example, the word 'resolve' could mean withdrawal, settled, or not settled, but they are not clearly defined and nor does it have a globally negotiated meaning. It makes data comparison difficult and might be read with caution.

The second aspect relates to the level of transparency and utilisation. One obvious example is the FOS where detailed data is available both on the website, in Excel spreadsheets, and in annual reports across the year. We can see that their number of enquiries has drastically decreased by 64%, the eligible rate increased by 41%, and the success rate increased by 6% to 90% between 2012 and 2020. It could indicate that there may be an increased awareness and usage of the mechanism. Unfortunately, there is no further data to validate this proposition, but this early evidence is provided by our interview with Mr Young (Chapter 5, Section 5.3.2).

The available data shows that the rate of increase in the number of enquiries grows much slower than the rate of increase in new cases. For example, in Hong Kong, between 2012 and 2022, the FDRC records a 10% increase in the number of enquiries, but only a 2% increase in new cases – that is contrasted with a 175% increase in complaints received by HKMA. In Singapore, the same figures between 2015 and 2020 are a 133% increase and an 18% increase, with only a 14% eligible rate (i.e., a 14% reduction), which indicates that grievance might not be transformed. Contrast with the FOS where respective data was a 64% decrease in enquiries, a 5% increase in new cases, and with 61% of eligible rate (i.e., a 41% increase). The eligible rate is much higher than that of FDRC (18.3%) and FIDReC (14%), the FOS appears to facilitate a healthier dispute transformation process from grievance (which is represented by the number of enquiries) to dispute (which is represented by the eligible rate), and it does not increase the enquiries rate, but on the other hand, a decrease in enquiries are observed.

It is notable that the Swiss Banking Ombudsman (SBO) also has transparent data available; it starts providing an English summary in 2013 detailing the number of cases handled. Although we do not have the data on the number of enquiries, notably SBO accepts oral complaints which consist of more than half on average for new cases. This data is not specified in other documents, and the flexibility to allow verbal complaints might have improved the success rate as it has the highest success rate of case completion within 1 year at 98% (Table 3.2).

Despite the lack of data from public sources, three observations are useful to our analysis: first, there is a clear lack of transparency in terms of the efficacy of arbitration institutions, and clients are not able to choose the best available option by themselves; the choices might not be clear to them even if it is presented, and this will be further discussed in Section 4.3.2, Chapter 4 by relating it to the tree and forest metaphor (Albiston et al., 2013) where clients might have to look at all the options but don't know where to start. Second, an ombudsman model appears to perform better in terms of dispute transformation and utilisation although this point shall not be fully supported by available data because this comparison might have omitted the court cases related to finance. Third, a much higher increasing rate of enquiries than that of the new cases received by FDRC and FIDRec indicates that the formation of the dispute might be stopped, or clients might not choose to resolve their dispute with external parties. Perhaps clients still prefer to make a complaint to the regulator which is supported by data in HK (note that similar data is not publicly available in Singapore). This further supports the notion that mediation and arbitration might not be viable options from the clients' perspective, further justifying our hypothesis and the need to conduct further research in the subsequent chapters.

3.4 The rule and power balance in arbitration

3.4.1 The procedure rules in the arbitration centre designed for banks

It is important to study the procedural rules of the arbitration centre designed for banks for the following three reasons: the first is to contrast their rules with the complaint-handling guidelines issued by Hong Kong regulators (Section 3.2.2); the second is to examine the important features of these rules for the purpose of the survey and interviews at later stages of the empirical study. The third is to understand any similarities and differences among these rules, specifically for banks. To facilitate the analysis, five arbitration centres from around the world were identified and studied arbitral rules were studied. These arbitration centres claimed to have a focus on handling finance-related disputes. They are the FDRC, the FIDReC, the CIETAC, the P.R.I.M.E., and the HKIAC.

Following the analysis of FDRC in Section 3.3 of this chapter, the FDRC will be used as the basis for the comparison. By comparing the FDRC with four other major arbitral institutions, some very distinct features can be observed, which illustrates a potential gap between the services offered and which may impose further hurdles for private banking clients to engage in arbitration. The comparison is shown in Table 3.3, and there are three distinct features.

The FDRC has shorter descriptions of arbitration rules. The FDRS Mediation and Arbitration Rule has a 16-page Mediation and Arbitration rule, whereas 10 pages with 56 clauses specifically describe the arbitration process (including four clauses describing fees and costs applied with mediation). Only the CIETAC Financial Dispute Arbitration Rule (5 pages with 28 Articles) has a shorter length but this is read in conjunction with the CIETAC Arbitration Rule, which has 51 pages. The relative lack of length in terms of description in the FDRC might be explained by the scope of the FDRC, which is for 'document-only' hearings (with exceptions) and there are no pre-hearing conferences available for arbitration.

The FDRC also has a more restrictive scope of services available, with only monetary claims of no more than HK$1,000,000 applicable to clients. This threshold is not imposed by other institutions except the FIDReC, which imposes a SG$100,000 threshold for adjudication. It can be noted however that this threshold is not imposed for mediation, which implies a wider scope than the FDRC. The scope of the FDRC is further restricted by the fact that arbitration is only available if a financial institution requests it. On paper, it seems that individual clients would not have the scope to initiate arbitration once the case starts through the FDRC.

The FDRC also has further restrictions on arbitration that other institutions might not have. For example, under the FDRC, no legal representative is allowed and parties must have completed mediation first before the financial institution can request arbitration. Communication with arbitrators must be made in writing and passed to other parties by the FDRC. P.R.I.M.E. requests copies of any communication to be made available to all parties including the arbitration institution. FIDReC requests that communication be done without prejudice. Arbitrators in the FDRC can make monetary awards and enquiries related to the adjudication of the dispute and other procedural matters, whilst other arbitration institutions (except the FIDReC) allow arbitrators to also impose interim measures. One special feature of the FDRC is the possibility of an appeal. The FDRC allows an appeal on a point of law against arbitral awards with the legal costs involved limited to HK$25,000. Without criticising the significance of HK$25,000, this rule allows for more leeway when compared to other arbitral institutions, whereas the HKIAC has made it clear that decisions made are not subject to appeal. This area is not mentioned by other arbitral institutions.

One small note is that the arbitral rules appear to be much more comprehensive than the respective HKMA's guidelines relating to complaint-handling. It has offered clarity on the procedures related to how the dispute will be handled. Clients are also given more autonomy, such as in how they can choose their own arbitrators, which banks do not let clients do (the best a bank can do is avoid conflict when selecting an investigator).

The findings will be subject to further validation through empirical studies to avoid pre-made conclusions as to whether these features attract or discourage the use of arbitration of FDRC. They will be discussed further in Chapter 4.

3.4.2 The role of the bank as arbitrator

Although it is acknowledged that there are limitations associated with this simple comparison between the different arbitral rules among different arbitration service providers, these rules (when compared to the HKMA guidelines and the process of handling customer complaints) seem to place the bank as an arbitrator in a dispute. This section examines the relevant features to explain this observation.

The IC-4 Complaint-Handling Procedures appears to be an arbitration process in substance. The HKMA strictly requires banks to ensure complaints are handled swiftly within a specific timeframe, and for banks to acknowledge receipt of the complaints and the outcomes of any investigation. Banks are required to put in place appropriate and effective mechanisms and procedures to handle customer complaints about banking products or services, making sure that individual cases are followed up in a fair and expeditious manner. All these features place the bank in a position as arbitrator, as the bank is the institution to investigate, hear, and adjudicate the case. In essence, the bank is both the investigator and arbitrator, who arbitrates the materials submitted by the complainant and collected by the bank.

There might be some shortfalls associated with this model. First, is *impartiality* which is otherwise available in an arbitration centre. Impartiality is not seen or perceived in this arrangement. Even though there are explicit requirements to ensure independence, it is the bank that is investigating its own claim. Even though the department responsible for the investigation is supposed to be independent, whether there exists a Chinese Wall between the complaint-handling department and the department being complained about is in question. Second, is the lack of disclosure and transparency of the actual procedures available to the public. It is questionable as to whether banks really have the incentive to unveil any significant shortfalls discovered, and there is also no clear guidance of what should or should not be disclosed when it comes to a complaint. Third, is the issue of consistency of outcome. Given that investigations and resolutions are private information, complainants are unlikely to identify what to expect from the complaints. Neither can complainants evaluate whether the complaint has grounds in the first place, which is particularly a concern because the information possessed by clients from the account opening forms focuses on clients' obligations instead of their rights or the bank's obligations (Chapter 2, Section 2.4). This could either discourage the clients to launch a complaint or just complain if clients feel a grievance regardless of the grounds of the complaint. Despite this, many issues associated with ADR discussed in the literature review (Chapter 1, Section 1.2.3) have been resolved. There is no need to identify a capable arbitrator as the bank itself must have experts to understand the situation. With the banks handling their own issues, there is no floodgate problem consuming the resources of society. The consistency and perception of the results within the bank are likely to be better ensured. The consistency issue deserves further discussion – whether different banks provide the same results for the same disputes is questionable and there is no way to ensure this, given the fact that it is often a commercial decision in which the HKMA would not intervene. A bank's own dispute-resolution mechanism appears to exist within the banking industry already. The clients are not involved except at the beginning of the process.

A special reference is identified in this process. This perceived role as arbitrator of the bank might be quite similar to a hybrid approach between litigation and arbitration, called 'modified litigation', which has been observed in the literature (e.g., Noyes, 2006, pp. 640–642). This allows contracting parties to construct the rule of litigation in a contract to accomplish nearly all of the procedural benefits of arbitration by setting their own rules. Modified litigation appears to be a better choice than arbitration as the parties are more likely to obtain unbiased judgments compared to that from judges (e.g., arbitrators), who would like to be hired again from repeated disputants. It should be noted that the power inherent to the court to control the litigation process cannot be waived. Parties can only waive their own litigation rights in the drafting. The waiver of constitutional rights may be subject to stricter scrutiny (Noyes, 2006, pp. 638–645). However, this model might not be ideal for private banking disputes because of the issues of a one-sided contract. The procedural rules of complaint-handling within the bank are only decided in a one-sided manner by the bank and are not disclosed to the complainants. Whether there exists common features found in litigation, such as due process and other procedures on discovery, evidence collection, and interim orders, is questionable. Even if it exists, it is not known to the clients. Without any mutual exchange of dialogue to the complaint-handling process, from this perspective, the current process appears similar to the modified litigation approach, but it is probably not comparable.

3.4.3 A case study: The role of the HKMA and power balance in a dispute

Although the involvement of the HKMA does bring in some, but not all, elements of both mediation and arbitration, it might be helpful to associate the role of regulators with a power balance under a client's perception. In other words, does the regulator play a positive role during the process of dispute resolution in maintaining the power balance between banks and clients when they handle the dispute directly? If the HKMA has played an efficient role in doing so, arbitration will not be necessary because reliance on the bank's internal process will suffice and could explain the under-utilisation of arbitration as well. Notably, since we are looking at perception in this thesis, the content has been analysed and assessed together with the source of power by Waldman and a case study from my own experience.

It is best to analyse these observations using a real case example, relating to my making a complaint to a bank. One limitation is that it was not a private banking dispute but, considering the purpose of the study which is to relate the role of the bank and the HKMA in resolving a dispute to the power theory, the process is identical, perhaps except if the banker had cared more if I had been a private bank client. This case is still relevant for the purposes of this study.

The incident can be described as follows: one day I noticed that there had been a regular charge of HK$200 in my current account, and I called my banker to enquire. The banker told me that it was the monthly charge imposed by the bank and my waiver period had ended, hence unless I had a HK$1 million balance in my account, this charge would continue. I could lower the account status but would still need HK$200,000 or above or a HK$100 monthly charge will be incurred. As usual, I sought a waiver because I used to work in this bank and having this bank account was not an option in the sense that I might still get a residual salary even if I had resigned. But no waiver was allowed, and I asked the banker to reconsider. I waited for a few days in vain and decided to walk into a branch to enquire. I received the same answer, and hence I filed a complaint to the bank directly and decided to see how the bank and subsequently the regulator would handle my complaint.

Initially, the bank responded and said they had waived the charge and would give me three more months to move in more money to avoid the charge. I subsequently closed the account to avoid more charges and wrote back on 3 May 2021 that I was not satisfied with their response because of a potential breach of relevant HKMA guidelines. After failing to get an acknowledgement within two weeks, I wrote to the HKMA through its online complaint channel. It was very easy to use and involved only four steps. Clients are asked to provide information about the things they are not satisfied with – I wrote to the HKMA that (a) I was worried that they would not address my further concerns because I was no longer their client; (b) I was of the view that the bank had been unreasonable in excluding the public to use basic banking services and discriminate against non-vulnerable groups and those less financially capable to pay for basic banking services.

One month following the complaint to the HKMA, on 18 June 2021 the bank wrote back to me again with a response. The response first started with an apology as they were not sure why I did not get their acknowledgement email on 5 May 2021, followed by drawing my attention to the fact that they did send me a notification letter in June 2020 notifying me of the changes to the terms and conditions, subsequently confirming compliance with a few provisions under the Code of Banking Practice. Without commenting as to whether their replies were legitimate (which in my opinion were not), there are a few observations that can be made: first, the interaction continues to be one-sided as the client has no choice but to either accept the explanation (and compensation, if any) or continue to rebut. Second, between 3 May and 18 June, which had passed the usual turnaround time of 30 days, the client also had no choice but to wait and it is suspicious that the bank might have chosen to ignore my email because I had already closed the bank account. Third, whilst the bank's reply was copied to the HKMA, it is unclear whether the client's reply was also forwarded to the HKMA. It is uncertain whether the HKMA kept track of our dialogue or assessed whether the response provided by the bank and the client were reasonable. Fourth, the bank seems to have the authority to say they have complied with the relevant codes of banking practice. With these observations, I wrote back on 21 June to request further clarification and asked them to assist me to forward my reply to the HKMA. On 5 July 2021, the bank wrote back and restated its position that they were in full compliance, without explaining how such conduct had followed the relevant rules and regulations.

It might be helpful to reflect on this phenomenon based on the factors that create power (im)balance (see Chapter 1, Section 1.2.1).

'The ability to shape the process and outcome'. It is apparent clients do not really have too much discretion to contribute to the process once they have escalated their complaint to the bank. The fact is that, if clients decide not to go to court directly, the first channel *must* be the bank first. The bank will receive the complaint, make an investigation, and decide what to do without involving the client. Upon making the complaint, I immediately received an email acknowledgement that my complaint had been received. I was not contacted in the next four working days until they emailed stating that actually (a) the bank has the right to make any commercial decision, and (b) the bank has done whatever it could to inform the clients that such a decision has been made. Nevertheless, in response to a good customer relationship and as a matter of goodwill, the bank was willing to give me a waiver of those fees for three months and by then I should move HK$1,000,000 cash or more into the account. If I failed to do so, I would need to downgrade my account and in any event, my account would still be subject to a monthly fee unless I could prove that I was in a particularly vulnerable group under financial stress. Strikingly, the bank did not respond as to how such a decision complies with the respective regulation and hence I wrote back again demanding an explanation.

This case study reflects the following: First the bank officers in the branch do not have relevant detail about the case. They either waive the fee for clients or if they are unable to, they simply ask the clients to file a complaint. Second, once the complaint is filed there is nothing much for the clients to do. I was not contacted by any bank officer to understand why I had these concerns (which in my case, is the fact that I was instructed by the bank to open a wealth management account as a staff member before I resigned from my position). They did not ask for more information or evidence which I might have been able to provide. Finally, the decision was made when I received a response and, unsurprisingly, it was to offer a monetary buffer. This experience reflects the fact that the clients are in a very passive position in this process, which is one distinct difference when compared to arbitration, as the only involvement clients have would be when they decide to file a complaint, which seems to have been welcomed by the bank officer in my experience with them. Possibly because it is not their decision to make this call, and they do not have the discretion to do so.

'Resources, knowledge, merits in the eyes of the law, moral conviction, personal traits.' The complainant relied totally on the bank's information. When I first received a reply from the bank, I was informed that it is their policy to charge a monthly service fee for those accounts below the minimum threshold. What was lacking was how these measures comply with the regulatory requirements. The bank told me what the correct conduct was. For example, they told me they had the right to charge a fee. It was their discretion to waive the fee only for vulnerable customers (and hence I was not entitled to a waiver). The first email I received did not offer any explanation in the eyes of the law. In my opinion, it was not a response supported by a valid argument supported by the law or regulation. There were a few more rounds of enquiries asking for the rationale behind their view of compliance, for example, whether this was approved by the HKMA or whether their in-house lawyers had ensured compliance with this practice. Yet, there was no further response. It seems that the bank did not owe a duty to explain after they had adjudicated the case.

'Ability to inflict pain.' During the complaint process, the bank followed all the HKMA requirements but in fact the interactions were close to minimal. To avoid being charged further, before I could wait for a response from the bank, I had already closed the account. This is the only thing I could do to 'inflict pain' on the bank, but given that my account only had a very small amount, and the fact that I was no longer the bank's customer, such 'pain' may actually be a relief and the bank might not have been obliged to respond to my questions any further. **Would banks be obliged to respond to a non-customer?** Thus far, HKMA regulations have only addressed bank customers. What if in this situation, a customer is not willing to engage with a bank as a customer because of a policy they do not agree with and, in fact, that policy might not be justified after a full trial? Would those customers have the right to make a complaint to the bank directly, or must this complaint be made to the HKMA? Would my exit to the bank inflict any pain on the bank, or would it be a relief to the bank as I might not be the type of customer they prefer? My grievance arose from this newly found policy of bank charges which did not occur to me until after three payments were automatically charged to my bank account. It seems that the bank did want me to exit so that I would no longer be concerned with the charge.

'State involvement.' Since I was so worried about my complaint not being addressed once the bank had found out that I was no longer a customer, I lodged a complaint using the HKMA complaint channel alleging that I was forced to close a bank account because I needed to avoid the monthly charge. The HKMA responded to my complaint and said that they 'have instructed the bank to handle my complaint properly' and I was given the same general email with a suggested title if I was not satisfied with their reply. But the purpose of informing them seems to 'allow them to facilitate a more efficient complaint-handling process' (email communication with HKMA, 21 May 2021). The HKMA appears to be determined to ensure banks continue to manage their own complaints.

'Perception (of customers)'. In this context, this refers to customer satisfaction with the bank's response. I was given an email and a three-month notice to top up my asset size. Why would they not give me a permanent waiver this time? To understand my perception, it may be helpful to take a step back by looking at the client's perception. Some disputes between banks and clients come from the imposition of a fee. Riding on my own experiences in the banking industry, Hong Kong depositors are very price sensitive. Customers might be used to enjoying the free banking services provided by banks and believe that the bank should earn their money based on the interest spread (the difference between the deposit rate banks offer to depositors and the lending rate charged to borrowers). Yet with the trend of a low-interest rate environment, banks are very active to earn non-interest income to catch up with the revenue they used to make and to also reduce the reliance on interest rates. I was given a clear signal by the bank that I was not their target customer. In reality, the bank does have the right to not bank a customer.

In addition, it creates an impression that, as long as the bank responds to you, no matter how unsatisfactory the answer, there may be nothing much the complainant can do. This observation seems to align with our observation of the FDRC which may have imposed a closed door to the complaint. These two observations seem to push the clients to not make a complaint in the first place. The long process (of going to the bank first, which only investigates itself, then to the HKMA, which will only facilitate, and later the FDRC, which is very restrictive) makes it not worthwhile for clients to start a dispute in the first place. These factors might discourage the clients from going that far.

3.4.4 The role of the HKMA as mediator

As we have seen in Section 3.2.2.3, individual clients can rely on the HKMA complaint channel should they not achieve their expected results when trying to resolve a dispute with a bank. Nevertheless, the role of the HKMA is to facilitate the process without any intervention in terms of both the substance and the process of the dispute. With the intervention of the non-contractual party into this informal dispute-resolution process, it has arguably resolved the informalism issue described in Richael Abel (1982) (see Chapter 1, Section 1.2.3) where there are official elements involved in the unofficial process, given that state power has now been involved. This might create more pressure on the bank because the HKMA could have launched a formal investigation against the bank. Nevertheless, the issue of procedural justice in the context of mediation as described in Welsh (2001) remains, because HKMA guidelines appear to be only outcome-based, meaning that the bank is only told of what the outcome of the respective system should be designed by the bank, instead of the specific requirement of how each process is to be conducted. Although this approach may cater to the consideration of how different banks handle their complaints, the public is kept as an outsider and only regulators and the bank are aware of the actual process. In fact, based on my own experiences as a private banker, the banker would not know what the process is, except when interviewed by staff from another department.

The HKMA seems to take the role of mediator because it only facilitates the resolution of disputes, yet it is unclear how the HKMA would do so. There are two ways the HKMA will facilitate a speedy settlement. First, the HKMA will ask the bank directly, indicating that the HKMA is aware of the current complaint, and in this way, the bank will be aware that a possible investigation may be launched against the bank. The bank might not want to draw regulatory attention. The fact that HKMA might have launched an investigation against the entire bank might create a second facilitative element for banks to offer a speedy resolution. However, the second approach might not be effective because based on my own experience, the HKMA would always want to give the bank a chance to resolve the dispute itself (Section 3.2.2.1). It is unclear how big the issues would have to be to draw regulatory attention. A lack of transparency in this area is not resolved by the issues of regulation because they are written in a board language (Chapter 2, Section 2.4.5.1).

With or without the HKMA to facilitate the dispute-resolution process, the procedure of handling the complaint and the outcome is still under the sole discretion of the bank. Neither is the expert knowledge of HKMA brought into the dispute between the parties, but instead, it is the general practice that affects the bank itself. This brings us back to earlier concerns on whether individual clients would have the commercial incentive to assist the HKMA to reveal a bank's shortfall for the benefit of the entire banking system. With the HKMA serving as a mediator yet lacking some power of a mediator to facilitate the resolution of disputes – except through imposing potentially undesirable consequences for a bank through the imposition of a bank-wide investigation – it does not seem to help clients as much. It is unclear whether a bank will just settle with clients to avoid such an investigation.

As a mediator, the HKMA seems to only facilitate from the bank's side. It does not (based on the description on the HKMA website) work for the client's side. There is no instruction of what kind of information is requested to facilitate the investigation, no information about how to follow up with the HKMA if clients have further information to provide, nor does the HKMA report progress to the complainant. The complainant simply sends an email or submits an online application form and the HKMA will then work with the bank directly. It does not bridge the power gap and clients remain on the less informative side.

3.5 Conclusion: When banks start to adjudicate their own dispute

Chapter 3 has reviewed the importance of ADR in resolving finance disputes by revisiting global standards and analysing the three major bodies of guidance from the HKMA in handling banking complaints. These guidelines were contrasted with the arbitral rules issued by arbitration centres. Chapter 3 has also involved a thorough investigation of the function and performance of the FDRC in an attempt to validate the hypothesis of low utilisation of arbitration for banking disputes in general, of which private banking is included as evidenced by the findings from the 2016 ICC report. An evaluation of the role of the bank and the HKMA in dispute resolution has been made, together with an analysis of the researcher's experience of two direct complaints made to the bank and the HKMA as stated in Section 3.2.2.1 and Section 3.3 in this chapter, as well as referring to existing power theory notably from Fiss (1984), Mayer (1987) and Waldman (2011). It suggests that the bank has a dominant position to control the complaint-handling process, which makes a client the weaker party in a dispute-resolution process. If an internal process is already that difficult, any external out-of-court process (arbitration included) would not be easier. This makes arbitration not a viable option and hence the under-utilisation for any banking dispute – as evidenced by the low utilisation of FDRC.

Although the regulatory environment following the Lehman crisis has been tightened, the method of compliance, including the process of handling complaints, is still largely at the discretion of banks. The regulators only maintain an oversight of the process. As a result, clients' interests and needs are often ignored unless clients make the effort to escalate the complaint to the regulators. In the private banking industry, the use of ADR mechanisms is still uncommon and even in some circumstances, the availability of such mechanisms is unknown. Regulators prefer banking disputes to be handled internally between the bank and clients, however, there are insufficient guidelines from both regulators and the banks for clients to provide them with the equal ground to resolve a dispute. This phenomenon appears to be global as shown in the comparative analysis of the selected jurisdictions, especially when regulators do not have jurisdictions to intervene with the bank decisions. In the case of Hong Kong, the HKMA appears to adopt a relatively hands-off approach by offering relatively broad guidance which focuses only on the timeliness of the response instead of the outcomes. It is arguably problematic due to possible conflicts of interest when banks are investigating and adjudicating their own disputes. It has also been discovered that banks tend not to provide any reason in their responses to complainants. There is no obvious end to this procedure, and hence it could turn out to be a 'persistency game' in which clients usually give up because there seems to be nothing else clients could do. These observations could explain the low utilisation of the FDRC, because clients may not have the 'energy' to further escalate their complaint externally after going through the internal process. This might render arbitration no longer a viable option because the disputes have been handled internally between banks ad clients. It further implies that even if arbitration rules are preferred by clients, they may not prefer using arbitration.

The findings are synthesised with the theory of powers and a case study of HKMA involvement to support the argument that existing dispute-resolution mechanisms might have failed to resolve power imbalance issues. It concludes by laying down the factors that hinder the use of arbitration from clients' perspectives by relating the power theory and the naming, blaming, and claiming model. There are no guidelines or standards on how a dispute should be properly resolved. The entire process forces the clients to passively wait for the bank's decision. Existing features of arbitration might have been incorporated in the complaint-handling process already, hence the under-utilisation of arbitration is only a reflection of the high utilisation (or reliance) of internal bank complaint channels. Nevertheless, the contextual analysis might not be directly applicable to private banking disputes, and hence empirical analysis is necessary.

A closer look at the process shows that a bank acts as an arbitrator in this internal procedure and has external power to investigate and adjudicate its own dispute. The HKMA acts as a mediator but only facilitates the bank's side by reminding them to actively respond or risk a full-scale investigation. Yet, the HKMA does not intervene as much as it could, although the BO might entitle them to do so. With regulators outsourcing dispute-resolution processes back to the banks, private banking clients may never consider arbitration as a dispute-resolution channel.

CHAPTER 4

Unfolding the clients' perspective: Knowledge versus experience

4.1 Introduction: do clients know the law?

Chapter 4 analyses the results of the survey. The survey questions were drafted based on the findings from the contextual analysis of relevant laws and regulations governing private banking, as well as the arbitral rules. The survey serves two purposes. The first is to assess clients' knowledge of their rights when banking with private banks. The results indicate whether clients are really put into a weaker position when it comes to knowing their legal rights contrasts with their actual experiences. The second is to identify clients' preferences in the arbitration process. The knowledge questions required specific answers in order to be marked as correct. There were no designated answers on clients' experiences with private banks and preferences in the arbitration process. An online survey required participants to answer a set of questions without any aid from a third party. The design of the survey produced categorical data which are independent and random. There were 58 respondents with 32 completed surveys. Given the small sample size, a descriptive analysis should be sufficient for the purposes of this study.

Most of the clients generally answered the questions correctly. This indicates that they had adequate knowledge of the law and regulations governing the private banking industry in Hong Kong. Clients' experiences were also largely aligned with the laws and regulations, as well as their expected scope of regulated activities. This indicates that they had not been mistreated, which supports the phenomenon of a small number of disputes as discussed in Chapter 3. Data also show that these results do not vary among different groups of clients categorised based on their wealth, experience with private banks, or whether they had experienced a dispute with private banks. However, the lack of demographic differences could be caused by the small sample size. The survey also shows that most of the existing arbitration processes are preferred by private banking clients, which aligns with the existing literature advocating the suitability of arbitration. It should be noted that the results are generated by clients who did not have many disputes with their banks, nor had they experienced arbitration, and therefore their responses were largely based on pure instinct.

DOI: 10.4324/9781003407591-4

This chapter partially explains why private banking has a relatively small number of disputes. In other words, clients might have little occasion to mention their grievances when engaging with their private bank. It may not be that arbitration is under-utilised but rather may not be needed in the first place. The survey results show that most features in arbitration are preferred by the clients, so it could be a viable option to resolve any private banking dispute. However, this chapter cannot explain why the number of disputes is small, which leads to the need to examine the clients' perspectives through interviews, as seen in Chapter 5, to examine why there were so few disputes escalated, particularly whether it is really due to perfect harmony between banks and clients, or if there are other factors that led to genuine claims not making their way to formal and informal dispute resolution mechanisms.

4.2 Clients' knowledge and experience

4.2.1 Set A: Clients' knowledge of the laws and regulations for private banks

4.2.1.1 Clients' knowledge: Account opening stage

Table 4.1 shows that most of the respondents answered the questions correctly, except for Qa5. For Qa2 and Qa4, almost all the respondents correctly acknowledged that private bankers have an obligation to explain the terms and conditions of the services provided and they have a duty to verify the client's identity. In terms of proving wealth status in Qa1, 81% of respondents thought it was regulated, and some respondents (16%) were not sure about it. This could be explained by the practice that clients are not usually formally asked to provide this information, but the private bankers would obtain such information through informal chats instead, leading to clients not being aware of such a requirement. We revisit this practice in subsequent chapters. Another possibility is that there are close personal relationships between the private bankers and clients, which means the private banker already has sufficient knowledge of the background of the clients and hence a formal question-and-answer scenario is not necessary (Chapter 2, Section 2.2.3).

For Qa5, signing a blank form is not encouraged by bank policy, but it is not directly regulated by the HKMA or SFC. There is a split in the results between 'no' (44%) and 'not sure' (41%), which indicates the uncertainty arising from this conduct. In the researcher's own experience, this happens often when onboarding a client, because no banker wants to fill in the form in front of clients as this can take a long time.

4.2.1.2 Clients' knowledge: Product knowledge and risk appetite stage

Similar to the results of Qa1 to Qa5, **Table 4.2** shows that clients had strong knowledge of the laws and regulations governing product knowledge and risk

Table 4.1 Clients' knowledge of laws and regulations on account opening form

			This conduct is complied with relevant regulation?						Correct Answers	
			YES		NO		Not regulated		Not sure	
1	(a) Account Opening	You are asked to prove how you generate your wealth.	26	81%	1	3%	0	0%	5	16%
2	(a) Account Opening	The Private banker explains to you the terms and conditions in the account opening forms.	31	97%	0	0%	0	0%	1	3%
3	(a) Account Opening	The bank amends the terms in the account opening forms without your consent, but simply send you a letter and said the terms and conditions will change 1 month later.	14	44%	5	16%	0	0%	13	41%
4	(a) Account Opening	Private banker requires to see your ID card for account opening.	31	97%	0	0%	0	0%	1	3%
5	(a) Account Opening	You sign the blank account opening forms; the private banker fills in details after.	5	16%	14	44%	0	0%	13	41%

Source: Online survey conducted by researcher, October 2020.

Table 4.2 Clients' knowledge of laws and regulations on product knowledge and risk appetite

			This conduct is complied with relevant regulation?						T	
			YES		NO		Not regulated		Not sure	
6	(b) Product Knowledge and Risk Appetite of the Client	Private bank explains the key product features and risks associated before placing an order.	29	91%	1	3%	0	0%	2	6%
7	(b) Product Knowledge and Risk Appetite of the Client	Private bank discloses conflict of interest before your investment order is executed.	25	78%	1	3%	0	0%	6	19%
8	(b) Product Knowledge and Risk Appetite of the Client	A private banker offers you his own view in an investment.	9	28%	6	19%	0	0%	17	53%
9	(b) Product Knowledge and Risk Appetite of the Client	You are asked to update your product knowledge and investment risk appetite regularly.	27	84%	1	3%	0	0%	4	13%
10	(b) Product Knowledge and Risk Appetite of the Client	You are asked to explicitly say you understand the product features before you place an investment order.	27	84%	1	3%	0	0%	4	13%

Source: Online survey conducted by researcher, October 2020.

appetite. In Qb6, Qb7 and Qb9, the proportion of clients who answered the question correctly is 91%, 78%, and 84% respectively. There are two questions which were mostly answered incorrectly by the respondents, which deserve further discussion.

Qb8 highlights the situation of a private banker offering his/her own view of an investment, instead of providing advice prepared by their banks. There was a split response. Only 28% correctly believed that private bankers were in compliance when offering their own investment views, 19% of them thought otherwise, and the remaining 53%, which was the majority of respondents, were not sure about it. This result provides an early indication of the unclear role of the private banker from the client's point of view. Questions such as the following should be explored. What kind of conduct of private bankers is regulated? How do we ensure their conduct is in line with the bank's policy? In this regard, the role of the private banker will be examined further in stage 3, in Chapter 5, Sections 5.5.2 and 5.5.3.

In Qb10, regarding the prior express consent before placing an investment order, it is actually not compulsory for the clients to explicitly say they understand the product features before placing an order. Nearly 84% of the respondents thought that it is regulated and complies with regulations in doing so. This is likely to be caused by a bank's usual practice. Based on my own experience from the three private banks I worked for, the bank would always request clients to explicitly, under voice recording, confirm verbally that they understand everything before a trade is allowed. This common practice makes clients believe it is a regulatory practice but in fact, the HKMA and SFC do not explicitly request such a practice. In this case, measures imposed by bank policy are stricter than the regulatory requirements, which may impose unnecessary barriers to the business even if it means clients are more certain and cautious about their understanding concerning the investment before making an investment decision. It also offers more protection to the bank, as it has ensured that clients understand the product's nature and cannot accuse the bank of misrepresentation. This phenomenon will be further discussed in Chapter 5, Section 5.2.

4.2.1.3 Clients' knowledge: Client communication between bank and client

Table 4.3 shows a different trend when compared to those of Table 4.1 and 4.2. Out of the total five questions in relation to the communication channel, only one question (Qc14) received correct responses from most respondents. Qc14 concerns the requirement for the bank to send written advice to the clients after an investment is executed. For the rest of the responses apart from Qc14, the answers from the clients are very different. It is observed that the clients expected some unregulated activities to be regulated; for example, in Qc11 88% of the respondents answered that it is a regulatory requirement to receive an informed letter from the bank when an account is opened, but

Table 4.3 Clients' knowledge of laws and regulations on client communication channel

			This conduct is complied with relevant regulation?						Correct Answers	
			YES		NO		Not regulated		Not sure	
11	(c) Communication Channel Between Bank and Client	You receive a letter to inform you that your private bank account is opened.	28	88%	0	0%	0	0%	4	13%
12	(c) Communication Channel Between Bank and Client	Your Private Banker is registered as a Certified Private Wealth Professional (CPWP) certified by the Private Wealth Management Association (PWMA).	19	59%	3	9%	0	0%	10	31%
13	(c) Communication Channel Between Bank and Client	You are asked to place an investment instruction through email.	6	19%	4	13%	0	0%	22	69%
14	(c) Communication Channel Between Bank and Client	The bank sends you a written advice after an investment is executed.	28	88%	0	0%	0	0%	4	13%
15	(c) Communication Channel Between Bank and Client	The investment product brochure shows expected future performance.	21	66%	1	3%	0	0%	10	31%

Source: Online survey conducted by researcher, October 2020.

in fact, there is no such direct requirement. For Qc12, despite most of the respondents holding the view that their private banker is a registered professional qualification, the Certified Private Wealth Professional (CPWP) is actually not yet a mandatory requirement, although it is highly encouraged by the HKMA. The possible reasons are that nearly all banks send a letter to a client informing them that an account has been opened and most private bankers would have obtained the CPWP already, hence creating an impression that these are mandatory.

For Qc13, 69% of the respondents were not sure whether placing an instruction through email is allowed, whilst the rest of their opinions were split between 'yes' and 'no'. From the researcher's own experience, banks do not allow clients to place instructions through email, but sometimes when clients sent an email instruction, the banker calls back the client to confirm. This may create an impression that a voice recording is always needed. In fact, it is not. Clients can provide written instructions to confirm their order. For example, the bank can witness the signature and write a report afterwards to validate the instruction.

For the correct answer to Qc15, it is clearly against the regulations to show expected future performance in any investment brochure, yet two-thirds (66%) of the respondents thought that it is allowed, and 30% of them were not sure. Two possible explanations are offered. The first is that clients might be confused with past performance and future performance as shown in the brochure. The second is that clients might be confused with a banker's own opinion, which is not part of the written documents. In the second explanation, in the process of advising the clients, it is usual practice for the banks and bankers to offer their perspectives with reference to past performance of the respective or similar products, so this allows the clients to take this as a reference for facilitating their investment decision-making. In the second explanation, clients have two channels to communicate with the bank – the official written documents and the banker's own opinion, which once again relate back to the role of private bankers in communication with clients. On a minor note, it can also be inferred that clients might rely on the bankers to learn about the regulatory requirement and the bank's practice.

Contrary to the strong trend in clients' knowledge in Qa and Qb, Qc shows a larger discrepancy. It reveals that clients were generally confused about what is regulated and what is not when it comes to communication, but generally, clients believed that most bank conduct is regulated and hence complied with. In fact, most of this conduct is self-imposed by the banks which indicates the bank's policy could be more stringent than the regulatory requirements. There are two possible explanations: the first is that the bank has adopted a stricter approach for the purpose of fulfilling the regulatory requirements and avoiding the possibility of non-compliance, given that the regulations are written in a generic manner as shown in Section 2.3.2 of Chapter 2. The second is related to the role of the private banker in this communication process, especially in how they explain the terms and conditions. It is also noted that communication between clients and banks is not consistently regulated when compared with the KYC requirement in account opening and investment execution. This will be further discussed in Chapters 5 and 6.

4.2.1.4 Clients' knowledge: Dispute resolution channel

Table 4.4 shows a split response when it comes to the dispute resolution channel. Responses to Qd16 show half (50%) gave a wrong answer (with 34% replying 'not sure' and 16% of them answering 'yes'). A similar pattern is also found in the responses to other questions in Question Set (d). In Qd17, half of the respondents (50%) wrongly believed that a private bank does not need to have a complaint-handling department. In Qd18, nearly 53% were not sure, or a portion of them even wrongly believed that receiving compensation from bankers complies with regulations. In Qd19, whilst 56% of the respondents correctly believed that banks must assist clients to file and handle a complaint, there is still a large portion (44%) who think otherwise. Qd20 then continues the same pattern with 41% of respondents not being sure about the formalities of making complaints, whilst nearly 20% of them thought the private bank is entitled to accept only a written complaint. Only 41% correctly stated that it is not the case.

The above analysis of the responses to Set Qd has led to the following two general observations. First, no one responded to the question with the answer 'not regulated', which means the clients generally believed that the bank's complaint-handling system is regulated. Second, the clients did not know how the complaint process is regulated. An explanation is that the clients believed that it is mainly the bank's discretion on how a complaint should be handled, as long as it fulfils the regulatory requirements as shown in Chapter 3, even though it was unclear to clients how banks would handle the complaints

4.2.1.5 Implications: clients know the law and regulation

This section implies that clients were well acquainted with the laws and regulations related to account opening, product knowledge and risk appetite, which are part of the process of client onboarding and when where investments are executed. The clients, however, were not too so familiar with issues related to communication and dispute resolution, or the clients seemed to either have very little experience in this regard, did not pay attention to them, or this process has been largely executed by the private bank by its own method and hence the scope and practice were not clear to the clients. The clients also had a perception that nearly all activities are regulated, indicating a strong perception of tight regulation and governance imposed on banks.

Table 4.4 Clients' knowledge of laws and regulations on dispute resolution channel

			This conduct is complied with relevant regulation?						Correct Answers	
			YES		NO		Not regulated		Not sure	
16	(d) Dispute Resolution Channel	You send a complaint letter to the private bank, but get no reply.	5	16%	16	50%	0	0%	11	34%
17	(d) Dispute Resolution Channel	Your private banker tells you that the private bank has no complaint handling department.	4	13%	16	50%	0	0%	12	38%
18	(d) Dispute Resolution Channel	You receive compensation directly from private banker to resolve a dispute.	4	13%	15	47%	0	0%	13	41%
19	(d) Dispute Resolution Channel	The private bank says they are not obliged to tell you how you can complaint against the bank internally.	4	13%	18	56%	0	0%	10	31%
20	(d) Dispute Resolution Channel	Your private bank tells you that your complaint can only be written in a letter can be followed up.	6	19%	13	41%	0	0%	13	41%

Source: Online survey conducted by researcher, October 2020.

4.2.2 Set B: Clients' experiences when interacting with a private bank

With regard to clients' experiences, this section observes whether the clients had experienced the described conducts; their experience is cross-compared with the results on whether the respective conducts complied with the respective laws and regulations. The correct answers are shaded in green, with 'yes' meaning complied and 'no' meaning not complied. If neither the 'yes' nor the 'no' field is green-shaded, the conduct is not directly regulated by the HKMA or SFC.

4.2.2.1 Clients' Experience: Account opening stage

Table 4.5 shows the account opening experience of the clients. In Qa1, most of the clients (69%) had the experience of being asked to prove how they generated their wealth, whilst there is still a significant portion (31%) not being asked this question when opening an account. This is possibly due to the fact that the bankers already know their clients well, thus such questioning is not necessary. In my own experience, usually bankers personally know the clients well and do not need to ask questions about the SOW, or this information could be extracted through casual conversation and research from the news. Hence, clients may not know that their bankers have already conducted the KYC instead of this process not being complied with. A similar pattern is shown in Qa4 where private bankers correctly request to check the client's ID card, where 9% of the respondents were required to provide their ID card. Instead, clients might be asked to provide a copy of their ID card through email, and the banker just certifies it. This practice might not be correct, but it is unlikely for a frontline banker to receive training to verify an authentic ID card, so the authenticity confirmation process would be carried out by back-office staff.

Table 4.5 Clients' experiences of laws and regulations on account opening form

		You have experienced this before? (Correct Answer)			
		YES		NO	
1	You are asked to prove how you generate your wealth.	22	69%	10	31%
2	The Private banker explains to you the terms and conditions in the account opening forms.	27	84%	5	16%
3	The bank amends the terms in the account opening forms without your consent, but simply send you a letter and said the terms and conditions will change 1 month later.	18	56%	14	44%
4	Private banker requires to see your ID card for account opening.	29	91%	3	9%
5	You sign the blank account opening forms; the private banker fills in details after.	12	38%	20	63%

Source: Online survey conducted by researcher, October 2020.

In Qa3, there is a split in the responses of getting notification from the banks with regards to any change of terms and conditions. Whilst the responses to Qa2 indicate that most bankers do explain the terms and conditions to their clients, responses to Qa3 reveal that 44% of the respondents had never been notified when there was a change to the terms and conditions. This is unusual because banks often change their terms and conditions, and they usually send out letters to inform clients of the changes. There is a high possibility that the clients did not pay attention to these kinds of letters, or the clients might have engaged the 'hold mail' service where they request the statement to not be posted to them for security reasons (for example, they would worry about burglary if someone realised the clients were rich, based on the private bank they are banking with). Yet, an alarming observation is that the clients do not pay sufficient attention to the changes in terms, hence they might not be aware of the scope of the banking services provided to them.

For Qa5, 38% of the respondents experienced signing a blank form, thus indicating bankers may cut corners for convenience. Although, based on my own experience, the clients do not mind signing a blank form to solve time.

4.2.2.2 Clients' Experience: Product knowledge and risk appetite stage

Table 4.6 shows clients' experiences of how their product knowledge and risk appetite are assessed. For Qb6–Qb10, the clients experienced all complying conducts, except Qb7 where the private bank discloses conflicts of interest before an investment order is executed. The responses to Qb10 show that 78% of the clients were asked to explicitly indicate that they understand the product. It is a more prudent measure adopted by the bank although it is not directly regulated.

However, in Qb7, 59% of the respondents had not experienced disclosure of a conflict of interest. Based on my own experience, there are two possibilities.

Table 4.6 Clients' experiences of laws and regulations on product knowledge and risk appetite

		Correct Answer You have experienced this before?			
		YES		NO	
6	Private bank explains the key product features and risks associated before placing an order.	25	78%	7	22%
7	Private bank discloses conflict of interest before your investment order is executed.	13	41%	19	59%
8	A private banker offers you his own view in an investment.	25	78%	7	22%
9	You are asked to update your product knowledge and investment risk appetite regularly.	22	69%	10	31%
10	You are asked to explicitly say you understand the product features before you place an investment order.	25	78%	7	22%

Source: Online survey conducted by researcher, October 2020.

First, is that the disclosure is usually written in the product brochures, and they are emailed to the clients before they place an order through the recorded phone call. Then, in a tele-conversation, the clients would be explicitly asked this question: 'have you received the emails describing the products and relevant disclosure made by the bank?', and clients would need to consent before the private bankers execute any investment order. Sometimes, the time span between the email and the phone call is very short because the banker would have explained everything to the clients via phone first. However, it is questionable whether the clients would really read through the documents and hence may not be aware of the disclosure of the conflict of interest statement. Another possibility is that banks usually have strict guidelines for conflicts of interest; for example, bankers must follow existing approval procedures in the buying, holding, and selling of clients' investments. In addition, banks have dedicated teams to conduct a product's due diligence before onboarding a product for recommendation to clients. Most of the products recommended or are available for investment in private banking have already gone through this due diligence process, and it involves enormous effort if clients would like to buy other products which are yet to be vetted by the bank.

Admittedly, banks will usually only offer products that have already been vetted internally by the banks. Qb7 might indicate that clients are obliged to understand what they have invested in, and it occurs often that they would not read those product brochures thoroughly. Because the clients trust the bank's profession and decisions in advertising those investment products, they mostly do not spend the extra time needed to go through the product brochures in detail. This could have had huge implications for this study, because when a dispute happens, the clients may blame themselves, which will be further examined in Chapter 5, Section 5.3.

4.2.2.3 Clients' Experience: Client communication between bank and client

Table 4.7 shows clients' experiences when they communicate with their private banks. When it comes to the official communication between banks and clients, the pattern is more consistent with my expectations based on my own experience. In Qc11, most clients (94%) received a letter from the bank to inform them when their account is opened. In Qc12, 66% of respondents indicated that their private banker is a CPWP. Within the banking industry, there is an upward trend in which more and more bankers are expected to be registered as certified professionals, either through examination or through a grandfathering arrangement (i.e., exemption of the examination requirement in light of their years of experience in the field). In Qc13, only 19% of clients were asked to place investment instructions through email, which could be explained by a strict approach of receiving instruction through voice recordings Qc14 reflects that 81% of clients had experienced receiving written

Table 4.7 Clients' experiences of laws and regulations on client communication channel

		You have experienced this before? (Correct Answer)			
		YES		NO	
11	You receive a letter to inform you that your private bank account is opened.	30	94%	2	6%
12	Your Private Banker is registered as a Certified Private Wealth Professional (CPWP) certified by the Private Wealth Management Association (PWMA).	21	66%	11	34%
13	You are asked to place an investment instruction through email.	6	19%	26	81%
14	The bank sends you a written advice after an investment is executed.	26	81%	6	19%
15	The investment product brochure shows expected future performance.	22	69%	10	31%

Source: Online survey conducted by researcher, October 2020.

advice after their investment order was executed. Whilst for the remaining 19% of respondents who had not experienced such practice, a possible explanation is that the advice might have been uploaded to the bank's website and hence clients might not be aware of it.

What comes as a surprise is the responses to Qc15, where 69% of respondents reflected that they did find the investment product brochure predicting the future performance of the products, in which the provision of such information in the investment product brochure is clearly against the Advertising Guidelines Applicable to Collective Investment Schemes Authorized under the Product Codes. So far, there is no evidence that the investment product brochure indicated expected future performance, but private bankers might have shared their views with their clients on the anticipated performance of the investment products, which might create an impression to the clients that future performance is indicated in the investment brochure.

4.2.2.4 Clients' Experience: Dispute resolution channel

Table 4.8 shows an almost one-sided response of 'no' when it comes to experiences in dispute resolution. The percentage of 'no' from Qd16 to Qd20 ranges from 84% to 94%. It is, nevertheless, believed that the response is driven by the lack of dispute experience, as only one out of 32 respondents had experienced a dispute with his/her private bank. Qd18 shows that 13% of respondents received compensation from their private bank before, and Qd20 shows that 16% of respondents got a message from their private banker that only written complaints would receive attention. This offers the early sight of a private banker's involvement to manage clients in the disputing process.

Table 4.8 Clients' experiences of laws and regulations on dispute resolution channel

		Correct Answers			
		You have experienced this before?			
		YES		NO	
16	(d) Dispute Resolution Channel	2	6%	30	94%
17	(d) Dispute Resolution Channel	2	6%	30	94%
18	(d) Dispute Resolution Channel	4	13%	28	88%
19	(d) Dispute Resolution Channel	2	6%	30	94%
20	(d) Dispute Resolution Channel	5	16%	27	84%

Source: Online survey conducted by researcher, October 2020.

4.2.2.5 Implications: Clients have different approaches to communicating with their banks

This section has indicated that clients' experience is very much in line with the regulated practices when it comes to account opening, the assessment of product knowledge; and risk disclosure, as revealed by the responses to Question Set (a) and (b). However, their experiences in communication with the banks, as found in the responses to Question Set (c), start to be more divergent. For the dispute resolution channel, there is insufficient evidence to infer whether a dispute has been handled properly by the bank because only one respondent in our sample population indicated that s/he had experienced a dispute before, and we have interviewed this client to understand further his/her transformation process. In addition, as we have seen in Chapter 2, the account opening form does not perform all the legal and regulatory functions; it indicates that clients possibly acquire the related knowledge from other sources or based on existing practices by the banks.

4.2.3 The relationship between clients' knowledge and experience

This section associates the clients' experience with their knowledge. To aid the analysis, a summary and comparison table, Table 4.9, has been created. In Table 4.9, the column of Set A responses states 'You (the clients) have experienced this before?'. And the column of Set B responses denotes 'This conduct is complied with relevant regulation?'. The field is coloured green for the correct answers. For ease of analysis, since no respondent provided the

Table 4.9 Divergence and alignment between clients' experience and knowledge

			majority answers SET A You have experienced this before?				correct answers SET B this conduct is complied with relevant regulation?				Align / Diverge
			YES		NO		YES		NO / Not regulated / Not sure		
1	(a) Account Opening	You are asked to prove how you generate your wealth.	22	69%	10	31%	26	81%	6	19%	Align
2	(a) Account Opening	The Private banker explains to you the terms and	27	84%	5	16%	31	97%	1	3%	Align
3	(a) Account Opening	The bank amends the terms in the account opening forms without your consent, but simply send you a letter	18	56%	14	44%	14	44%	18	56%	Align
4	(a) Account Opening	Private banker requires to see your ID card for account	29	91%	3	9%	31	97%	1	3%	Align
5	(a) Account Opening	You sign the blank account opening forms; the private	12	38%	20	63%	5	16%	27	84%	Align
6	(b) Product Knowledge and Risk	Private bank explains the key product features and risks	25	78%	7	22%	29	91%	3	9%	Align
7	(b) Product Knowledge and Risk	Private bank discloses conflict of interest before your	13	41%	19	59%	25	78%	7	22%	Diverge
8	(b) Product Knowledge and Risk	A private banker offers you his own view in an	25	78%	7	22%	9	28%	23	72%	Align
9	(b) Product Knowledge and Risk	You are asked to update your product knowledge and	22	69%	10	31%	27	84%	5	16%	Align
10	(b) Product Knowledge and Risk	You are asked to explicitly say you understand the	25	78%	7	22%	27	84%	5	16%	Diverge
11	(c) Communication Channel	You receive a letter to inform you that your private bank	30	94%	2	6%	28	88%	4	13%	Diverge
12	(c) Communication Channel Between Bank and Client	Your Private Banker is registered as a Certified Private Wealth Professional (CPWP) certified by the Private	21	66%	11	34%	19	59%	13	41%	Diverge
13	(c) Communication Channel	You are asked to place an investment instruction through	6	19%	26	81%	6	19%	26	81%	Align
14	(c) Communication Channel	The bank sends you a written advice after an investment	26	81%	6	19%	28	88%	4	13%	Align
15	(c) Communication Channel	The investment product brochure shows expected future	22	69%	10	31%	21	66%	11	34%	Diverge
16	(d) Dispute Resolution Channel	You send a complaint letter to the private bank, but get	2	6%	30	94%	5	16%	27	84%	Align
17	(d) Dispute Resolution Channel	Your private banker tells you that the private bank has no	2	6%	30	94%	4	13%	28	88%	Align
18	(d) Dispute Resolution Channel	You receive compensation directly from private banker to	4	13%	28	88%	4	13%	28	88%	Align
19	(d) Dispute Resolution Channel	The private bank says they are not obliged to tell you how	2	6%	30	94%	4	13%	28	88%	Align
20	(d) Dispute Resolution Channel	Your private bank tells you that your complaint can only	5	16%	27	84%	6	19%	26	81%	Align

Source: Online Survey conducted by researcher, October 2020.

answer of 'not regulated' in Set B responses, the responses of 'no', 'not sure', and 'not regulated' are grouped together. The survey questions are drafted in a manner that the 'yes' answers between Set A and B responses are aligned (i.e., the questions were not drafted as a negative sentence). The data in Set A are associated with the data in Set B to examine an alignment or divergence based on descriptive analysis.

An alignment is identified when the majority of clients experience conduct that is in accordance with the law. Take Qa4 from Table 4.9 as an example, Set A responses show that 91% of the clients (respective data field filled with dark yellow colour) had the experience of being asked to provide an ID card when opening an account, and Set B shows that such practice is performed in accordance with the law (respective data field filled with green colour). In addition, 97% of the clients correctly understood that this is a regulatory requirement.

On the other hand, a divergence means that the majority of the clients experienced conduct that is not aligned with their understanding of the laws and regulations. For example, in Qc12 of Table 4.9, 66% of the respondents mentioned that their private banker is registered as a CPWP, and 59% of respondents believed that this is a regulatory requirement. In this case, although the clients' experience is aligned with their understanding of the law, their understanding of the law is inaccurate (i.e., there is no regulatory requirement to make a private banker a CPWP).

Table 4.9 demonstrates the number of questions between Set A and B that are aligned or divergent. The observations are as follows:

1. The 'account opening stage' shows no divergence. Qa1 to Qa4 show that clients have experienced the standard account opening procedures (Set A) and they are in compliance with the regulation. In addition, the clients know this conduct falls within the regulation (Set B). Qa5 shows that most clients (63%) had not signed any blank form before, and 84% believed that this conduct did not comply with the regulations.
2. The 'product knowledge and risk appetite' stage has two divergent results. Qb7 shows that there are nearly 60% of clients who did not receive banks' disclosure of conflict of interest before their investment orders were executed, whilst 78% of the clients knew, correctly, that disclosure of conflict of interest is a regulatory requirement. Similarly, Qb10 shows nearly 80% of clients were asked to explicitly confirm their understanding of the product features before placing an investment order, whilst only a few of them knew it is not an explicit regulatory requirement. Indeed, it is good practice to increase the customer's confidence, which is why the banks/bankers might be willing to do so, although it is not required.

3. The 'communication' stage shows three divergences. Qc11 shows that 94% of clients received a letter from their private bank when an account was opened. Qc12 shows 66% of clients had been served by private bankers who are registered as CPWP and believe that they are regulated, when in fact this is not regulated at present. Qc15 shows that almost 70% of clients saw an investment product brochure showing expected future performance and incorrectly believed that they are in compliance (66%).
4. There is no divergence under the 'dispute resolution' stage. All answers in Qd16 to Qd20 show the respondents had not experienced dispute resolution channels (Set A), and most of them (81% to 88%) thought either that this conduct was not regulated or they were not sure about the compliance status (Set B). The results in Set A and Set B are consistent. The answers are likely to be driven by the lack of dispute experience.

There are three major observations and implications.

First, there is a good alignment between knowledge and experience in terms of account opening, product knowledge and risk appetite. This means that clients have been served in accordance with the laws and regulations, and clients knew clearly about the laws and regulations. The trend is very strong with only a few exceptions, such as clients signing a blank page in Qb10, and the disclosure of conflicts of interest in Qb7. On the other hand, the clients' experiences in terms of communication channels are more diverse (Qc11 to Qc15), and most of the clients did not have any disputing experience with their banks (Qd16 to Qd20).

Second, most of the divergences appear to be driven by more prudent bank practices, for example, Qb10 with regards to requesting clients to explicitly confirm their understanding of product features before placing an investment order, which further ensures clients' understanding; Qc11 concerning the receipt of a bank letter stating that an account is being opened; and Qc12 regarding the CPWP qualification. Whilst for other divergences which have been explained before, take Qb7 for instance, it is likely due to pre-set disclosure (Section 4.2.2.2, this chapter).

Third, the understanding of whether a professional qualification is required for a private banker is worth paying more attention to. Whilst 66% of clients reflected that their private banker is qualified as a CPWP (Table 4.9), nearly 40% of clients were not affirmative or were unsure when asked whether it is a regulatory requirement to be qualified as a CPWP (Table 4.3). This indicates a certain degree of bias against the less experienced private bankers, where new private bankers require examination but the grandfathering system allows for a group of more experienced bankers to be exempted from examinations. This means that we have two groups of bankers: one more technical and one more 'experience-driven' (interview, Mr Peterson).

4.2.4 Clients' preferences for arbitration process

Part III of the survey laid down 12 processes extracted from different arbitral rules as per Table 11 in Chapter 3. The results are shown in Table 4.10. The respondents were required to select their preferences for respective arbitration processes and indicate whether they preferred, not preferred, or had no preference for the process. The questions were distributed in the same online survey form to the same group of participants. This approach faced two key limitations. First, the survey shows that only one respondent had experienced arbitration before. Clients' preferences do not come from their actual experiences of the process. The interpretation of meanings could have been different based on how they understood the literal understanding of the process. This limitation is acceptable given the scope of the survey on clients' perceptions and actual experiences. Second, the survey did not ask for the degree of their preference (e.g., strongly or least preferred). The answers provided might be too simple and might be subject to further elaboration.

4.2.5 What are the clients' preferences?

Out of the 12 major procedures, 7 were preferred by the majority of clients. The clients preferred to argue the case directly with the bank without any judge involved (66%) and if a judge is needed, they would prefer to choose their own judge (78%). Furthermore, the clients would also hope to appoint a private institution to organise the arbitration for them (78%), choose their own venue and law (75%), design their own process (69%), arrange their own schedule and timeline (84%), and have the entire hearing held in private (84%).

In general, the responses reveal that the clients prefer to have a dispute resolution hearing to be held in private, aligning with the conventional benefits of having a private and confidential hearing so that the disputants could maintain their privacy (see Chapter 1, Section 1.2.3). The clients also show a high preference to have the autonomy to decide the process of dispute resolution, which may not be supported by the case studies of this thesis where the clients just need transparency instead of becoming involved in deciding the process (interview Mr Peterson and Mr Young).

4.2.6 Procedures not preferred by clients

There are two features that were not preferred by the clients. First, the award/ judgement offering no reason (Q11, with 66% of respondents choosing 'not

Table 4.10 Clients' preference on arbitration process

Imagine you have a dispute with your private bank, and are asked to resolve it privately (i.e., not going to the court) -		Prefer		Not Prefer		No Preference	
1	You argue the case directly with the bank (i.e., no judge involved).	21	66%	5	16%	6	19%
2	If a judge is requested, you choose your own judge.	25	78%	0	0%	7	22%
3	You handle the dispute directly with the bank without a lawyer.	14	44%	15	47%	3	9%
4	You argue the case by written submission and no need for personal hearing.	9	28%	15	47%	8	25%
5	You appoint a private institution to organize the arbitration for you.	25	78%	2	6%	5	16%
6	You organize the arbitration privately between yourself and the bank.	9	28%	18	56%	5	16%
7	You choose you own venue and law to hear and adjudicate your case.	24	75%	1	3%	7	22%
8	You design your own process (e.g., which evidence is acceptable, how to collect).	22	69%	3	9%	7	22%
9	You design your own schedule and timeline to process the case.	27	84%	2	6%	3	9%
10	You have the entire hearing process held in private.	27	84%	1	3%	4	13%
11	The award (i.e., the judgment) offers no reason.	5	16%	21	66%	6	19%
12	After the issue of award, no appeal is allowed.	6	19%	22	69%	4	13%

Source: Online survey conducted by researcher, October 2020.

prefer') and second, no appeal being allowed (Q12, with 69% of respondents choosing 'not prefer'). This is aligned with most arguments or findings in the literature, as the mechanism will lose its attractiveness if these features are missing.

4.2.7 Procedures with a split view

The other three remaining items received relatively split views.

Responses to Q3 have 44% of respondents indicating their preference to have a lawyer engaged in the dispute, whilst 47% of them did not prefer this. This implies that most clients would perceive that the bank is a highly regulated industry, and it is almost impossible for them to conduct business against the regulations. Also, the clients may not be in a better position even if they had a lawyer. This is because the bank as a well-structured organisation would have a team of its own lawyers to defend itself, and the legal documents would be in favour of the bank.

Q4 shows a relatively split view in terms of submitting the dispute cases in paper form only. Whilst 28% of respondents preferred to have this due to convenience, 47% of them did not prefer this, but another 25% had no preference. This rounds up to a half-half situation about having a dispute with or without a hearing. This leads to an important implication of whether arbitration could be a suitable process for them because the clients appear to be quite flexible in terms of how their cases could be brought up.

Q6 shows the clients' preferences for organising arbitration with the bank directly. Although 56% of the clients indicated that they did not prefer to organise arbitration just between themselves and the bank, 28% indicated such a preference, and 16% had no preference. The observation is again around a half-half split. This implies that the clients would expect the bank to provide a clear direction of a complaint-handling procedure, whilst the others might think that they, as clients, could only either ask the bank to consider a complaint or close the bank accounts. It is then shown in the case studies that the clients do prefer to exit, hence the under-utilised ADR mechanism for banking disputes.

4.2.8 Implications: Clients may or may not prefer arbitration

A majority of the arbitration process appears to be preferred by clients, although there are some split views on the involvement of lawyers and arbitration organisations in a dispute. The clients did not prefer an unreasoned award, the unavailability of an appeal, as well as the ability to organise an arbitration privately with the bank. The results might to some extent support the argument that arbitration can be preferred by clients, but the mixed results indicate that whether it is a viable option is still inconclusive. The under-utilisation of arbitration may not be explained by clients' not preferring the arbitration process.

4.3 What is hindering the use of arbitration?

Similar factors impacting the formation of a dispute could also explain why arbitration is not widely adopted. We could only derive these possibilities from our case studies: These factors come from the perceptions of those clients who did not attend arbitration or probably were not aware of what arbitration is. Neither do these reflections come from a comparison with the experiences in court. It comes from their perceptions as to whether there was a dispute to start with and how this would affect their use of an out-of-court adjudication mechanism (that is, arbitration). It is argued that similar reasons why disputes are not formed appear to coincide with the reasons why arbitration is not used even if there is a dispute. Under this, there are four observations.

4.3.1 Uncertain legal obligation and clients' rights

Clients do not have a single source of the law as a reference. The legal basis can be associated with the bank account opening forms, which is a *one-sided contract*. In the contract between individual clients and banks, usually only the bank drafts the agreement, and the other party is left with a 'take it or leave it' situation. A bank will ask potential clients to sign the forms with little chance to negotiate the terms and conditions. Once the form is signed the bank will undergo due diligence to open an account for the client. Successful opening of the account means that the contract is effective, and before that can happen the potential client would need to provide their personal and other necessary information for the bank to go through various assessments for client onboarding, which includes, but is not limited to, their SOW, their knowledge of financial assets, and their experiences in financial investment. Potential clients also need to agree to the terms and conditions set by the bank. The contract is drafted in a way that complies with the regulations. The content has two distinct features: the first is that the content focuses mainly on clients' obligations and banks' scope, without mentioning in detail the bank's obligations or clients' rights; and the second is that different banks have different requirements, which means different clients play by slightly different rules under the same regulatory framework. The content is written in a more elaborative way than what the regulations require (Chapter 2, Section 2.4).

The contract may not provide meaningful consent. The entire account opening process involving contract signing is a one-way communication where clients are assessed for eligibility, but it implicitly means that clients have agreed with whatever the banks have proposed. More often, clients do not read the details but simply believe the bankers (Section 5.5.2, Chapter 5). This raises the issue of meaningful consent to the contract. Is it a real commitment? Do clients know what they have committed to? Would they acknowledge those terms in a dispute where clients should read and understand by themselves (for example, in Selina Kwok vs HSBC)? All these questions make the benefits of arbitration questionable as it relies on mutual agreement not only to the use of arbitration but also to the terms and conditions embedded in it, which does not impose any (fiduciary) duties on banks.

Reynolds (2014) wrote about 'consent fictions' by using adhesion contracts which bind consumers to agreements that they were unaware they were making. It is often associated with the use of boilerplate provisions which do not carry any meaningful consent. Most people do not read boilerplate provisions, and even when they do, there is evidence to show that they do not understand them (Nolan-Haley, 2018). In our context, private banking clients seem to fall into the category of not reading any provisions at all, regardless of how they had been written. The design of arbitration clauses might become problematic because they can be drafted in a way that the other party would not pay attention to them, or prevent them from properly evaluating the costs and benefits of accepting such clauses. Sternlight (2004) argued that it is fundamentally wrong and unfair to deprive consumers and employees of their access to court on an involuntary, unknowing basis – with or without reading the contract. The non-consensual nature of mandatory consumer arbitration is itself a problem. Empirical studies have shown that only a small percentage of consumers read their agreements, and of these, only a small number understand what they read. Some companies may even deliberately design their arbitration clauses in a manner geared to decrease the likelihood that the consumer will focus on the arbitration clause. Psychologists have shown that predictable irrational biases will prevent them from properly evaluating the costs and benefits of accepting such a clause (e.g., being overly optimistic, underpredicting the processes, or undervaluing what they are losing by giving up a right to sue). Companies may seek to take advantage of consumers' irrational behaviour by manipulating arbitration clauses together with other aspects of consumer contracts (Sternlight, 2004). Our observations offer insight from a step before a consumer reaches that situation, as it appears that the contract was never the core of the legal relationship, even at the time of a dispute. When adhesion contracts are part of arbitration and accepted by the courts, it creates an effect where arbitration displaces voluntary dispute resolution. Hence, compulsory arbitration provisions that eliminate a party's access to court are often prohibited, as clients might want the case to be heard by court, as confirmed in Mr Collins' interview.

The account opening form would still act as a contract when necessary, although the account opening forms seem not to serve the purpose of a contract from a practical point of view. The relationship between a bank and its clients is often a relational one. This can be explained in the context of relational contract theory, where the legal relationship does not cover the actual transaction between parties (Macneil, 1999). Whilst private banking disputes come from actual transactions that are subject to other sets of contracts, the account opening form does play its role. For example, In *Selina Kwok v HSBC*, HSBC successfully disclaimed their duty to explain an accumulator transaction by referring to a provision stated in the master agreement put forward at the account opening stage, even though another agreement had been signed for the accumulator transaction. It can be confusing when the sources of legal obligation are scattered across different documents. With uncertain legal obligations and rights on the clients' side, engaging in arbitration can be risky. The matter is further complicated by the involvement of private bankers who may or may not be part of the contractual relationship, which deserves further research attention.

4.3.2 Lack of understanding of what arbitration is

The existing literature has offered numerous insights on whether arbitration is a suitable platform for banking and finance disputes in the context of power balance and informalism, contract formation, and the arbitration process. However, the literature has mainly focused on the relationship between two institutions, instead of between institutions and individual clients. Arbitration should address market-specific needs (Dugue, 2000), and the insights from the current literature are unlikely to apply to private banking disputes.

Whether clients correctly understand arbitration is another issue. For example, they may be overly optimistic, undermine the engagement of the process, or undervalue what they are losing by giving up the right to sue. Banks could be in a stronger position to direct their clients to opt for a channel that is more favourable to themselves, be it negotiation in private and settling, or going to court so that banks could set a precedent. Mr Collins's case further confirms the issue of familiarity. Mr Collins is a senior counsel in Hong Kong, and he described his understanding of arbitration in a manner that did not relate to the reality of arbitration. Nevertheless, it could be the actual experience under the term 'arbitration':

> What I know about arbitration is that both parties sit down to discuss a claim in order to find a way to resolve the dispute.
>
> *(Mr Collins, Interview)*

In fact, after Mr Collins filed a writ in court, he negotiated with the bank. The case was later settled to Mr Collins's satisfaction, and hence he did not proceed with the case in court. The accusation of operating without a licence or proper authorisation was no longer his concern. He believed that he had put the reputation of the bank at stake through his actions. He did not opt for arbitration because he did need the publicity offered by the open court. His experience did not align with the results of the online survey where respondents indicated that they would hope to resolve any dispute in private. This further illustrates that the lack of understanding of arbitration might have driven different perceptions of what arbitration can do. Mr Young also had similar experiences with his involvement in arbitration, where the process was not like the arbitration we are used to.

4.3.3 The dispute can easily be resolved with monetary compensation

As we have seen, private banking disputes can usually be resolved by providing monetary compensation (e.g., Chapter 5, Section 5.3.3). Any form of ADR mechanism may be inefficient as a bank will settle with private banking clients in consideration of 'goodwill' and 'relationship'. It is unlikely to be meaningful to seek legal remedies from the bank as the issue in a dispute is usually due to the misconduct of a private banker who has deviated from the bank's policy. For clients, compared to engaging with ADR, it appears more appealing to just accept and settle. The ADR process might be as complex as the court process. Clients have a very clear agenda of asking for their money bank. They do not have other legal or extra-legal needs (Vidmar, 1984). Direct negotiation with banks is more straightforward. Also, once a grievance starts to form, the bankers are quite heavily involved to resolve it because it is usually perceived as being related to the banker's conduct. Therefore, private banking clients would not rely on the contract to name the grievance. In a dispute, the client's perception is that there is no real obligation for banks to be responsible for their bankers' conduct – be it an over commitment or a mistake made. If this is the case, banks simply settle if they wanted to retain the client.

Some well-established arguments to promote the use of arbitration may not be applicable to private banking disputes, as they do not often involve the application of law but instead financial and accounting principles, speed, reduced expenses and expertise of the neutral, which are mainly business decision, as per Ms Emily's interview in Chapter 5, Section 5.4. The benefits of arbitration, such as having a proper discovery process, better use of evidence, addressing power imbalances and asymmetric information, and eliminating repeated user advantages (Ali, 2013), might not be as prominent in private banking disputes because, for one, the clients probably do not want to position themselves in a dispute. If a dispute is formed, the best way to resolve it may be to sue the bank as per Mr Collins's interview in Chapter 5, Section 5.4.2. There are additional efforts needed to engage in arbitration which clients might not prefer (Section 4.2.6 in this chapter). Clients may prefer to use the court as a tool to impose a threat to the bank's reputation to gain the bank's attention and force the bank to negotiate. Banks can either just settle or simply go to court to defend their reputation. For both parties, ADR is unlikely to be an option. The two extremes between negotiating with the banks and going to court highlight the need to properly govern how banks handle complaints. A transparent procedure needs to be in place that is perceived to handle the complaint objectively and without conflict. The clients should also be educated and encouraged to engage in ADR first before going to court (Ali, 2013). These proposals would apply to banking disputes in general.

4.3.4 Lack of precedent and publicity

Legal uncertainties in arbitration arise from the fact that it produces unpublished awards and hence a lack of precedent to follow, unlike in the public court system which publishes its judgments. Nevertheless, Weidemaier (2010) explained how precedent can arise in arbitration from a theoretical perspective. By reviewing a set of agendas that aim to make arbitration a mechanism of 'generating robust systems of privately made law', he identified three factors: (a) whether the arbitration institution allows arbitration awards to be accessible if not published; (b) benefits to the parties in terms of filling in gaps in state-supplied laws through setting precedent in arbitration and (c) concerns from arbitrators to be seen as lawmakers or, on the contrary, too heavily reliant on the decisions of other arbitrators. Weidemaier (2009) further examined the citation practice of arbitrators by comparing the awards written by arbitrators in arbitration and judgments written by judges in public courts. The published awards in labour, employment, class action, and securities arbitration show a clear trend that arbitrators cite more judicial opinions and only use past awards to fill in obvious gaps created by the law. This supports arbitrators' behaviour of using precedent, which in turn creates legal certainty. However, in securities arbitration, out of 203 awards between 1995 and 2009, only two awards cited judicial or arbitral precedent whilst most of them were non-reasoned. Hence, it is inconclusive as to whether precedent can be a reliable source when resolving banking disputes in arbitration. Ali and Huang (2012) identified several practical and court-related factors that could make arbitration a generally preferable to in-court litigation for securities-related disputes and low utilisation of CIEAC.

The survey results show that all the factors identified above appear to apply to applications of arbitration in private banking disputes, with the exception of fee concerns. Clients may feel more uncertain about whether arbitration is just another procedural hurdle against the resolution of the dispute. Such a perception could be related to the issue of publicity. Arbitration is as complex as the court, but the court has more positive publicity favouring the clients. Clients might be more than aware of their weak position when negotiating a dispute with a bank privately. According to our case studies, Mr Collins' grievance and his reaction echo the above arguments. He simply went to the court first to gain more bargaining power. During the Lehman Brother's breakdown in 2008, when a number of investors made miss-selling claims, most of those investors simply went to the courts. Mr Collins went a step further by accusing the bank of conducting SFC-regulated activities without a proper SFC licence. He filed a writ, the case was reported in the newspaper, and he then went back and talked to the bank. This gained him significant bargaining power to blame and claim. The case was settled by the bank almost immediately. Mr Young's case was published in the newspaper, but he did not go to court; still, the bank insisted they had no liability. This suggests that the threat to take the issue through a legal process could make a difference, but again it depends on the merit of the case. Nevertheless, it should be noted that one bank may be more ready to fight in court than another.

4.4 Discussion: Do clients perceive that they could challenge a bank in a dispute?

4.4.1 Clients generally believed that everything is regulated

The interaction between a bank and a client has largely echoed the regulatory framework described in Chapter 2. Furthermore, although the laws and regulations are not written in the account opening form (Chapter 2, Section 2.4), the clients displayed adequate knowledge of their rights and banks' obligations. However, we have seen evidence from the survey that the clients might simply perceive that the banking procedures they have experienced should have been regulated. Therefore, clients generally presume that whatever they have experienced is well-regulated and monitored. In addition, banks usually do more than what is required, and when banks do not do this, it could imply that this conduct is not regulated in the first place.

This lays an important foundation to answer our overarching question of 'whether arbitration is perceived to be a suitable process'. A possible answer is that it really depends on who is adjudicating the arbitral settings. If banks follow regulators' directions strictly and the clients are made aware of this, it might mean that the most obvious candidate to adjudicate the arbitration would be the regulator alone. Yet, as discussed in Chapter 3, regulators do not play a very active role in resolving disputes between banks and clients, but most of the decision-making process relies solely on the bank's own handling. There is a chance that the bank becomes a 'hidden' arbitrator of the case. In other words, one of the disputants (i.e., the bank) is adjudicating their own disputes with an invisible hand at the back from the regulators to ensure that this process is 'just and proper'. This could lead to potential conflicts of interest and render all benefits of arbitration or features of arbitration within a dispute resolution process useless. This concern is further evaluated in Chapter 6, Section 6.3.3.

4.4.2 Clients' experiences generally do not deviate from the regulated boundaries

With a perception that every activity is monitored and regulated, the clients' responses reveal that (with only a few exceptions) they have been properly served. However, little is correlated with specific features of the private banking business (Chapter 2, Sections 2.2 and 2.3.2). This provides further affirmation that the bank-customer relationship has been at peace even if it is not bound by contract but bound by laws, regulations, and codes of conduct (Chapter 2, Sections 2.3.1 and 2.3.2). Yet, it is uncertain about where clients obtain this knowledge – do the public educate the clients, or do they simply relate their experiences as per the regulation? This is where case studies can give us further insight (Chapter 5). In our case studies, it seems that clients with more than one private bank account would cross-check banks' practices in the same or similar bank services, for example, if they heard of an investment idea from one bank, the clients would not make the decision immediately. Instead of reading the information on their own, the clients might go to another bank and ask it to verify the information and seek a second opinion. Nevertheless, clients could often find different experiences in the same services provided by different banks. The most obvious one is the practice of account opening, where just because a client can open an account in Bank A does not mean that they could do the same in Bank B, even if they are subject to the same set of regulations in Hong Kong.

This phenomenon has further weakened the basis of having arbitration as the dispute resolution channel because clients seem to regard that the activities are regulated and complied with. It might be difficult to legally accuse the bank of being in a wrongful position. The bank can refuse clients' requests and, even if it upsets the client, the client would not be able to 'blame' the bank. This phenomenon is also explained by the survey results in Qc11 to Qc15. Clients have diverse experiences when communicating with banks. This can be explained by two possibilities: the first is that there are different handling practices by different banks as each bank is entitled to offer what suits the bank's internal processing procedures as long as the practices are in compliance with the laws and regulations. This is clearly indicated by the different comprehensiveness of their account opening forms (Chapter 2, Section 2.4). The second is the conduct of the private bankers and the close relationship between private bankers and clients (Chapter 2, Section 2.3.1). Different bankers could have different ways of handling their clients. This could lead to a huge divergence between clients' actual experiences versus their understanding of the laws and regulations.

4.4.3 Generally, there are few disputes between private bank and their clients

Another important observation is that there are very few disputes. As we have seen in our survey results, there was only one response indicating that the respondent had experienced a dispute with his/her private bank. This notably low number of disputes might explain our observation in Section 3.3 of Chapter 3, where after the Lehman Brothers crisis, very few disputes occurred. However, using the FDRC to estimate the demand for private banking disputes is not entirely accurate, because the FDRC has literally excluded private banking disputes due to its low maximum claimable amount (Chapter 3, Section 3.3.1), hence the need to conduct the survey.

Based only on the survey results, the reasons for few disputes happening (and hence the under-utilisation of arbitration) would be due to the perfect harmony of clients' experiences in accordance with the laws and regulations, but the diverse range of communication experienced by different clients creates a gap because the role of the banker is unclear in this context. This will be further examined in subsequent chapters (Chapter 2, Section 2.5.1).

4.4.4 Key features in arbitration are preferred by clients

Based on the survey results, seven out of the twelve processes preferred by clients might indicate that clients generally do not resist the adoption of arbitration to resolve any dispute between them and their banks. This might, at least, suggest that arbitration is not regarded as a non-viable option to resolve private banking disputes. However, there are two very important caveats: the first is that most clients had not experienced arbitration before, and their preferences mainly arose from their own imaginative perceptions of what could or could not be proper. When it comes to reality, they might have very different feelings and perceptions about what arbitration could do. The second is the low utilisation rate of the FDRC, as discussed in Chapter 3. Although the FDRC does not cover private banking disputes, preferences for the arbitration procedure could not explain low utilisation in general. There might be other reasons – either because there were not many disputes escalating to such a level, or because clients do not trust any ADR platform, so clients' preferences in favour of arbitration might only reflect part of the reality if the analysis is based on the survey results alone.

Another important implication is the issue of confidentiality. Most clients prefer the hearings to be held in private, although our case studies might offer a different view. Yet the literature has mainly focused on organisation-to-organisation disputes and investment or lending agreements, so the dispute parties would want to protect commercial secrets in any dispute-handling process. However, this is not the case for individual clients. Between clients and private banks, it seems that only the private bank (ICC report) would prefer to keep the dispute private whilst the clients might prefer to 'create a scene' instead. Also, by disclosing the dispute to the public, the power balance could be positively skewed towards the clients, who might use the media or other pressure to ensure banks take their views seriously. This point will be further illustrated in the subsequent chapters. Nevertheless, there is little evidence to infer that clients would prefer an informal setting, although they might want the flexibility to appeal and know the rationale behind the judgment. This view is later confirmed by our case studies in Chapter 5.

4.5 Conclusion: The more I know, the more I find out what I don't have

Chapter 4 describes clients' knowledge or perceived knowledge of the laws and regulations of private banking, versus their actual experiences. It also describes clients' preferences on arbitration and presents the dilemma that whilst most features of arbitration are preferred by clients, the process itself is not perceived to be viable.

The descriptive analysis shows that, despite the lack of relevant information provided in the account opening form, clients seem to know the laws and regulations governing the private banking industry well. Clients have also been treated in accordance with the legal and regulatory boundaries. This may explain the few disputes in the private banking sector and hence the low utilisation of arbitration can be implied because they are simply not needed.

The alignment between clients' knowledge and experience is more solid in the account opening stage and the product knowledge and risk appetite stage. More divergences appear in the communication channel stage. Although there is no divergence in the dispute resolution channel, this is largely due to the lack of dispute experience to start with, and it does not necessarily mean that the banks are complying. The result of the descriptive analysis reveals that clients' knowledge is largely correctly matched with their experiences with their private banks. A notable divergence is knowledge and experience with regards to the qualification of their private bankers: clients wrongly perceived that private bankers need professional qualifications, whilst in fact, the qualification (namely, the Certified Private Wealth Professionals in Hong Kong) is not yet a mandatory requirement. This gap might suggest that the role of a private banker might have undergone changes that deserve closer attention.

Clients' preferences on the arbitration process show that seven out of the twelve listed arbitration procedures are preferred by the clients. Features not preferred by clients are no appeal and no reason given in the award. Split views are observed in preferences to the document-only hearings, engagement of a lawyer, and a third party to organise an arbitration. There is no specific pattern which suggests that arbitration is not a viable option. Instead, there is a slight trend to be in favour of arbitration. However, our observations are based on the respondents who have not had a dispute with a private bank before. The pattern might not be generalised. Nevertheless, it supports the notion that the under-utilisation of arbitration is due to the lack of private banking disputes. Hence, even if the survey results show that the clients do prefer an arbitration process and it is a viable option, arbitration (or any other form of ADR platform) might not be necessary in the first place. To examine this notion, it is important to explore further why there are so few disputes. Is there a perfect harmony between banks and clients? Are all grievances properly resolved internally before they are formed officially? Do clients know that they could complain or have a dispute? These will be addressed through the case studies examined in Chapter 5.

CHAPTER 5

The transformation of disputes

5.1 Introduction: The importance of the client's perspective

This chapter analyses the findings that emerged from the face-to-face interviews. It first explains the interview structure and then examines clients' insights in the context of each dispute transformation stage in the 'naming, blaming, and claiming' framework. The central issue is to examine why there have been few disputes from examining clients' own experiences and perceptions of their grievances, and whether these experiences have positively or negatively impacted dispute formation. The notion is that if a dispute could not be formed, discussing the suitability of a dispute resolution mechanism would be premature. The subject and agent factors in the 'naming, blaming, and claiming' framework are applied to critically examine clients' insights, in particular the dynamics involved.

The interviewees must have first-hand experience with disputes with their private banks. There were 12 face-to-face interviews conducted with private banking clients, but only four of the interviewees were willing to put their experiences on record. The remaining eight interviewees were bound by confidentiality agreements made with their private banks and were of the view that even if the incidents were mentioned on an anonymous basis, readers might be able to identify the actual incident, which could breach the confidentiality agreements signed upon the resolution of the dispute. The four private banking clients were interviewed through an interactive exchange of dialogue. They were selected based on my own personal network, and there is no mention of the identity of the banks and the individuals themselves. It is believed that the insights generated are genuine and representative. Last, given that I was a private banker for nearly seven years between 2012 and 2019 in Hong Kong, my own views as an observer are also adopted to aid analysis.

The case studies are described in a first-person narrative to facilitate the first-person understanding of participants' dispute experiences, opinions, and chains of thought. The face-to-face interviews will be analysed under the three stages of dispute transformation, and this chapter will explore how each

DOI: 10.4324/9781003407591-5

stage was impacted by the clients' own experiences. Chapter 5 explains sub-research question 2 by offering possible reasons as to why there have been so few formal disputes in the private banking industry.

5.2 Clients prevent naming

The concept of naming refers to whether an individual can identify whether a violation of his rights has taken place, such that the clients would 'name' the violation. Naturally, we identify these rights from the contract so that once the clients have started the grievance the basis of naming would be referred to the terms and conditions in the contract. The interviews aimed to identify whether the clients had acquired the relevant knowledge from the contract signed between themselves and the private banks. It should be noted that in Chapter 4 we established that clients know the regulatory requirements quite well and have generally been well-treated. In this section, it appears that clients spent enormous efforts by themselves to equip themselves with the knowledge.

5.2.1 The dispute is unlikely to happen within the scope of the contract

This relates to the 'scope' factor, in particular the context and circumstances of the dispute. The grievance does not come from the contract. When clients have grievances over a decision or action from the bank's side, clients and banks do not go back to check what was signed and agreed upon; instead, they have an immediate dialogue to see what the bank can do to make the clients feel less upset. Mr Peterson described this process by detailing how clients and banks usually handle grievances, and contracts only come at a very late stage, if at all:

> Well, I think they will eventually [use the contract], depending on the seriousness and the stage of resolution of the case. If the case is getting ugly and serious, more at the later stage of the resolution, the signed account document is clearly one of the pieces of evidence. I am not saying that they won't [use the contract]. The bank will, or otherwise, they won't sign it. **It is about when is it going to be used.** I think most of the time, most of the reputable banks or mature type of bankers would like to handle client dispute on the first level whether [they] can resolve it without getting to further stage, [which] tends to get ugly. When you take out the client documents and say, 'this is what you sign', I think that's a point of no return already.
>
> *(Mr Peterson, interview)*

One of the reasons why discussing contracts is not so popular is that most of the grievances/disputes may not arise from what was written in the contract. In Mr Peterson's experience as a manager of private bankers, the top reason for grievance is not mis-selling/misrepresentation. The top reason is the handling of corporate actions. One example of corporate action is when a publicly listed company distributes dividends, and shareholders can choose to receive their dividend by cash or in kind (i.e., the number of shares based on a pre-set share price); another example is when an event happens in a corporation that issues a bond, for example, a change of ownership of a company, delays, or failure to pay interest on a scheduled date. In these circumstances, bondholders might have the right to either accept or sue the bondholder or deliver a proxy to the destinated agent to manage the matter. Corporate action is the communication between the investors/creditor and the company issuing the shares/bonds. Mr Peterson described, in the 'Corporate Action Incident' to be described later, a situation when he received a complaint from a client of one of the bankers he managed:

> [the client] had a holding of a bond where the issuer will have corporate action very soon. In that corporate action, the bondholder (i.e., that client) is asked to decide whether he wants to 'do nothing' or 'sell the bond'. If he decides to do nothing, the bond will be converted into public shares. However, the communication broke down. Client wanted to sell the bond, but it was not done and later it was converted into shares. Share price dropped and the value of his investment dropped dramatically.
>
> *(Mr Peterson, interview)*

In such a situation, there is no need to draw the contract out and explain what clauses have been broken. Technically, according to Mr Peterson, the responsibility still lay with clients because it was the communication between clients and the issuers directly. The bank served as the middleman, and it was the responsibility of the clients to ensure such communication was thoroughly delivered, as per the contract signed by another contract not in the account opening form. Nevertheless, clients only reacted to what banks and bankers did. Clients thought the cause of the grievance came from the bank, even though strictly speaking it was the clients' own responsibility, even though it was the banker who failed to acknowledge the instruction.

5.2.2 Clients contribute significantly to ensure grievances do not happen

This relates largely to the 'attribution' factors, referring to the perception of the experience. It seems that clients do acknowledge their own responsibilities in engaging with the bank, and they have been very careful when dealing with the bank/bankers. We see that clients tend to engage with the bank proactively to ensure things go in the right order. All four interviewees told me that they had significantly acted to ensure that things would not go wrong. Mr Young described what he did as follows:

> Now what I do is: when Banker A at Bank A recommends me a product, if I cannot understand it after hearing him for five minutes, I will just give up and it is definitely going to be too complicated for me.

If I understand the product from the description, the next thing I will do is to tell Banker A I need to think about it and ask him to send me some materials about this product. Then I will go to another banker at a different bank to hear what he says.

(Mr Young, interview)

There was a clear reason why he did that, which is rooted back to two very unhappy events when he was trying to resolve the disputes privately with the bank, namely, the 'FX accumulator event' and 'risky shares event'.

5.2.2.1 Incident 1: The FX accumulator event

Mr Young's business involves exchanges of AUD and HKD monthly. His banker identified this pattern and, given that the currency value of AUD was very volatile, she advised him to 'regularise' this pattern with a more stable exchange rate every month. It later turned out to be the infamous accumulator and if the market exchange rate traded outside the agreed range, Mr Young needed to buy double the amount. The market did not favour Mr Young, and he ended up compensating USD3 million to the bank and buying up more than he told the bank he would need. He did not feel that this was what he signed up for. He went to talk to the bank first, and it was not easy to get a response. Finally, he consulted a lawyer and reported the case to the press.

Here is what happened: I have been with Bank A for about 5 or 6 years, and I do not have any lending facility with the bank at that time, everything is just cash. There was a new manager that came onboard and started taking care my account, she observed that I had a lot of trades in AUD and EURO – every month I had to trade AUD500 thousands and close to EUR 1 million. We had a meeting introducing herself as a new banker and understand my business. During the meeting, she said to me, 'I know you do trades in AUD and EURO dollars. Our bank can structure some special tailor-made structured products for you'. So, what she did was she structured the product for me, and I finally realised that was what they call 'accumulator'.

Then the size of the accumulator was double or three times as big as what I really need. The lady knew that I did not know Chinese very well. The contract was in plain English, but then the next page was written in Chinese with different context. It is not the translation of the English version. It is, later I was told, the very crucial points of that case.

Then Lehman Brothers blew up. I was told to deposit USD5 million into the bank to make sure that I have the available funds to continue to service this structured product. I said no way. Then I started having a discussion with her and I realised the size would be in fact AUD6 million and EUR16 million to fulfil the whole contract. It was bigger than my actual trade. I did not realise the size of the contract because she told me I only needed to buy once. I did not know I needed to buy it for the whole 12 months because the knock-out price was never touched, and my contract never expired and I was obliged to keep trading EURO and AUD, at double the size since the rate fell below the favourable range

I called the manager and the manager had left the bank already. So another person in the bank handled the case. He told me that the bank had investigated

> the case, the terms of the contract were stated very clearly and the trade was clearly stated in the contract and did not deviate from that. Yet, the contract was in English and Chinese and I initialled the Chinese one, so the bank had a copy of it.
>
> Hence, I was told I was obliged to the contract, or else we need to unwind it. I told the manager that I would not put money into the account. The bank froze my account at that time where I had USD800,000 in the account. The bank said unless I have sufficient money in the bank to fulfil the contract, it is not able to trade anymore.
>
> Hence, I took legal action and engaged a lawyer to study the case and write a legal letter, which has cost me HKD100,000 already. But it does not get any response as quickly as I wish.
>
> Later, I talked to the press. Once the story broke, a bank's senior manager initiated a meeting and promised to escalate the case to the head office and re-negotiated.
>
> *(Mr Young, the FX accumulator event)*

After all conversations, three months later, Mr Young engaged a lawyer who advised him that the key issue of Mr Young's case was to do with the contract. Different content in the same contract was written in Chinese and English interchangeably whilst the bankers involved knew Mr Young did not understand Chinese. However, Mr Young did initial each page. Later, the bank invited him for an 'arbitration', which started with the bank representative telling Mr Young that he had signed the contract already and refused to grant any compensation. Mr Young was also very irritated by the fact that the representative reiterated repeatedly that 'he had to confirm that with the senior' for whatever requests he made. Five minutes later, he slapped the table and left. He wanted to go to court, but in the end, his family members advised him not to start litigation because of potential high cost involved. Finally, he accepted the compensation offered by the bank. The case was then closed but he never banked with them again.

> Finally, we settled on a 60–40% discount, in which the bank paid 60% whilst I paid 40%. At the end, I lost close to USD3 million.
>
> *(Mr. Young, the FX accumulator event)*

5.2.2.2 Incident 2: The risky shares event

This relates to another bank which Mr Young traded in his own capacity. He was advised to invest in a share, but later that share was unlisted. He lost USD300,000. Later he found out that the risk profile of that share was much higher than the level of risk that Mr Young wanted to take on, which he had indicated to the bank. He called the banker, but the banker did not work for the bank anymore. The banker who had taken over Mr Young's account had trouble understanding and following the case. What followed was quite like the FX accumulator event, and three months of chasing resulted in the bank finally offering compensation equivalent to 80% of the invested value and another opportunity to invest in a bond at a discounted price, which ultimately made up the losses incurred.

There are three things in common in these two events with regard to how Mr Young reacted to the grievance. First, the grievance was only identified when a loss was incurred. Second, Mr Young acted on the advice of the banker and called the banker first when things went wrong, but coincidentally both bankers involved had left the bank when the grievance occurred. Third, he only got the attention he looked for when he threatened legal action or adverse publicity; the bank seemed to only react to certain pressure at the time. In the FX accumulator event, one may observe that the 'arbitration' mentioned does not look like the usual arbitration setting at all, based on the description from Mr Young. I now incorporate these three common features into the transformation factors to further articulate these observations. We can see how new grievances and disputes are created due to the people involved.

5.2.3 The conduct of the private banker is the source of grievance

This relates to the 'parties' factor, in particular the identity and type of action associated with the relationship and interaction between the parties. Whilst the private banker may arguably not be the contractual party between the bank and clients, based on the observation from Mr Peterson and Mr Young, the grievance seems to have been caused by bankers. In Mr Peterson's case, the banker forgot to place the order upon the client's instruction. In Mr Young's case, the banker asked Mr Young to trust the banker. It is also evidenced by the fact that when the next banker handled the complaints, they were not quite able to follow up with what had happened to their predecessor.

This research also reveals specifically how clients give consent to what is promised by the private banker, instead of just relying on what the bank documents say, by considering the involvement of a private banker in the signing process and their impact on informed consent. Clients interact with private bankers who very often have personal relationships prior to clients engaging with the private banks. They play a key role in coordinating clients' onboarding, which involves a thorough review of clients' SOW, investment knowledge, and investment experience for onboarding. Clients interact highly with private bankers when they sign contracts with private banks. Private bankers are also the day-to-day point of contact for the clients and are very often the 'source of dispute'. The role of the private banker is crucial as it could affect what clients think they have consented to, as a banker's word could outweigh the content of the contract. When it comes to blame, clients also blame themselves for trusting the private banker so much (Section 5.3).

It should be noted, however, that the conduct of the private banker is not included in the scope of the signing agreement (Chapter 2, Section 2.2.2 and Table 2.2). There is an unclear role between the private banker and clients, which will be discussed further in Section 5.5 in this chapter.

5.3 Clients take the blame

As we will see in Section 5.3, clients are powerless, as they do not know who or what to blame. It appears that they blame themselves. The banks regard themselves to be served in accordance with the laws and regulations. Clients also tend to believe that most of the activities are regulated and that the bank has done more than is necessary under the law. Against this background, when things do not go as expected, the client might think they have been asking for something more than what can be committed to by the bank. It weakens their confidence to proceed with their dispute and might further widen the perceived power imbalance between the bank and the clients before a dispute is formed. It would make *any* form of dispute resolution mechanism unviable (sub-research question 2), as the chance for clients to win is nil.

Clients also blame themselves for not reading the one-sided contract they signed. This further puts clients into a weaker position in both the contractual relationship as well as in the dispute. Clients do not regret not reading the agreement because it is not possible to thoroughly read it, and even if they read the contract, only very few would understand it; even fewer would have the power to change the terms and conditions. This is why it is forbidden to deprive consumers and employees of their access to court on an involuntary, unknowing basis and hence making the non-consensual nature of mandatory consumer arbitration itself a problem. Some companies may deliberately design their arbitration clauses in a manner geared to decrease the likelihood that a consumer will focus on the arbitration clause. Psychologists have shown that predictable irrationality biases will prevent people from properly evaluating the costs and benefits of accepting such a clause (e.g., being overly optimistic) or underpredicting the processes, or undervaluing what they are losing by giving up a right to sue. Companies may seek to take advantage of consumers' irrational behaviour by manipulating arbitration clauses together with other aspects of consumer contracts (Sternlight, 2004). With clients knowingly not reading the contracts, naturally when things do not go as planned, they blame themselves first.

Hence, as a grievance starts to form, clients might not know who to blame except themselves. They could find themselves powerless to blame someone else. This argument is confirmed by Mr Young's and Ms Emily's experiences that when things turned sour, they believed that it was also their own fault. They blamed themselves for either trusting the bankers too much, or deep down they believed somehow that there was nothing clients could do, as it was the bank's own business decision. Their perception of their own power against the bank was further weakened before a dispute could even start.

5.3.1 Clients do not rely on one single bank

The 'ideology' factor comes from a legal victory that someone can 'legislate morality', and the sense of entitlement to enjoy certain experiences and be free from others (Felstiner et al., 1980, p. 643). In Mr Young's case, his sense of entitlement did not come from victory in a legal case but instead to avoid the occurrence of grievance and avoid getting the wrong information. He developed his own routine to govern his banking relationship with the banker after the two incidents. His sense of entitlement comes from his ability to be free from the influence of bankers from one bank:

> It was my fault as well. My fault for trusting the bank too much by their interpretation over the table roughly what it means. I trusted the bank and the banker and signed the contract.
>
> Interviewer: In this case, when you open a private banking account, would you read all the terms and conditions before you sign anything?
>
> Mr Young: Not really, I don't read 100% of the 60 pages of the whole thing. The print was too small. I would not bother trying to know what the bank could do, or not do.
>
> Interviewer: Then how do you make sure you understand what you have agreed with?
>
> Mr Young: Every possible way! When they ask you to sign the risk disclosure, what type of risk you can take, they will make it in such a way that if you tick Option C but not Option A, you are not able to buy any products because it shows you are a risk-averse client. Sometimes, to buy a certain product for the profile, I must tick Option A. Now, I will be very careful.
>
> *(Mr. Young, the FX accumulator event)*

He made sure that his risk appetite level would not allow the bank to advise him to invest in a high-risk product he could not understand. However, as shown in the FX accumulator event, Mr Young did not know about the risk profile mismatch when the banker advised him to invest in high-risk shares. He did not ask the banker whether the share was categorised at a risk level higher than indicated in his risk profile. He only listened to what the bankers had told him when making the investment decision, and so, it appeared that he might have no or very little knowledge about what was written in the prospectus or what he had signed in the account opening form relating to the role of banks when he made an investment decision. Hence, the risky shares event should not have happened if he had been told that the shares were categorised at a risk higher than his profile before the investment. At that time, he was not explicitly asked whether he accepted this risk mismatch (which was then not a regulatory requirement, but now is). The risk share events should also have not happened if he did not have to respond to a margin call when the values of the currency went against his investment. If the investment made a profit, he might not even have noticed that it was the case. Learning from this experience, Mr Young appeared to have a closer look at himself:

> *Interviewer:* How do you gate keep yourself? Do you seek advice from the banker or conduct your own research?

Mr Young: After my experience with past banks, I do not invest in anything that I don't understand. If it takes the banker more than five minutes to explain the product is, it is too complicated for me. I do not buy it. Very simple way… I get offered a lot of products too. SEN, ELN, accumulators etc. all these types of things I still get offered and will not touch them anymore.

Interviewer: So, you just do not touch things that gave you a bad experience before.

Mr Young: Frankly speaking sometimes, the people who sell it to me, they don't understand it. They pretend they understand it and try to sell you this product. Then they bring in another so-called professional to join the conference call to sell you the products. It takes 30 minutes to sell you the products and at the end of the day, it has no meaning. I just buy the bond, which is easier to understand.

Interviewer: On that ground, who you are more engaged with in the relationship? Do you feel yourself engaging more with the bank, or with the bankers?

Mr Young: Now, I don't deal with the banker. Frankly speaking, I have not spoken to the bank relationship manager for two years now.

Interviewer: Why not?

Mr Young: Any products that her junior introduces to me. I take to another bank and ask, 'Is it okay?', 'does it look good to you?'. They would persuade me not to buy from them, but I also got their opinion on it. That is how I balance my thinking now. Because what happened is, they want to get my business, the other bank would tell me the best thing and bad thing of this contract. For example, Bank A gives me a contract, then I take it to Bank B for their opinion, then I realised how bad it is. Then I go back to Bank A and say it is too risky for me. I have gone to this stage whereby I don't trust the bank anymore.

(Mr Young, the FX accumulator event)

Mr Young's behaviour is *complicated*, and it involves *ambiguous behaviour*. He could have set a lower risk appetite threshold in the first place, but he did not because it would greatly restrict his choice of making an investment. The risk appetite was already the second highest for simple investments in shares in cash, and when it involves applying a credit line for leveraged investment (even secured) it would be the highest risk appetite. Whilst he said he would not trust a banker anymore, he would ask for opinions from different bankers from different banks. His strategy is to let 'banks fight each other'. One banker would have attacked and identified as many risks and problems as possible from the recommendation of another banker in the view of gaining the business. Mr Young wanted them to contradict each other so he could be alerted of any abnormality and gather reasons to reject one banker with a reason validated by another banker. In order to do this, he must have more than one private bank account in HK to create this additional source of information, or a channel to exit the bank if the bank could not offer what the clients wanted, which is confirmed by Ms Emily's experience where she was always prepared to leave her current private bank if things could not be resolved (Section 5.4.3).

5.3.2 Lack of transparency of bank's internal dispute resolution mechanism

> The bank should be the party who tells me how this could be handled, how much they should compensate, and how it would not happen anymore. It is the bank's responsibility to tell me how to follow up. The bank should clarify what are my next steps and give me some ideas what to do.
>
> *(Mr Young, the FX accumulator event)*

In Felstiner et al. (1980), the 'choice of mechanisms' factor refers to where the person voices a complaint. This factor is related to the 'dispute institutions' factor, which describes the substantive norms, rules, and customs that influence the transformation process. These two factors would clearly be impacted by and influence the 'objective sought' in the transformation process. These three interrelated factors clearly impacted Mr Young's expectations in the dispute resolution process after the bank reacted to the situation. However, the experience he had was different from what he could have expected. For clarity, it would be useful to evaluate his experience and articulate the phenomenon through the 'choice of mechanisms' and 'dispute institutions' factors, whilst leaving the 'objective sought' factor aside, as has been analysed in a prior section. Mr Young's objective was clear – he needed to be compensated for the loss incurred. He left it to the bank to decide how this could be done. This thought circles back to the 'choice of mechanisms' and 'dispute institution' factors.

Mr Young made a complaint directly to the bank, but he only got the attention he needed after months of chasing and threatening publicity and legal action. Mr Young stated that the entire process was, and should be, driven by the bank. He did not provide any evidence to the bank except to tell the bank officer what he had experienced. He did not mention what he needed. He hoped that he would only be *reacting* to the bank's proposal of resolution. The bank came back to him, and the experience was not pleasant at all, which will be described later in this section. Concurrently, Mr Young went to the SFC and lodged a complaint, but at that time Mr Young reflected that the SFC was too busy to handle his complaint. Therefore, he did not hold any hope in that channel and did not bother to escalate the risky shares event to the regulators, given the amount involved which was smaller than the FX accumulator event. It left him in a situation of either referring to the bank or the court. He hired a lawyer for both the FX Accumulator Event and Risky Shares Event:

> I am sure they had more important cases to deal with and therefore my case had to wait… I would not bother going to them because the involved amount was ten times less (than the FX accumulator event). Maybe I should have gone to HKMA and would have got a completely different treatment? I don't know.
>
> *(Mr Young, the risky shares event)*

Back to the experience he had with the FX accumulator event where he finally got the attention he asked for, the bank proposed to have an 'arbitration'. Below was how Mr Young reacted to the arbitration process:

> I slapped the table and left five minutes after it started…
>
> The room was very small. There was me, my lawyer, the other side and a middle person sitting between us. The arbitration starts with the bank representative explaining the bank's position. It was a lot of nonsense and all I could hear was the following two messages: First, I had signed the contract already. Second, the involved banker had left already and there was no way I could not find out exactly what happened that day.
>
> I interrupted and pointed to them the problematic contract prepared with intermittent use of Chinese and English. They told me they had to go back and confirm.
>
> They were not the one in charge! They were here just to tell me there was nothing they could do besides telling me nothing they could do.
>
> *(Mr Young, the FX accumulator event)*

During the interview, I double-checked with Mr Young that he was sure that it was an arbitration that he had attended. He confirmed positively as he clearly remembered it was the term used by the bank and the lawyer had told him so. But he was not told about the process of the 'arbitration' and was not given the chance to share his views. But Mr Young did not find it useful even if he had been able to present his case because he soon realised the banker appeared to have only one purpose of being in arbitration – to deliver a message to Mr Young. It was not the platform to talk about the case and decide who made the mistake. Mr Young stated:

> [The people] were not there to settle. They were there to tell you what you did wrongly and you are liable for everything that you did; and you are liable for everything you signed. They were not the one in charge! They were here just to tell me there was nothing they could do besides telling me nothing they could do.
>
> It wasn't fair…
>
> [to make it fair] All parties that were involved in signing the contract, everybody including the bank manager, should be there, but not the representative of that person or the company… the representatives cannot make decisions… not that they didn't care, but the bank representatives can't make decision. What they said was that they just inherited the problem because I signed the contract

with the previous manager. We have to have clarification before we proceed or before the bank get back to the client.

I will bring back to the bank and will discuss further' is what I heard most but it was not what I want to hear. When I heard that I already realised I should leave. I signed the contract with the bank and the bank is speaking with me now, but what about the relationship manager who dealt with me?

Every other second, they said they needed to get back for clarification. They know nothing. That is why after their speech, I slapped the table and ran away because they were not here to discuss. They don't know the problem.

Also, before meeting for arbitration, the bank's lawyer and my lawyers should come to a close 80–90% agreement and formalise it in a close-door, private, settlement.

(Mr Young, the FX accumulator event)

His experience of arbitration did not seem to align with arbitration as it is generally understood as we see under Section 1.2.3 of Chapter 1. It indicat es the confusion associated with the use of terminology at that time. Yet Mr Young stated quite clearly what he could have expected in a dispute resolution setting. His experience of being put in the dark during the resolution process further made him believe that it was not ideal to rely on the bank to resolve a dispute as it had occurred, and it appeared in his dialogue that he found it a bad idea to rely on the bank at all. The only function of the bank was to act as a platform allowing him to assess the investment market, but it had been limited with regard to its execution function. He used the platform and it appeared to him to be his own problem that he could not master the platform well by himself, leading him to blame himself when things started to turn against his own expectations.

5.3.3 Clients may not blame if the mistakes result in benefiting clients

This appears to be a form of manipulation by the bank or the clients to eliminate a dispute – by waiting or delaying the handling in case the loss incurred in the dispute becomes a benefit. For the bank, if it is an investment-related loss, the market price might turn in favour and clients would not be upset. For the clients, such a mistake can become a stake to ask for other discounts in future transactions. This echoes the 'naming, blaming, and claiming' model that the dispute transformation stage could be unstable. It would be particularly true for investment-related private banking disputes where the remedies could have changed. This is briefly mentioned by Mr Peterson that in the 'corporate action' incident, the remedies kept changing. Mr Peterson explained that the loss incurred in this incident changed every day due to share price fluctuation. It is also affected by how the bank calculated the value of the position:

The client basically looks at two factors: first had this transaction be placed as instructed? Then, what should have been the value of the position if it is

> correctly placed. Whereas the bank's calculation averages out the value by also considering the timing of the complaint and existing market value.
>
> *(Mr Peterson, interview)*

This happens in most disputes, but in a banking dispute related to investment or corporate action, it is more obvious. Imagine a scenario when the client had been mistakenly vested in some shares that s/he did not want, but the price of the share value rose significantly and the client ended up gaining more than what s/he could have earned otherwise. The client is unlikely to feel wronged, and based on my own observation, this happens all the time when a bank or bankers are saved from a dispute because the market turns in favour of the clients. Now imagine the market favours the bank one day but the tide turns the next day.

This relates back to how clients' experiences and feelings are largely reactive to bankers' behaviour and the complicated attribution process clients go through. It appears that the grievance itself is not really a grievance but how the grievance is managed determines how it is named (if a client decides to name it in the first place). Mr Peterson emphasised a number of times that a dispute is not an issue in the industry, as it is about how the banker handles it in a humanised way:

> However, the one who deals with the dispute is the banker, and that should be personal. How you humanise this process, making the client feels like their concern is being heard and they are really working on it. But skeleton, however, is very mechanic and intuitional. When client dispute happens, how do the person or banker follow this mechanism to make it more humane, and let client feel that they are engaged, no matter what the outcome is. I think the problem most of the time is how the front-line people humanise the skeleton. The problem happens, most of the dissatisfaction is the way they poorly handle the process.
>
> *(Mr Peterson, Interview)*

Although a clear direction on the client complaint hearing process is what the client wants, a bank usually lacks transparency in such a process, which is clearly illustrated in the two case studies with Mr Young.

The bank told Mr Young that it was very worried about the floodgate problem, that all other clients who signed similar contracts would come to make a claim against the bank. Then, it could be time to take real legal action. Mr Young considered with his lawyer and his family whether a USD3 million claim was worth the effort and hassle. They decided it was not because the bank also told them they would be ready to fight until the end once it went to court.

Mr Young did not have a preference on how the problem could be resolved. But Mr Young was not happy with what he had experienced because the bank did not send the right person who either understood the incident or had the authority to make a decision on the spot. However, this did not further provoke Mr Young to go to court, but instead, he became tired and started thinking about how much more would it take. He gave up:

> Once it went to the court, I would not be so sure anymore.
>
> *(Mr Young, the FX accumulator event)*

Mr Young was not too keen to go to the courtroom because of how little he could achieve there (Felstiner et al., 1980, p. 648). He was also concerned about the enormous efforts needed to spend time in the courtroom with little certainty of the outcome. This echoes the findings of the online survey (Chapter 4, Section 4.2) that clients do have a perception that banks comply with everything and every activity is regulated. Therefore the feeling of uncertainty about going to court would have grown stronger especially due to the client's perception that the law is always on the bank's side. Even if Mr Young did have the financial resources to fight the bank in court, he did not have the time or energy to fight the case, and the best remedy was to leave the bank, which is also what happened with Ms Emily, to be described in Section 5.4.1.

5.4 Clients ask, or leave

With clients' strong preference to prevent naming (Section 5.2) and the fact that clients blame themselves when a grievance is named (Section 5.3), it can be observed that not only the bank but also the clients would want to sweep the dispute away (Edelman et al., 2014). In this internal dispute resolution perspective, clients appear to be part of the managerial team of the bank, and the details become an internal issue that the dispute is being handled, managed, and disposed of, rather than litigated to claim civil rights or justice. This could be potentially dangerous because if internal resolution does not work, the clients would go straight to the courtroom because the ADR channel has already become part of the internal resolution mechanism.

5.4.1 Clients rely on the bank's reactions in resolving a dispute

If we set aside the situation where a person is not a client or has decided to exit the bank until the disputes have been resolved (Chapter 3, Section 3.5.3), the case studies show us that clients appear to still rely on the bank in the resolution of a dispute, somehow like making an application to the bank and waiting for the results, which is quite similar to applying for a credit card (as clients ask), and if the application fails, then the client would close the account (as clients leave) or sue in court.

The *scope* of banking services will not allow a dispute. This is the general perception of Ms Emily. Before we examine Ms Emily's case, it might be useful to review the scope factor and incorporate it into Ms Emily's case.

'The scope of conflict – the extent of relevant discourse about grievances and claims – is affected both by the objectives and behaviour of disputants and by the processual characteristics of dispute institutions'. The scope of the conflict is perhaps *complicated* by the fact that Ms Emily did not believe she stood a chance against the bank, as she was a corporate lawyer herself and knew the bank's position was unlikely to be challengeable. However, she still escalated her grievance and fought to challenge the requirements imposed on her to re-submit all the documents when her initial private bank was acquired by another bank. Ms Emily was very careful with the meaning of the word 'dispute' when I applied this term. She did not want to mix this with the word 'disagreement' (Felstiner et al., 1980, p. 641):

> A dispute is where you think your legal rights are breached. A disagreement is where you do not agree with a term and conditions in a contract.
>
> *(Ms Emily, interview)*

Ms Emily was of the view that it was almost impossible to make a bank liable in a *dispute*. She reasoned that even if one does not agree with the requirements of the bank, in essence, the bank is unlikely to breach the contract or the law, especially when it is required by the bank and not the banker. With her incident, she did not know why she had to prepare all the documents again just because Bank A was acquired by Bank B, but she could not say that the bank had breached the law or the contract.

> It is very unclear to me why I had to re-do all the documentation again just because Bank A was being acquired by Bank B. They requested exactly the same set of documents, but I had to request those documents again at a cost because they only accepted documentation being valid within a short period of time.
>
> I raised my concern and asked if I could re-use the certificate of incumbency requested six months ago, and I could vouch that there was no change of ownership or directorship. My banker told me no, they only accepted certificate within the three-month period. Then I asked what the difference between three months is and six months; the banker tried hard to explain but it still did not make sense to me.
>
> At great expense, I had to figure out how to set up the same structure at a different jurisdiction that the bank was willing to open account for. It costed many thousands of dollars to do so. But without a bank account at each LLC (Limited Liability Company), of course that irrevocable trust would become practically useless, so I was forced to do that by the bank at that time.
>
> Again, I had no way to really challenge that decision. That was something told to me as a conclusion. I was given a time limit. I was told the account was going to be shut. There was no way to object it. That was it. It was all final. So, at that time, I was obviously not happy with it, but I still went ahead and at great expense and great deal of time to change the account setup and to move that structure jurisdiction.
>
> Happened a year later when all the information was relevant and up to date, I felt it was unreasonable [to request the documents from scratch again]. I also felt like we had very legitimate reasons to have these set up in this way even though it was sort of complex that you don't see very often, but again I am a trained lawyer,

> and I spent many years in structuring bank deals. Therefore, I was very familiar with the use of structure. For me, I was very familiar with the process and I didn't see that it is complex. It makes a lot of sense. For the bank specifically their compliance department, they felt it may not be used very often, they didn't understand the rationale and they were afraid of the structure. So, I felt like there was in doubt of the structure and it was starting from a claim of legitimacy. It was set up for some illegal purpose, and then I had to convince the bank that it is legitimate. There was lot of money and time that I spent to deal with this problem which first came up from Bank A and then Bank B just because of this complex structure.
>
> But it is their own policy. There is nothing you can do about it.
>
> *(Ms Emily, the interview)*

Ms Emily was already very frustrated with the policy because this documentation process should not have happened given that it was an acquisition. Bank B should not need to re-do everything Bank A had done. It was clearly inefficient and created unnecessary burdens for the client. Yet, one could not really argue against the bank's policy, which was that it was the bank's own discretion to do so.

Nevertheless, there was one occasion in which she had the opportunity to fix what she disagreed with. On that occasion, a banker at Bank C told her that she could not conduct a foreign exchange with a same-day settlement, and she had to wait for two days for the trade to happen. She did not think this was true. She argued against it and, similar to Mr Young's experience, the banker could not address the client's problem because the banker was not the one involved. Ms Emily escalated the situation to the banker's manager and then it was resolved. It was apparent that the banker was not familiar with the process whilst the problem was not associated with the bank policy. Therefore, any exception would be a mistake made by bankers. This is also confirmed by Mr Peterson's incident on corporate action, where the banker failed to follow the instruction made by clients.

But neither Ms Emily nor Mr Peterson would believe that the mistakes from the private banker would cause problems for the bank, as the way the complaints were handled seemed to be quite similar to 'taking a shot' by 'asking' the bank to offer a 'leeway' or 'exception' to each situation, without accusing the bank of making a mistake. And if banks refused to give way, the best they could do is to walk away and move all the assets to another private bank. It was confirmed by Ms Emily that once she was asked to re-submit all the documents of the investment companies again, she opened another private banking account using the same sets of documents, just to make sure she had a choice. Clients are always ready to leave if the ask has failed.

5.4.2 Clients prefer courtroom resolution

This relates back to the 'dispute resolution mechanism' factor where clients would find making a complaint to the bank or HKMA meaningless.

Knowing that the grievance is usually caused by the conduct of the banker (Section 5.2.3), there is no point in escalating a dispute with the bank. In Mr Collins's case, his grievance was only identified when the banker's conduct went against the banker's description, and although the content of the contract favoured the bank, the banker's conduct did not. Mr Collins immediately went to court after realising the uselessness of hearing the bank blaming the banker involved.

Mr Collins had a joint account with his wife in a private bank. The day-to-day operation of the banking relationship was done through his wife. Mrs Collins was an active member of high society and had good friends in many sectors, including banking. When it came to banking or investment advice, she only believed her friends' advice as she believed her friends would not trick her given the relationships built:

> I discovered what had happened when its [the bank's] staff rang to ask for topping up of a margin deal. I never 'invest' with margin and thus asked why I was asked to top up margin. Then when they explained, I discovered that my wife had said yes to a staff who was a close 'friend' without knowing what it [this investment] was.
>
> *(Mr Collins, interview)*

Nevertheless, things did go wrong. The bank appeared to have the authority to operate their joint account and make investments through borrowing from the same bank, using the invested assets placed in the bank as collateral to support the loan. It was simply not the arrangement they recalled, as they had not authorised the bank to borrow throughout those years. They did not confirm because no statement had been sent to them. Mr Collins did not answer when I further asked whether Mrs Collins had read the contract before signing it in the first place. But apparently, it did not stop him from acting immediately after checking the relevant facts when the bank failed to address why the borrowing had happened:

> Having checked all the bank statements (which were not sent to us because this 'friend' had used the 'hold mail' and kept all bank correspondence to us with the bank) it was discovered that we were having weekly borrowing from the bank to invest in various deals although what we had with the bank was more than enough to cover all these deals. This weekly borrowing generated bank charges and interest payments to the bank which was deducted from the monies we had with the bank...
>
> When I asked the bank to explain why this weekly borrowing happened instead of using the monies we had with them, they could not answer.
>
> *(Mr Collins, interview)*

It turned out, after the bank's investigation, that this operation had been going for six years until they were margin-called, a call for extra collateral to cover existing borrowing, which Mr and Mrs Collins never authorised. Mrs Collins contacted her banker immediately, but the banker had left the bank without telling her. Like the situation of Mr Young, the bank told Mr and Mrs Collins that they now found it difficult to validate their complaint, but this did not affect Mr and Mrs Collins at all when it comes to requesting the bank to take full responsibilities:

> However, this 'friend' had already left the bank and we were not even told by her about it. We did not know whether she was dismissed by the bank although we suspect that she was, and the bank was left with no witness to explain all the dealings and why there were such dealings.
>
> The first thing we did was to write a letter to the bank to put everything we complained of on record. Then we issued a writ against it but without filing a statement of claim because I had in mind the claim for fraud.
>
> *(Mr Collins, interview)*

What Mr Collins did not tell me was that the writ was reported in the news as well. It was not what he intended, but he expected this given the attention he had already had, at least within the legal community, and the court reporter would have noticed his case immediately. Also, notably, according to the news, the writ contained more. The writ also accused the bank of operating a banking business, securities business, and asset management business without a licence or proper authorisation in a specific period, which was at the early stage of their engagement with the bank. Note that the writ was issued without a statement, and therefore Mr and Mrs Collins did not respond further what has been written in the statement.

Mr Collins knew very little about the complaint channel offered by the HKMA, and hence never filed a complaint to it and would not have considered this. When it came to helping a client to resolve the dispute with the bank, he only said, 'All that HKMA can do is within its powers'. It reflects his high expectation of HKMA but also his lack of understanding, or enthusiasm, of what the HKMA can do. To him, the best process to resolve his private banking dispute was:

> Issue a writ and then talk
>
> It was indeed reported in the newspapers that I had issued a writ against this bank. That was part of the reason why the bank was willing to settle in the end. It wanted to keep its reputation and not let the public know that its staff had committed fraud.
>
> *(Mr Collins, interview)*

Whilst Mr Collins's case was very straightforward, one important observation should be noted. At that time, they did not pay attention to their bank statements nor did they regularly check their investment portfolio. This is now impossible within the current regulatory landscape because private bankers are now obliged to meet the clients and go through the investment portfolio regularly to ensure clients understand their financial position (Hong Kong Monetary Authority, 2017). But this measure may not be useful because if the portfolio is making money, any wrongdoing is unlikely to cause a grievance and will eliminate the grievance quite instantly, such as the risky shares event with Mr Young.

5.4.3 Leaving the bank is a better choice than challenging the bank

The only *choice of mechanism* is to negotiate with the bank directly. Ms Emily made it very clear that there was no point in debating with the bank unless the execution was obviously wrong. Near the end of the interview, she told me that she went through the bank's internal process to complain about the request to change the country of incorporation of a corporate account she had with another bank. She was asked to fill in a form to start with, which she described as follows:

> I filled out a form, maybe two pages long, and I listed why I felt that their concern (of tax evasion) did not apply to my accounts. I explained the legitimacy of setting up the company in that jurisdiction, etc. My case was very straightforward and did not contain any issues relating to tax evasion other company setup might have been exposed to when trying to structure them like such. I filled the two pages for them to discuss internally and then I was told that we still had to change and I had to redomicile. It didn't go anywhere else but instead just went through a formal complaint process internally with the bank.
>
> *(Ms Emily, interview)*

Before that, she repeatedly explained why there was no point in going through any mechanism other than talking to the bank directly. When I asked her about arbitration, she regarded 'arbitration' as either a legal process not much different from a court process or a place where she might have equal grounds for escalating the argument and discussion informally. She responded:

> It depends. I guess in terms of the arbitration like you are required to have legal counsel and is made to feel like it is a very formal arbitration process, then I probably wouldn't really distinguish it that much from a court process.
>
> If I felt it was like the Small Claim Tribunal sort of process where no one has legal representation and it was a discussion decided to produce some kind of compromised outcome and suppose to based just on legal merit alone, then I would be more open to it. So, I think it was less formal and wasn't required to get legal representation. I felt like the bank also would not go and spend lots of money on getting a powerful lawyer to argue that case, and the purpose wasn't just to argue at specific legal point but it was specifically decided to ensure that all laws will be in comply with that the customers went through arbitration process, so that they felt more happy with the outcome, then that's something I would have been prepared to do.
>
> *(Ms Emily, interview)*

The bank is in a favourable situation because legally there seems to have been no chance for Ms Emily to win a case. It is the bank's legal right to decide how they conduct their own business. They had more resources to fight against their clients and only if the bank wants to improve customer satisfaction will the bank discuss the disagreement with the client concerned. She explained what she would have expected if she were in arbitration with the bank, which turned out to be nothing like arbitration at all. It is quite similar to Mr Young's experience in using the word 'arbitration' but the process being nothing like it.

> Specifically, it relates to arguing the legal point of a terms and conditions contract. If it was in a formal setting and it was specifically just to argue the legal point whether or not you signed the contract, I would have thought that it's more likely that the bank would win in a sense that whichever legal point that was being argued, it would be upheld by the judge. So, I think you are asking me if I would agree to an arbitration process, I think it depends on the purpose and process, like I wouldn't want to take a bank to court to argue whether or not I was bounded by the terms and conditions of the account opening documentations because I feel like based on a pure legal review of arguments, and maybe they would have a stronger argument and the judge might from a policy standpoint want to uphold the contract. Otherwise, it would open up all kinds of 'worms' in terms of people who joined later and try to form an argument based on that precedent.
>
> Secondly, I would feel like the legal resources available to the bank and amount they are willing to spend to prove that their terms and conditions contract is upheld would be huge, including the staff and resources put in their legal team. And as an individual or company taking them to the court, we wouldn't have the same legal resources and wouldn't have the same situation in terms of subsequence precedent, so no, I wouldn't go that far.
>
> When I enter into informal arbitration where the purpose was not just to argue a legal point, where the purpose was to discuss the disagreement and see if a compromise or some kind of outcome that would increase customer satisfaction was possible without jeopardising whatever the legal right, remedy or stand the bank was trying to adhere to, then yes. If it was a case of not requiring me to get legal representation, I felt like it would be more than just an argument based on the law.
>
> If I thought it was going to be raising a disagreement where there was more than just a legal point of state, what is the purpose and rationale of arbitration if one of the goals was to improve customer satisfaction and see if the outcome was possible where the customer could be satisfied and could be happy? That means the bank may depart from their legal right to apply that policy, then maybe I would do it, but it kind of depends on the purpose and the proceeding. Again, it takes a lot of customer time and so if you feel like it is not gonna be fair, and it is not gonna change anything, then why go through that process?
>
> *(Ms Emily, interview)*

The day the bank rejected her request became the day she left the bank. Because there was no point arguing with a bank that would not listen to its customers,

> I would just leave the bank if I could not be satisfied anymore. As a matter of fact, the reason why I was willing to go through the same process at Bank B was that I was also opening another account with another bank. I was very ready to leave.

> There is no point to go to arbitration when the purpose is to discuss any legal argument. I will only go to an arbitration when we're sitting down to talk about possibility to make the bank policy more flexible from status quo.
>
> Actually, if I have doubt, I just go to another private bank and set up an account with them. It is such that I would never be in the situation where I only have one private bank relationship and therefore if they decided to appoint some random policy change to shut the account, I will not be in the situation where the whole structure was made impractical because I had no banking relationship there. The way I deal with this was to diversify my private bank exposure and private bank relationships. Till this day, I have multiple private banking relationships. That's what this taught me. It taught me I cannot rely on one institution and I need to go on a mixture of multiple relationships, so that if one ever had some random change on policy and that impacts me, then I can easily move my assets, I can easily say goodbye and shut the account so that this not going to impact me.
>
> *(Ms Emily, interview)*

She then talked about the role of the regulator – in her opinion, going to the regulator was not going to help either. She described that the role of HKMA, similar to how Mr Peterson commented on the organisation, was not to help customers but only to safeguard the banking system – although making a complaint to HKMA may also allow customers to be heard:

> I would expect that there would be like a more formal record in the HKMA. I expect that there would be some kind of follow-up and maybe an in-person meeting where they document who they have spoken to and what their complaint process went through, and then maybe a discussion of the outcome. Yea, I feel like it would be a more formal process but I don't know, just my guess.
>
> In these cases where just involved the bank implementing their policies, I feel like HKMA does not really want to intervene because it is just a policy disagreement and the customer feels the burden. HKMA again is probably there to make a point for you and remind you that you can shut your account and go elsewhere. For them they are implementing a broader policy and concern, and they would not want to create precedent all these sorts of things, so yea, I just feel like unless all of the sudden the bank has ten thousands of complaints, then HKMA would have thirty thousand complaints. So they are going to be thinking about the broader industry implementations but not just to a bank, and so… it may be even less likely to get any change through that path.
>
> I don't think they want to intervene a policy that a bank applied. I just don't feel like it is what they will do. They are going to feel like violating the bank's autonomy. But if it is about setting up fraudulent accounts then I think the HKMA would be more likely to get involved as it is related to the reputation of the banking industry as a whole. I personally feel that it is very extreme behaviour.
>
> I think it's a good idea to get the customer a whole spectrum of choices in the situation, and it would be a good thing. For example, maybe the bank offers a less formal alternative, say a full-blown court process which is expensive and public, and maybe it would involve HKMA with your complaints being made to HKMA because it gives customers everything, and they feel like it's more than just a legal proceeding, then maybe that's something they would participate in. Obviously, it's important that customers feel like there is an independent

> arbitrator, or moderator or mediator, and their goal is more than just to uphold the law. That will be pretty cool. It's an optional process by the bank that would potentially have the benefit to the customer reducing the chance of them making it to a more extreme way of mediating the situation, for example going to HKMA.
>
> *(Ms Emily, Interview)*

Ms Emily indicated quite clearly that clients would not be bothered to launch a formal dispute against the bank. Any informal dispute resolution mechanism would be too formal if it must rely on written documents assessing the merit of the law. It seems the ADR mechanism itself has already put the clients off, and what clients need is a real informal channel to discuss with the bank how business could be delivered in a way more aligned with their needs. But Ms Emily was convinced that banks would not cater to her needs.

5.5 What hinders the formation of a dispute?

5.5.1 Grievance does not come from a breach of contractual terms

Mr Peterson shared how a grievance arose due to a banker's failure to execute the client's instruction. In his experience and observation as both a private banker, manager of private bankers, and private banking client himself, he emphasised that the only relevant matter is how bankers, the *representatives* of the bank, manage the relationship in the event of a dispute, as clients usually only *react* to what a banker has said, instead of relying on what has been written down in the signed contract. Neither the bank nor the clients handle their disputes based on what was signed unless absolutely necessary in the event of litigation in court. Clients are reactive to the bank's response because clients also place a burden on themselves to avoid the formation of any injurious experiences. This could be regarded as a *self-attribution* process because, should a grievance start to happen, a client would blame themselves, discouraging them from standing firm in their dispute with the bank. Yet, this *self-attribution process* is itself *complicated* because clients also *attribute* the faults to the bank when a grievance starts to occur. At this point, the attitude of private bankers could become important because clients have complicated feelings of both feeling guilty (of not being able to prevent the wrong and hoping that the bank will 'rule in their favour') and angry at this mistake occurring in the first place. Finally, the *objective sought* by clients is unstable. Clients might not know what to expect whilst escalating a complaint, but as confirmed by the Corporate Action Incident described by Mr Peterson, the usual objective is to cover the monetary loss. Time appears to often be the best medicine in banking disputes when the market value is involved. Clients generally do not care about the mistake anymore if it does not incur a monetary loss. Mr Young's experience in accepting the offer proposed by the bank in the risky shares event confirms this observation, as Mr

Young did not continue the complaint because the proposed remedy made him better off.

Ms Emily's grievance came from her disagreement with the bank's policy. This further illustrates how the *representative* of the bank (not directly related to the dispute) could form or resolve the grievance. In Ms Emily's case, she mentioned that the banker followed up diligently, but her banker did not resolve the issues because it was a strict bank policy that was not easy to amend. She thought negotiating with the bank directly was the only *choice of mechanism* because the bank had the legal right to decide how it conducted the business if it fit into the regulatory landscape. The regulator was not going to be helpful as the *scope* had already been confirmed when she engaged with the private bank, and any legal argument would be unlikely to win a case. Even if she was not happy with what she had experienced, because of the way the grievance was formed, she knew that there was nothing she could do. She was only able to be certain that the fault had been due to the bank, which, in Ms Emily's case, stemmed from an inexperienced banker handling foreign exchange transactions.

5.5.2 The role of the regulator in building bank–customer relationships

The role of regulation and regulator needs to be examined in the context of unequal contractual relations and information asymmetry skewed towards the bank, as well as the procedural power in handling the dispute resolution process. Arguably, this places clients in an unfavourable situation in an arbitration process. It can be assumed that unequal contractual relations exist between consumers and corporations, and these may be carried through to any dispute resolution process, making arbitration unfavourable to clients in the eyes of the process and laws (Nader, 1980). The private bank also has procedural power over private banking clients, as private banks have information and expert knowledge of the specific details in the content of the account opening forms and other contracts signed with clients, which are otherwise not obvious to clients. This creates a power imbalance between the parties, and hence clients might not want to engage in informal processes they believe they are bound to lose. Even if there are arbitration clauses in their contract, the consent might not be meaningful.

Regulation protects banks, not individual clients. As self-regulation may have been proven to have failed after the Lehman crisis, more regulation may not necessarily be the answer. A bank is required to ensure individual clients fully understand the risk. Yet with issues concerning unequal bargaining powers, information asymmetry, resources and economies of scale between the two parties, clients are led into a 'take it or leave it' situation before signing. This means that even if clients do not fully understand, or do not agree, they will only have the choice between accepting the conditions or exiting the process. With no commercial incentive but enormous efforts to make a complaint to the regulator, it is hard to say that regulation protects individual clients. More accurately, regulation protects the integrity of the banking system by requesting banks to handle all complaints internally. The banks are also not in a better position to protect individual clients: due to keen competition and the desire to reduce the homogeneity of products, bankers may need to gain business 'in the shadows' by stepping along the borderlines all the time. This is particularly applicable in a situation where written policy is proven to be impractical from a business perspective. It opens more gaps for a dispute when the bankers' conduct deviates from what they should have done. There is a risk of generating unresolvable disputes if such conduct is inevitable due to the gap between business reality and regulatory standards.

I have first-hand experience in under-the-table negotiations when engaging with a potential client. He told me that if there was a loss of investment made due to my advice, the banker should compensate for the loss, and he said that he did the same with other private bankers he engaged with. I later confirmed this practice with other bankers and realised that it was the 'hidden rule' that clients are willing to keep their eyes closed. Whilst I was prepared to make this personal commitment, it was not uncommon for bankers to have 'under-the-table' negotiations. Hence, whilst banks are in a good position to behave properly due to tight regulations, the bankers might not and are likely to conduct their business not only on behalf of the bank but also on behalf of themselves. They might be forced to handle clients 'at the borderline', otherwise bankers may find that they are less competitive when trying to acquire new clients. When a dispute happens, it is the banker's fault if they behave outside of the contractual scope, and hence clients soon realise filing a complaint against the bank might not help.

Regulators govern banks with powers to impose penalties or to revoke licences upon violation, whilst the relationship between banks and clients is governed mainly by a one-sided contract and agreement on the scope of services and responsibility (hence liabilities) associated. These two levels of governance do not interact; their inter-relationships are often not addressed. Banks are more concerned with the regulators than their clients, as banks' relationship with the regulator will affect the very existence of the bank whilst the banks' relationship with the clients will be rescued by the bankers whose career depend on it. Banks ensure that all regulatory requirements are followed and careful documentation is provided to prove that. Yet, as we have seen in Chapter 2, Section 2.3.2.1, the HKMA does not have a direct mandate to protect individual clients but rather the overall stability of the banking system. With a policy tending towards protecting banks from failing by ensuring that clients 'understand' their own obligations, banks would be in a strong position in any dispute if the rules were followed on paper and signed by clients. In such circumstances, banks and individual clients have an even higher chance to get into a deadlock when negotiating in a dispute resolution process because the source of the grievance comes from the banker. In this situation, even the court at present would not be an ideal platform to resolve the issue, as clients, who have stated they 'understand' everything, would have no chance of winning, even if they were misled by the bankers as is often the case.

The implication derived from the role of the private banker in this bank–client relationship is that establishing an effective ADR mechanism would be more imminent, but the focus should be on the conduct of the banker and how we make banks more accountable. We have seen in Chapter 4, Section 4.2.2.3, clients' communication experiences with the bankers are diverse. This is worrying, because it appears that bankers may not interact with the clients in accordance with clients' understanding or with the regulations themselves. Different clients play by slightly different sets of rules. There is initial evidence to suggest that clients presume all conduct from bankers is regulated, which is not the case. The reverse would be more worrying. The gap between different communication methods is based on different bankers' styles of communication, which is hard to govern because the ethical codes are written in a more principle-based manner (Chapter 2, Section 2.3.2.1). The conduct of bankers becomes extremely influential, as it appears to be the source of clients' grievances as confirmed in our case studies.

5.5.3 The role of the private banker in dispute formation

The *representative* turns grievance into business. In Ms Emily's case, she was ready to leave because she had other private banking accounts. During the transition from Bank A to Bank B, despite her dissatisfaction and the desire to close the accounts, Ms Emily continued with the process with Bank B because her banker there (Banker B) tried very hard to retain her. Banker B followed up on the matters very closely and addressed every question she had, seeking a solution or explaining why the bank could not fulfil the request:

> [Banker B] did not really address my question at the end of the day. I still needed to do all the process I did not want to go through.
>
> However, I was quite impressed with the follow-up work done by the banker. He tried very hard and addressed to my concern. When he could not make the answer I wanted, at least he explained with sincerity and clarity what he had done and what he could not do.
>
> If it was not due to his service, I would have closed the account already.
>
> *(Ms Emily, interview)*

At that time, Ms Emily was extremely upset. She argued fiercely. Every other day she brought out new arguments that the banker could not offer an answer to immediately. Most notably she did not understand why she had to go through the KYC process again when her previous bank was acquired. In her mind, all banks are subject to the same regulatory requirements and hence one bank should be able to trust the assessments from another bank. But what she heard from the private banker was that the acquiring bank needed to go through a process called the 're-papering process' to ensure that all the clients are onboarded to the same standard from the acquiring bank. During the re-papering process, all the newly acquired clients were regarded as completely new.

Ms Emily revealed that it was the most honest answer she had heard from a banker, when she was just expecting the banker to thank her for her patience and say that the bank would cover any monetary costs associated with the change. The difficult part, however, was not about the money but the fact that the banker had to make enquiries about their SOW and its corroboration (e.g., tax receipts). Ms Emily found it particularly offensive and annoying that she had to address issues again from another entity for the same purposes, whilst management or compliance officers would say that if the clients wanted to open an account, this was the process to go through, that it is for the benefit of the banks, the clients, and society that banks exercise careful due diligence when onboarding a client.

Ms Emily was not convinced but thought it might be easier to just comply and move on with the process. Then she found out that the questions asked on the KYC were quite different from those she was asked by previous banks. The level of detail for Bank B was so much deeper than that of Bank A. In her opinion, this was totally unreasonable. She challenged the banker as to whether this information was required by the banker, required by other internal staff members who were responsible for reviewing her work, or required by the regulator. The answer given to Ms Emily was that it was in the best interests of the client and the bank to have information about clients. However, this did not help because it meant that Ms Emily still needed to go through the same process again.

She complained, but nevertheless, the private banker tried very hard to keep her with Bank B. The private banker even mentioned that she was very important to him personally and showed continuous appreciation for her understanding and patience. In the end, she stayed with Bank B:

> I stayed only because I was impressed with the banker. He acted on my best interest although he could not resolve my question. He was also very clear about what I needed to do to comply with Bank B's requirement and that makes life slightly easier. If he was not so keen, I would have left Bank B already.
>
> *(Ms Emily, interview)*

This shows the importance of what a private banker can do to turn a grievance into business, and it also explains the survey results shown in Section 4.2.2 of Chapter 4 in which clients' experiences can be very different, as banking is a very personalised business (Chapter 2, Section 2.2.3; Hong Kong Monetary Authority, 2009).

5.6 Conclusion

Four case studies of private banking clients in Hong Kong, who had experienced a dispute with their private bank, have been evaluated using the subject/agent factors under the 'naming, blaming, and claiming' framework. Each shared their own perceptions of how they interacted with their private banks and revealed their preferences for dispute resolution mechanisms in the context of a dispute.

Clients perceived that the grievances experienced are usually out of contractual scope or due to mistakes made by their private bankers. In each of the cases, the bank made no mistake, and there was no point in escalating a dispute with the bank. Clients make enormous efforts ensuring their private bankers make no mistakes. Clients are actively engaged in the prevention of naming a grievance. If a grievance is named, clients take the blame because it seems to be their own mistake. Clients want to fix the wrong. Clients also perceive that the blaming stage is rather meaningless because filing a complaint to the bank is equivalent to making an application to the bank. Clients can only wait for the bank's decision as to whether they acknowledge their grievance. If so then it is resolved, and, if not, then clients would just lump it or close the bank account. Any of these events would not form a dispute, and these factors are *subjective*, *unstable*, *reactive*, and *complicated,* which work against dispute transformation.

Ms Emily revealed that clients are always in a weaker position because banks would not breach any law or regulation. Any grievance formed was caused by a mismatch in expectation between what she wanted from a bank and what a bank could offer. **Mr Young** wanted to avoid any dispute resolution platform due to the perceived fatigue in managing the process. Internally, the complaint handling process was dominated by the bank with staff who knew little about the dispute, whilst externally it was too expensive and time-consuming. **Mr Peterson** revealed that the only source of grievance was contributed to by clients' failure to manage their private bankers properly. These experiences created a perception that if any grievance is formed, it might be easier to go straight to litigation, as evidenced by the actions of **Mr Collins**. Our case studies indicate that the dispute transformation process was halted by the clients. The halt was not due to a lack of legal knowledge but fatigue in going through the process. Clients actively prevented naming by actively managing their private bankers, which made them feel responsible for avoiding any form of grievance.

A lack of autonomy, transparency, and predictability in the dispute resolution process might contribute to the above. Banks are not required to explain how an investigation is being carried out, nor do they need to provide reasons for their decisions, although they usually address the proposed action to avoid similar incidents from happening again. More importantly, there is no mechanism for when a complaint is concluded, except in the case when clients accept the reply or give up. The HKMA did not assist clients directly but instead discussed the issue with the bank to ensure a prompt response. This would mean that the low number of disputes and under-utilisation of arbitration are caused by discouraged clients who want to avoid the helplessness and nuisance arising during the dispute resolution process.

These findings reveal that the perception of clients regarding themselves as a weaker party in disputes has been shaped by clients' belief that it is not worthwhile to name a grievance in the first place. When the bank–client relationship is built on a one-sided contract, a lack of transparency in the internal complaint-handling process, and insufficient support from the regulator, it would be very difficult for clients to engage themselves with external dispute resolution channels again, especially *after* they have gone through the internal processes but failed. The viability of arbitration is difficult to confirm, even though clients might have already experienced an arbitration-like experience with the bank, without clients knowing about this, as discussed in Sections 3.5.2–3.5.4 of Chapter 3. Hence, it is essential to develop a theoretical implication to explain how these perceptions would explain the perceived viability of arbitration as a channel to resolve private banking disputes – be it appearing in the form of an internal complaint process managed by the bank entirely or arbitration organised by an external third party. Further analysis of the interviews would help us achieve this.

CHAPTER 6

The self-corrective mechanism for dispute 'elimination'

6.1 Introduction: The role of power in dispute transformation

Although it seems to be a less methodical approach, a case study approach to research allows us to observe interesting and important social phenomena (Luckham, 1981, p. 12). Given the small population of private banking clients in Hong Kong, as well as their general unwillingness to openly discuss in detail their experiences and concerns, case studies offer evidence to explain and identify the reasons for the low number of disputes in the private banking industry (Chapter 4). With the aid of the 'naming, blaming, and claiming' framework, the quantitative and qualitative analysis carried out in this book supplement each other and allow us to analyse clients' perceptions in the context of power balances and dispute transformations, identifying the social and political relevance (Chapter 5). This chapter lays a foundation to theorise about the specific characteristics of how potential disputants withdraw themselves from the dispute transformation stage. It further analyses the case studies within the NBC framework and relates these findings to the role of power, as well as the role of private bankers and regulators, in the business operation and dispute resolution processes.

This chapter also consolidates the insights generated and the answers from the sub-research questions by examining their theoretical implications. It explains the importance of understanding these dynamics and reveals that the outcome (a small number of disputes between banks and clients) might be triggered by the wrong cause. The small number of disputes might be caused by the fact that clients simply give up resolving the dispute. It also explores the factors causing this behaviour in the context of dispute formation, the perceptions of arbitration, and the power balance of the bank–client relationship under a dispute.

Since CJR in 2009, Hong Kong courts have advocated the use of ADR to resolve civil disputes. Nevertheless, arbitration is not widely adopted in the private banking industry. This is also a global phenomenon. A 2016 International Chamber of Commerce survey showed that in-house counsels of private banks around the world did not know that arbitration was

DOI: 10.4324/9781003407591-6

an option for resolving private banking disputes; for those who knew about arbitration, they had great reservations as to whether arbitration was suitable for resolving private banking disputes. This book is dedicated to explaining this phenomenon. A mixed methods approach has been conducted consisting of three stages: content analysis on relevant bank regulations and arbitral rules, quantitative analysis on data collected through surveys, and qualitative analysis through the use of interviews. Through applying the NBC model, this book has examined the suitability of arbitration for resolving private banking disputes from the client's perspective and has addressed three questions, namely: (a) how are banking clients' perceptions about engaging in arbitration shaped by their understanding of the power imbalance between the client and the bank?; (b) to what extent is arbitration perceived as a viable dispute resolution option by private banking clients in Hong Kong?, and (c) to what extent do such perceptions explain the under-utilisation of arbitration in the private banking context in Hong Kong?

The empirical studies show that while clients may perceive arbitration as a suitable channel to resolve private banking disputes, it may not be a necessary one. This is because clients have found themselves as a weaker party in a bank–client relationship, arising from one-sided contracts. Clients prevent naming by taking a lead from their private bankers in executing daily transactions. When grievances are formed, both private banking clients and private bankers facilitate the elimination of grievances to avoid the trouble of dealing directly with the banks. Also, regulators encourage clients to resolve disputes through a bank's internal complaint system. All these factors render arbitration unnecessary and under-utilised. Chapter 6 answers the ultimate question by addressing how the transformation process impacts private banking clients' decisions in choosing a dispute resolution platform. The findings suggest that clients embed a self-corrective process when interacting with their private bank. This self-corrective process might force clients into a binary option of either leaving the bank to eliminate the dispute or suing the bank. The chapter reviews the features of this self-corrective mechanism and its implications, and it concludes with this research's contribution to scholarship, the research limitations, and recommendations for future research.

6.2 A self-corrective mechanism and its prerequisites

6.2.1 Definition of the self-corrective mechanism

In a relationship governed by a consumer contract, an individual customer would actively prevent the formation of monetary-related disputes by engaging their agents, who execute the contract, to eliminate any grievance generated within or outside the scope of the contract.

Clients are hindered from forming a dispute due to this self-corrective mechanism. It has been illustrated that once private banking clients have signed the one-sided contract, they perceive themselves to be a weaker party in the context of any legal argument and contractual scope. Clients would tend to spend enormous efforts to prevent dispute formation because they perceive that it would be impossible to challenge the bank from a legal point of view. Any dispute formed is likely to be caused by services not meeting clients' expectations, which does not breach the contractual terms or any regulations. The weaker party finds that prevention is better than the cure, and if any grievance is formed, clients work to eliminate it by either accepting the status quo and exiting the relationship, or going to court to fight the case. Clients are unlikely to think that any ADR process would help.

6.2.2 Prerequisites of the self-corrective mechanism

6.2.2.1 There exists a gap between the terms signed by and the expectation of customers in a contractual relationship

There is a gap between what is signed by the customers and what is expected from them. Individual customers do not have the chance to review or amend the contract they sign. As a result, they can only influence the agent to get the service they want, which may not necessarily be part of the contract signed. If there is a dispute, it may not be within the scope of the contract signed by clients. This was confirmed by Mr Peterson's interview.

This can be explained by examining how the development of international commercial arbitration became a process involving business progression and human experiences. Dezalay and Garth (1996) have offered insights relating to Hong Kong. The starting point is that Hong Kong is featured with a 'growing role of legal profession and tension between different and competing legal profession' (Dezalay & Garth, 1996, ch 12). Among the historical and political development, such as the handover of Hong Kong to China, there are three notable features that could drive or deter the development of arbitration in society. The first is the dominant involvement of non-Chinese ethnic lawyers in the legal field. This feature has affected the impression of legal professionals and their experiences in handling legal matters both in and out of court. The second is the dominant involvement of expatriates in the law schools in Hong Kong, which is not regarded as a strong system as it does not help construct the requisite legal autonomy. The third is the lawyers' role in business transactions, whether they show sincerity in ensuring a transaction goes properly or if they are suspicious of the counterparties, making sure they protect the legality of their side. Disputes between individuals and banks/bankers could be triggered by some black swan event. Yves and Garth, citing Gunningham (1990), showed that events like Black

Monday in 1987 in Hong Kong (where the stock market suddenly crashed in one day leading to the closing of the Hong Kong Stock Exchange the next day) reflected the failure of the regulatory system to cater to the local and family orientation feature in the Hong Kong market. This does not fit with the norms of the cosmopolitan legal culture. The handover of Hong Kong to China further complicated matters, as each has a very different legal system and culture, representing a 'gap' between the two systems and triggering further review and reform, such as the disclosure requirement. Matters of arbitration also 'encompass very different experiences' such as the role of formal law, formal procedures, the approach, and the characteristics of an arbitrator, which should not be overlooked.

6.2.2.2 Disputes could be resolved by monetary compensation

Contrary to the possible argument that ADR provides a form of 'second class justice' to consumers and offers something less than what can be realised through courts (Menkel-Meadow, 1999), it turns out that in the context of private banking disputes (and possibly all banking related disputes), justice may not be the priority. As we have seen in the case studies, most of the disputes were resolved by the bank by covering the losses incurred by clients. Banks could exercise this discretion to make compensation so as to avoid the floodgate should the disputes go public. Through private settlement, banks do not need to disclose any wrongdoing. To clients, the question of justice might be equivalent to the question of covering their monetary loss.

In a private banking dispute, the formation of a grievance can largely depend on market movement. Mr Collins discovered he had been engaged in a loan without his authorisation only after the market value of his assets was revealed to not cover the cost of the loan and hence was margin-called, as was the case with Mr Young. This reflects the fact that disputes usually occur when clients incur a monetary loss. Hence, a dispute would not be identified or discovered if there is no monetary loss. Mr Peterson reflected that his client had stopped the complaint because later the market value in the mistaken execution of his order turned out to be profitable. These circumstances offer examples where experiences might not be perceived as injurious even if there were enacted against clients' instructions, as long as there is no adverse impact on clients' assets. In other words, grievances can be formed and disappear very quickly. This situation could be particularly true in a regulated industry like banking. As we have seen in Section 4.4.1 of Chapter 4, clients perceive that all activities are regulated. When there is a grievance, clients tend to believe that it is the fault of the bankers who took a personal stake in order to keep the relationship. The relationship is largely maintained through monetary compensation and hence the dispute that clients are trying to prevent would be restricted to what financial compensation can resolve.

6.2.2.3 Power imbalance between parties

The fundamental argument against a settlement is rooted in the following factors, as first described by Fiss (1984): power inequality between parties, the absence of authoritative consent in the process, a lack of continuing judicial involvement after settlement, and its damage to the public adjudicative process to exercise public value. In a private banking context, the case studies have shown that clients had already assessed these factors when they first started the banking relationship. In an extreme case in relation to Mr Young, he would have already assumed that the likelihood of winning in court was less than minimal and not worth the effort. Clients have a perception that there is a power inequality and appear to accept it. It would be safer for clients to prevent grievances from occurring on day zero through active engagement.

The findings from the case studies also align with another argument from Fiss in relation to how banks handle complaints internally. Clients did not consent to the bank complaint-handling procedure. Clients did not know how the complaint was handled and could only passively wait for the outcome. The HKMA also adopted a hands-off approach indicating a lack of regulatory involvement. The internal processes might have also exhausted the clients, and they might project similar experiences in public court, hence damaging the public administrative process. All these features do not appear to suggest that the banks' internal complaint-handling process is for clients and arguably in the best interests of the public.

6.2.2.4 Clients lack the ability to articulate specific harms

This prerequisite follows the power imbalance feature where a weaker party is unlikely to impose any specific harm to the other party. When one party is perceived to be weaker than another, then the only way to articulate harm is through the court, but the use of court equally hurts the weak party as well:

> The relationship between objectives and mechanisms is reciprocal: not only do objectives influence the choice of mechanisms, but mechanisms chosen may alter objective…because courts, for instance, often proceed by using a limited number of norms to evaluate an even more circumscribed universe of relevant facts, the needs of the parties, their wishes for the future, cease to be relevant to the solution
>
> *(Felstiner et al., 1980, pp. 642–643)*

Naming an event as harmful provides an impetus for future action. One party is more likely to initiate legal action if it can articulate specific harms upon a perceived wrongful terminated employment (Lind et al., 2000). In a private banking dispute, it is extremely difficult for clients to articulate specific harm to banks for reasons of a lack of disputable argument and unstable objectives, supported by Mr Peterson's experience where the clients withdrew the claim when the mistake turned out to benefit the clients. If the bank or banker has done something wrong but it turns out to be earning money for the clients, the clients might not form any grievance at all, or any dispute in transformation. In this sense, banks can easily get away from the claim and clients would end up having no remedy, leading towards the self-corrective mechanism.

6.2.3 Why the self-corrective mechanism occurs among the wealthy?

There are notably numerous studies relating to the theory of law that may offer insight to explain why clients would self-correct themselves, and it merits a thesis of its own. This section offers a preliminary insight benefited from my reflection on studies relating to legal theory, in particular the legal consciousness (e.g., Silbey, 2005) and procedure justice (e.g., Tyler, 2005), choice of dispute resolution mechanism (e.g., Engel, 2016), dispute transformation (e.g., Felstiner et al., 1980), power balance (e.g., Galanter, 1974; Galanter & Cahill, 1993); and the insights from this book. The reason for this leads to the answer to three important questions. The first question is: what is the purpose of the law? The second question is: who can execute the law? The third question is: is dispute a bad thing for the bank? This section will address these three questions using the insights generated in this book, noting existing doctrinal and empirical studies could also contribute to the observation but might be too numerous to cite all.

What is the purpose of the law? If there is a certain truth about the infamous quote, where it says, 'In Heaven there will be no law, and the lion will lie down with the lamb… In Hell there will be nothing but law, and due process will be meticulously observed' (Gilmore, 2015, p. 99), that law appears to exist only to prevent harm from happening, then parties must have anticipated the harm before the contractual relationship begins. The matter is further complicated by the fact that parties might have been tempted to cheat and hence a contract must be enforceable by law. Contrary to this apparently common-sense approach, the reverse seems to be true in the bank–customer relationship featured by a one-sided contract. Banks draft the contracts so that the law could not harm them, clients may find regulations not helpful because they are written at a rather high level, and hence different banks can do different things and still fulfil the requirement of the law and regulation (Chapter 2). It suggests that the repeated player advantage has been well applied before the dispute occurs because the rule of the game has been designed to almost dominantly favouring one side – which is the bank – and therefore the fear to expose the dispute in court seems to be a better strategy, as we can see from Mr Collins (Section 5.4.2, Chapter 5).

It leads to the next question of who can execute the law. From the case studies it is obvious that the parties themselves should execute the law and resolve any disputes among themselves. It is simpler in a football match, where if there is a breach of the rules of the game, you just need a referee to identify this and impose a penalty. But there is no independent referee in a bank–customer relationship because the regulatory requirements in Hong Kong and most jurisdictions only regulate the turnaround time and conflict of interests, which is resolved by having an independent third party within the bank to regulate (Section 3.2.2.2, Chapter 3). It appears problematic because it does not require the bank to offer a reason (Section 3.2.2, Chapter 3), and hence no matter how quickly the bank responds, the dispute may not be resolved. An independent department to handle disputes would not resolve the fundamental issue of conflict of interest because the person in charge of the dispute resolution still works for the bank, and we have seen from Mr Young's case how it delays the process because the party handling the dispute usually has little experience and incentives to handle somebody's else dispute (Section 5.3.2, Chapter 5).

Finally, is dispute necessarily a bad thing for the bank? For private bankers, it certainly is because if the bank is perceived to follow the law and regulation (Chapter 4). The only loophole would be the banker who fails to comply with what the bank requires of them. Therefore, we will see private bankers trying very hard to resolve or avoid the dispute from happening (Section 2.5.2, Chapter 2). For the bank it can be an opportunity. Ms Emily's case show that a crisis can be an opportunity for the bank to demonstrate the strength of the bank/banker, and win a client back if a grievance is handled properly. Ms Emily decided to give the bank another chance, as she was impressed by how the banker handled her grievance even if the banker did not resolve her issues (Section 5.4.1, Chapter 5). Ms Emily's case, however, is an exception; the norm appears to be in the case of Mr Peterson, where he advocated that the key is to 'pre-empt' and avoid the occurrence of a dispute, which we will discuss in Section 6.3.1 in this chapter.

The self-corrective mechanism would have triggered a lot of problems because it would render all dispute resolution mechanisms irrelevant because clients would not care how just the law is, how fair the process is, and how fast justice and fairness could be achieved through any dispute resolution mechanism – because clients are deemed to lose, and it has nothing to do with the wealth level of the disputants, and perhaps especially the wealthy ones as they would be able to evaluate all these possibilities before engaging themselves in a dispute resolution process. The implications will be carefully looked at in the next section.

6.3 Common mentalities concerning the self-corrective mechanism

6.3.1 Prevention is better than cure: Prevent naming

In the infamous Lehman Brothers incident in 2008, there were widespread complaints about 'misrepresentations, negligent advice and breaches of relevant regulatory rules and procedures on the part of the banks' when selling minibonds to clients (para. 1, Hon. Judge A Cheung judgment. *Shek Lai San v Securities and Futures Commission and Another [2010] HKCFI*). According to the Legislative Council Background Briefing Paper, the complaints focused on promoting the Minibond as a low-risk and capital-protected fixed-income product. Bank staff failed to advise investors who lacked the related financial knowledge of the risks associated with these types of structured products (LC Paper No. CB (1)113/08-09). Since then, there have been new and stricter requirements on the selling of investment products especially in the area relating to making adequate disclosure of relevant materials and the suitability obligation of investment advisers.[1] As we have seen in Chapter 4, some requirements are fulfilled in the account opening stage such as the signing of the ISDA agreement,[2] the client's declaration of investment experience and knowledge, and the assessment of a client's risk profile. With everything written clearly and signed by the clients, both parties are assumed to have a clear knowledge of what can and cannot be done in a legal relationship between banks and clients. This significantly impacts the naming stage because clients already have limited scope to claim misrepresentation as they have declared a clear understanding of the scope of banking services, clear knowledge of the investment product, and their obligations through signing the one-sided contract.

Chapter 2 showed that although clients signed the account opening forms, they do not necessarily obtain legal and regulatory knowledge from those forms because those forms do not seem to serve such a purpose. Instead, the high awareness of that knowledge is likely to be the result of clients' active engagement with their private bank. Mr Peterson confirmed this argument and showed that contracts might have played no role in establishing the bank–customer relationship from a business perspective. Clients protect themselves and instruct private bankers on requests within or outside the contractual scope. From the moment clients sign the contract, clients would hand-hold their bankers and take the lead in the relationship.

Clients seem to assume all the responsibilities onto themselves to prevent naming. Clients rely on information provided by the bank and their own sources to learn the regulatory landscape. However, the account opening form only has limited information and clients are overwhelmed in ensuring

1 For example the post-sale cooling off or unwind rights published in the Circular to Licensed Corporations and Registered Institutions Obligations Relating to Selling/Distribution of Investment Products on 28 May 2010, available at https://apps.sfc.hk/edistributionWeb/api/circular/openFile?lang=EN&refNo=H639 (last accessed 12 Dec 2020)

2 ISDA: International Swaps and Derivatives Association. Banks require clients to sign the ISDA agreement when clients intend to invest derivatives product with the bank, because in essence clients and banks are trading counterparties.

they are up-to-date with the situation of their accounts, instead of trusting the bank or their banker. As Mr Peterson indicated many times in the interview:

> The better way to prevent client dispute is to *pre-empt*
>
> *(Mr Peterson, interview)*

This may impose an unnecessary burden on the clients. Regulators should consider providing more easily accessible education materials or hotlines to support private banking clients in handling their relationship and also in supporting any action to prevent a dispute, on top of offering a channel for them to complain. Grievances would not flow towards any formal or informal dispute resolution process; using the dispute tree metaphor (Albiston et al., 2014), the branch may have never grown but instead died down from the root.

6.3.2 Clients blame themselves, not shame the bank

With clients working hard to prevent naming, when a grievance is formed naturally clients blame themselves for the injurious experience. This relates to the attribution theory mentioned under the naming, blaming, claiming model:

> Attribution theory asserts that the causes a person assigns for an injurious experience will be important determinants of the action he or she takes in response to it; those attributions will also presumably affect perception of the experience as injurious.
>
> *(Felstiner et al., 1980, p. 641)*

The court appears to hold a similar view and assumes a heavy duty on clients to ensure they are not misled by the banks. For example, in *Selina Kwok v HSBC Private Bank (2013)*, the CFI dismissed Ms Kwok's mis-selling claims. Ms Kwok claimed that she sustained heavy losses on her trading account with HSBC by investing in about 350 forward accumulator contracts and other structured products. The account opening documentation included a risk disclosure statement, signed by Ms Kwok, which clearly pointed out that HSBC did not offer investment advice, and investors should seek independent professional advice if they had doubts about the risk involved. While Ms Kwok sought to rely on statements made by HSBC bankers years after the accounts were opened, the judge relied on basic contract law to discuss this submission and stated that 'one cannot use the subsequent conduct of one or other party to an agreement to construe the terms of their contract' (para. 101, SA [2012] HKCFI 964). Also, 'one cannot imply obligations which are contrary to the express terms of an agreement' (para. 105, SA [2012] HKCFI 964). The 'regulatory standards in the Code of Conduct for Persons Licensed by or Registered with the Securities and Futures Commission' were of little assistance, (para. 133, SA [2012] HKCFI 964) and could not override express contractual provisions (para. 135, SA [2012] HKCFI 964). Kwok 'only has herself to blame' as she submitted that 'she was too unsophisticated, too busy, or too occupied by other matters, to look at the many papers being sent to her… she did not bother to read or understand them' (para. 115, SA [2012] HKCFI 964). Mr Young had a similar experience. He had invested in a very similar product to Ms Kwok. He signed a contract without reading the content, but he alleged that what he heard from the banker turned out to be different from what was written in the contract. When the losses were realised, Mr Young opted for a very different journey, although the efforts were in vain, just like Ms Kwok's in *Selina Kwo k v HSBC Private Bank (2013)*. Mr Young recognised the risk of going to court and decided to give up because he wanted to close the matter although he felt that it was the bank and banker's mistake (Chapter 5, Section 5.3.3).

It is essential to explore why Mr Young gave up – it is because whatever he did, if the bank decided to fight against the claim, nothing seems to hurt the bank. During the interview, Mr Young repeatedly mentioned that it was such a mistake to rely too much on his banker, as well as on the bank (Chapter 5, Section 5.3.1). This clear self-attribution has shown that the clients might also regard themselves as contributors to the injurious experience. This self-attribution was contradicted by his defending why he had to trust the bank and banker – it was not possible to read everything himself in the actual environment. He had, to a large extent, been relying on his luck because the dispute only arose due to a margin call. Otherwise, there would not be an issue.

'An injury moves through a sequence of steps before blame is affixed and demands for action are made' (Buzbee, 2003). This analysis visualises these steps by unveiling a possibility that blaming might not only mean blaming others, but also blaming themselves for trusting the private bank or private banker too much, or by signing the account opening form which meant they made a declaration that they were not aware of or exempted banks of certain duties. As a matter of fact, clients also have obligations to maintain the banking relationship. In *Greenwood v Martins Bank Ltd [1932] AC 51*, 'if the bank, to its detriment, then acts on, or fails to act because of, the implied representation that the signature is genuine, the customer will be estopped from denying that it is'. On top of defining a banking relationship, in this context, clients now also have an obligation to maintain the relationship on equal grounds (even though the contract is one-sided).

Tightening regulations would mean that it would be more difficult to challenge the bank, but this would not necessarily offer clients more protection. It would result in fewer complaints because clients essentially waive many liabilities that the bank could have been held accountable for. If it was then left entirely to how the private banker interacted with the clients using the platforms and resources provided by the bank, it would put the bank into a very strong position with a perception that the bank was unlikely to make mistakes. In this way, the clients have helped the bank to ensure compliance as well instead of victimising themselves and swallowing all the grievances when in fact the bank might be at fault, and the grievance is exactly how this mistake is discovered.

There is a risk that self-blame is the reason that a grievance does not ferment, hence their continuous efforts to stop the dispute transformation process. This is because clients might also need to maintain the relationship, avoid nuisance, save operational costs, and have little time to raise complaints. The existing 'complain and wait' approach could seem to reflect the blame on clients too. Support should be given to clients at the onboarding stage because the account opening form does not lay down all the information detailing a bank's obligations or a client's rights. For example, banks or regulators should provide a single document detailing the bank's obligations and the client's rights. More transparency on the complaint-handling procedure instead of simply ensuring that banks will seriously deal with them without engaging the clients in the process should be provided.

6.3.3 Fulfilling regulatory requirements vs protecting clients?

There are several observations associated with this: compliance with regulation is only seen between regulators and the banks, but not by the public. The laws and regulations are not written into the account opening forms, and different banks can impose different rules to fulfil the regulatory requirements due to the broad language adopted in the regulations. Banks can handle their own disputes, act as arbitrators and adjudicate without any obligation to provide a reason, which is clearly not aligned with clients' preferences, as per the results from the client survey (Chapter 4, Section 4.2.6). Although the survey results show that clients do know their rights and obligations, this is due to their own actions. Clients will not escalate the dispute against the bank. Clients either ask for resolution or close their accounts, as confirmed by Ms Emily (Chapter 5, Section 5.4). This regulatory requirement might have eliminated the disputes that require regulatory attention, as there is a leeway for the bank to cover up their dispute that would otherwise deserve regulatory or public attention (Edelman et al., 2014)

The relationship between private bankers and clients should be further regulated, as the close personal connection is influential in a bank–client relationship and in dispute formation/elimination. Hudson examines this relationship by stating that the normal relationship is governed *'entirely'* by the law of contract unless specific circumstances have arisen to justify the inference of a fiduciary relationship (Hudson, 2013). But, the contract is between clients and banks, yet the private banker might take over the relationship way beyond the original scope of the contract. The survey also showed that the only possible divergence comes from the professional qualifications of the private banker (Chapter 4, Section 4.2.3). It appears to be a norm for private bankers to dominate the relationship and it was unclear how compliant the relationship is. In Hong Kong, all private bankers are now required to obtain CPWP qualifications to ensure that client-facing private banking practitioners have sufficient knowledge and ethical awareness to conduct their business. This qualification is obtainable by exam, but private bankers with more than ten years of experience can obtain this qualification through grandfathering, which is arguably not appropriate. The regulatory landscape and framework are very different and are still rapidly changing. It is essential to equip all bankers with the basic and fundamental knowledge to ensure they are equipped with the proper technical skills to keep up with the rapidly changing requirement. On-the-job training would not serve this purpose.

Clients' needs do not seem to be considered in this regulatory requirement, and neither do banks actively disclose the regulatory requirements to their clients. This discourages clients from escalating a dispute, as they are often left alone without any involvement of a third party to assist. To resolve the dilemma between speedy resolution and justice, an enforceable and recognised platform to resolve financial disputes is needed. This will be particularly true for the private banking industry as a growing segment in the region and their clients are very capable of escalating matters given their ample resources to challenge banks.

6.3.4 Concern arising from a bank as arbitrator

Banks might act as arbitrators in disputes of their own. This means that one of the disputing parties is adjudicating its own dispute. This creates potential conflicts of interest, although there will be different departments within the same bank handling the alleged disputes.

William Park's observation on the arbitration process might help reflect this situation (Chapter 1, Section 1.2.3.2). In his literature, notable merits of arbitration to resolve financial disputes have been identified. They are arguably not directly applicable to disputes between individual clients and institutions due to a lack of emphasis on parties' features and how the adjudication process is conducted. In this analysis, the arbitration process has been internalised in a bank's complaint-handling process. This could affect the clients' perspective on the adjudication process, as it would be tiring for clients to go through the complaint process internally. Internal processes may influence a client's perception of the impartiality of arbitration. Banks have a dual identity of both being a disputing party and an arbitrator, which presents a potential conflict of interest.

To meet the rapid change in their needs to resolve disputes arising from different scenarios and ever-changing product offerings, a tailor-made dispute resolution process is also vital in promoting healthy interactions between banks and their individual clients and facilitating the much-needed incorporation into the regulatory framework, instead of the processes being conducted by the bank who is a party in a dispute. Although a bank would assign an independent party to handle the dispute (Hong Kong Monetary Authority, 2002, section 2.5), they still represent the bank. Mr Young's case reflects the fact that the third party is unlikely to take ownership to resolve the dispute. They told Mr Young that they were not involved in the dispute and did not know what actually happened. This further frustrated Mr Young. It is contrary to the common notion that the bank would have sufficient knowledge to handle the issue.

Another issue is consent. Clients have not given consent to their dispute being handled by the banks, especially under the situation of a one-sided contract prepared solely by the bank, with individual clients being left with a 'take it or leave it' situation. It is unclear whether there are legal grounds for banks to handle these disputes. Should clients know that a bank's internal complaint procedure is similar to that of arbitration, it is unlikely to be offered a positive alternative as a viable option, possibly due to a lack of transparency, a lack of meaningful consent, and potential conflicts of interest. There are important questions to ask before understanding the suitability of arbitration. Mr Peterson suggested that banks should enhance transparency in how they handle complaints. This would offer certainty as to how their complaints would be handled.

For these reasons, it is inconclusive how arbitral rules would be a suitable fit for resolving private banking disputes from the client's perspective. Clients may have already experienced a process similar to arbitration. Further support and education should be provided to clients to understand the functions and procedures involved in arbitration. These should be provided at the start of the relationship. The current framework might have over-relied on a bank's integrity, which is not visible to clients. Further scrutiny and transparency should be offered to clients.

6.4 Contribution to the scholarship

The content analysis, surveys, interviews and my own observations in the field hope to offer an empirical observation to the theoretical study of dispute transformation in the private banking industry in Hong Kong. To the best of my knowledge, this research is the first of its kind offering the perspectives of Hong Kong private banking clients to address the issue of suitability of the arbitration process to resolve private banking disputes. It also identifies potential impediments to the broader adoption of arbitration in the global private banking industry through understanding how clients' disputes are, or are not, transformed. The work proposes new methodologies which include the examination of end-to-end private banking business processes, the adoption of the theoretical context of the NBC framework in banking disputes, and a comparison of private banking clients' understandings of relevant laws and regulations and their actual experiences. The empirical nature of this study could also generate insights for policymakers and regulators. It hopes to contribute to both the private banking industry and the academic field.

The experience in Hong Kong offers a global reference to private banking as an international finance centre where most banks operating in Hong Kong are foreign banks subject to the laws and regulations of Hong Kong, their own jurisdictions, and international conventions. Specifically, this research contributes to the scholarship by discovering new mechanisms that further shape the dispute transformation processes and selection of an ADR platform. It also offers insights into how ADR fulfils legal and extra-legal needs and objectives. Finally, it identifies specific needs for arbitration for private banking disputes. These will be described in detail below.

6.4.1 Presenting the three-stage method

This book presents in detail the three-stage approach that has been applied to aid the analysis. Stage 1 shows the results of the content analysis of relevant laws, regulations, account opening forms, and arbitral rules associated with the private banking industry in Hong Kong, contributing to the question of how power imbalances might have already created unequal ground in the existing dispute resolution mechanism, which is negatively perceived by clients when it comes to the choice of ADR mechanisms. Stage 2 presents a quantitative analysis of the survey results to show and confirm the argument that arbitration is not perceived by clients as being a viable dispute resolution option even if most features of arbitration are preferred. It leads to the need to conduct the stage 3 qualitative analysis from four selected case studies in order to unveil clients' reflections of their experiences that forms the perception of power imbalances and dispute transformation process under the 'naming claiming, blaming' process, which contributes significantly to the under-utilisation of arbitration in private banking in Hong Kong. The results of stage 3 have been applied to explain the results of stages 1 and 2. This has presented an alternative method to conduct empirical studies in law and regulation by incorporating the clients' perspective. The incorporation of my own first-hand experience is also a feature that shall demonstrate how a sense of issues derived from a personal touch derived from a systematic methodology could further develop insights supported by data collected through the systematic methodology. The extended description of the literature review methodology in Section 1.4 of Chapter 1 deliberately lays down the details of this approach to present the thought process which could be useful for future research. The method could be applied to interdisciplinary research.

6.4.2 Uncovering the phenomenon of a client's self-corrective mechanism for dispute elimination

The philosophy of how the decision to select a dispute resolution mechanism is studied, and human experiences and progression in a dispute transformation process have been built upon with this research. Such reflection is supplemented with empirical studies of how the role of the law is being perceived by market participants, hence providing the much-needed evidence and insights into what can boost their confidence in ADR. First, it provides evidence of how the regulations are not clearly incorporated into the legal documents between banks and clients in practice and unveils the issue brought by one-sided contracts, diverse interpretations, execution of regulatory requirements written with a lack of specificity, and heavy involvement of private bankers who have a personal stake in the bank's business. These factors force clients into a weaker position in the legal relationship between them and the bank. Second, it identifies the four business stages which reflect the dynamics and framework to examine how power impacts dispute transformation at a pre-dispute stage, especially the legal relationship established through one-sided contracts. Third, it offers the experiences of market participants. It allows us to review their behaviour and perceptions that impact their decisions to choose a suitable ADR platform to adjudicate their disputes. Fourth, the application of the 'naming, blaming, claiming' model in dispute transformation has been further enriched by the self-corrective mechanism to explain how disputes might not be transformed. It would help society find the right cause to a dispute and hence ADR, preventing the disputants to regress to informal channels such as bribery or even violence. It provides evidence as to how human experiences and social progression transit in practice. For example, the new mechanism could now explain the interrelationship of the changes impacting businesses, society, and people; and in return how businesses respond and react to the law and to dispute resolution mechanisms.

It has further confirmed a lack of familiarity with the arbitration function, coupled with the need to provide more public information about the arbitration process, including public educational campaign[s] about the process and better judicial cooperation in appropriate cases and non-intervention (Ali, 2013, p. 174). This book offers an initial empirical framework to examine the perception (and reality) of the laws/regulations and businesses, between what is written and what is conducted in the eyes of private banking clients (i.e., the laymen's view), indicating in both formal and informal justice processes with all the benefits legal representation can offer, litigants are dominated throughout by lawyers and dependent on their expertise and paternalistic construction of what is best. The key is that it is often incongruous with the disputants' own understandings and needs.

The potential finding of the self-corrective mechanism could supplement the power theory and the NBC model, as it incorporates the role of non-contractual parties at a pre-dispute stage; in this study the private banker who represents the bank interacts with clients most of the time. It moves further away from the conventional dispute between two parties from the dispute resolution stage to the pre-dispute stage, particularly highlighting the power imbalance between disputants (or more accurately between business partners as disputes were not formed at that stage). It brings empirical evidence to guide the design of a dispute resolution process and offers initial empirical evidence that supplements Sternli's (2004) points of view, who stated:

> yet, does the manner in which arbitration is imposed affect the perceived procedural justice of the process? While I can offer no empirical studies in support of this proposition, I believe that it does. When one party designs a process and then imposes it on another, thereby depriving that party of access to the default dispute resolution mechanism chosen by society... I believe it will naturally, if not inevitably, raise concerns that the impost process is unfair.
>
> *(Sternlight, 2004, p. 1671)*

Although this book does not adopt Galanter's paradigm, the self-corrective mechanism can also explain Galanter's observation on different strategies and behaviour of disputants with their access to resources and their repeat experiences, and how they impact the success of their claims. Using a law school pedagogy, Galanter used two perspectives: (1) a ground or bottom-up perspective, from the point of view of the people who used the courts, as opposed to (2) a top-down perspective where the law and rules of such a system are taken as the starting point and a lens through which disputants and their interactions can be examined (Galanter, 1974). In the private banking context, the two perspectives turn out not to be relevant, as clients would not even consider whether they had the experience, and given the fact that those clients are financially well-resourced to bridge the disadvantages coming from lack of experience, the decision to select a proper resolution mechanism actually began much earlier. It might be less relevant to consider the impact of power within a dispute resolution mechanism. This can be seen also in the framework where the article states:

> To generalise, when clients encounter lawyers in one-shot relationships (e.g., divorce, criminal defense, personal injury), the lawyers' primary allegiance is often to others (insurance claims agents, police, judges, other lawyers), whereas clients who deal regularly with lawyers demand and receive greater loyalty... which may stimulate a participant to take steps to avoid similar disputes or structure his behaviour to place him into stronger position next time.
>
> *(Felstiner et al., 1980, pp. 642–643)*

6.4.3 Offer insights into how ADR is perceived by private banking clients

This is one of the pioneering works that examine whether arbitration is suitable for resolving private banking disputes by analysing the factors at a pre-dispute stage. It specifically examines the role of contract in the legal relationship between private banks and private bank clients, and when further dynamics are added this relationship becomes complicated. It offers an opportunity to explore existing practices in private banks and contrasts them with the issues of power imbalance, formal and informal justices, and the role of the regulator in affecting the decision to choose the right dispute resolution platform, in particular arbitration. It further widens the existing spectrum to aid the promotion and selection of an ADR platform when the entire legal relationship (not just the time when the dispute occurred) is being considered. It will be particularly relevant to explain why market practitioners still prefer the courtroom when they are unlikely to possess actual knowledge of the functionality of both public and private adjudication systems in the first place.

Specifically, the findings also contribute to the debates of formal versus informal justice by raising two important questions: (a) does justice or result matter more? and (b) what are the elements of justice in the eyes of private banks, private bankers, and private banking clients? Through drawing empirical studies in Hong Kong, one could now explore the features that matter to clients and help build a reputable, efficient, and transparent resolution mechanism that would consist of incorporating the views of clients. One would know better how to further engage with the private banking industry to use arbitration.

The empirical perspectives from the private banking industry provide insight into how arbitration could consider clients' both legal and extra-legal needs and objectives (Banakar, 2003, pp. 7–8; 74). It explains the phenomenon of 'litigation romanticism' which validates the claim that litigation is no longer likely to be the alternative platform to produce complete fairness in the context of a private banking dispute (Menkel-Meadow, 1994, p. 1173). This could be explained by the possibility that the perception of fairness might be jeopardised by clients' perception of unfair rules, due to a lack of equal power to negotiate the contract and a lack of engagement from the complainants' side when a bank is resolving the disputes internally. It also offers evidence to sustain the establishment of procedural fairness where such fairness could be affected not only by the law and respective regulations but also by business practices once a legal relationship is established (Menkel-Meadow, 2004).

6.4.4 Identify factors that hinder the use of arbitration

Hence, factors can be identified from a wider spectrum, for example, a new understanding of how confidentiality might have played a role. The perception factors identified in Chapters 5 and 6 have added new understanding from the client's perspective.

Arbitration is not an option for private banking disputes regardless of its features. Private banking clients are very resourceful to either engage in litigation or arbitration, but neither is preferred. Private banks should also participate in arbitration, but this does not happen, as an ADR clause is forbidden to be incorporated in bank consumer contracts by Hong Kong Law under section 15 of the *Control of Exemption Clause Ordinance* (Chapter 2, Section 2.3.1). Banks do not offer to use mediation/arbitration methods because they have a better option in adjudicating the case themselves. However, arbitration is not needed by either private bankers or private banking clients. To my knowledge, the existing literature mainly focuses on how to enhance the process of dispute handling but insights from lawyers, private bankers, and private banking clients bridge the gap in the common goal of consolidating the integrity of the financial system. It may also challenge the 'unqualified faith' in the benefit of confidentiality (Gitchell & Plattner, 1997, p. 443), which escalates disputes to be resolved at a private platform, which might not be as beneficial as the academic literature advocates. Keeping a dispute resolution process confidential might not be socially just. Therefore, my work prompts an ultimate question: is going to court really a bad thing?

This confirms an important notion that 'there is no one-size-fit-all arbitration model' in a private banking dispute (Park, 1990, pp. 1347–1348). It also offers an empirical test to support Sternlight's (2004) appeal to 'have an effort to think about ways to modify mandatory arbitration to make it more just' (Sternlight, 2004, p. 1673). The work has also reflected on an important question from a social perspective, in line with the public interest when ADR is only conducted against the backdrop of litigation. It contributes to important questions such as whether there exists a mutually recognised out-of-courtroom channel to handle private banking disputes. It is now understood that there is a possibility that during the global financial crisis, the lack of bank regulation made it difficult for individual customers to be successful in court against their banks. The alleged misbehaviour in advising and selling Lehman-related products may be difficult to justify legally and in a timely way in court due to a lack of legal grounds. Clients still reacted radically by most notably occupying the main financial streets or blockading bank entrances to force compensation. Investors ignored the legal basis in those cases, and therefore going to court does not always give clients what they want. If individual clients and banks could have settled the disputes privately through an efficient dispute resolution mechanism, such social unrest could have been avoided. As a matter of fact, most cases were eventually settled privately. Nowadays, with protection from tighter regulation governing the bank's side and from more careful contract drafting through imposing responsibility on individual clients, banks are in an even stronger position to close any door for dialogue. Extensive bank regulation does not seem to make it easier for customers to sue their bank, as the banks cannot be wrong, at least on paper. This added dynamic could be a warning signal that should a financial crisis occur again, similar social discontent might also occur again but for a different reason. Customers find the banks to be legitimate, but actually, the wronged party is a banker or client with ignorance of the rules and regulations. Customers by then could find themselves short of other channels to resolve their grievances, as they only blame themselves. Without a proper resolution mechanism, individual clients may either give up or trigger another 'scene' to force the bank to open up dialogue.

These deterrent factors identified in the self-corrective mechanism are important findings which help make necessary measures and incorporate them into the regulatory framework. It is expected that there is further room to cater for clients' needs from the contract, regulation, and arbitral process perspective in order to better fit the needs of the users. In addition, recent works have focused on the design of arbitration but often place too little emphasis on analysing how existing legal frameworks and regulatory preferences affect the choice dispute resolution channel. Therefore, resolving obstacles to ADR from a disputant perspective is of paramount importance and will supplement other studies relating to procedural matters that aim to make the ADR process fair, just, and efficient.

6.5 Recommendations for further research

6.5.1 Examine banker's behaviour

Chapter 2 unveiled that the account opening form does not contain all the necessary information for clients to base their disputes, affecting their intention to transform their grievance into a dispute, not to speak of handling any dispute. We only see that the account opening form seems to serve as a tool to collect data and declarations from clients, and does not seem to govern the subsequent conduct of the bank or banker. Questions such as whether the account opening form incorporates all regulatory requirements so clients can read them should be addressed. In another word, what is the impact of the regulatory framework in contract formation, interpretation, and the efficiency and effectiveness of incorporating these regulations into a contract? For example, shall we mandate the complaint-handling process into account opening forms so that clients would have easy guidance, instead of just relying on their bankers who seem to be most of the time the source of the grievance? For example, the impact of suitability requirements on account opening forms (while in this book we only extract the AML part to discuss in depth) or whether a more comprehensive code of conduct for private banking has arisen since 2018 needs some attention (Chapter 2, Section 2.3.2). What has not been incorporated is the conduct of private bankers. Their dual roles with both personal connections with clients and representatives of agents add dynamics to the banking relationship and deserve further study. The conduct of an individual cannot really be dissociated from that of the bank. Whether bankers' conduct and, more generically, the bank's obligations should be incorporated into the contract deserves further scrutiny.

Another angle is to associate the findings with the 'relational contract theory' where contracts are the outcomes of continuing or wider commercial relationships (Macneil, 1999). In this study, the private banking account opening form (aka the contract) appears to be irrelevant as more contracts will be needed for further transactions. They do not seem to serve any purpose except to confirm the relationship. How does this theory embed with the choice of dispute resolution? The real function of the account opening form should be further explored to re-explore the function of the account opening forms, which appears not to be a contract that establishes a legal relationship between banks and customers, but rather something more generic or even 'symbolic'.

In short, influence from others remains relevant even as early as the pre-dispute stage and throughout the disputing stage which increases the likelihood for the disputants to lump (Engle, 2016, p. 157).

6.5.2 Conduct comparative studies between different jurisdictions

This book focuses exclusively on Hong Kong with a comparative contextual analysis of other jurisdictions at stage 1. Although it is observed that regulators in Hong Kong have followed international standards and each foreign bank in Hong Kong would have followed the laws and regulations of their respective jurisdictions, human interactions in each country might be different. Each geographical location is subject to its own cultural, ethnic, and legal environments that might impact clients' expectations and perceptions of banking services and choice of dispute resolution mechanism. Another angle is how international standards have been applied locally, and how different local standards could interact/conflict/supplement with each other when transactions happen among them. These questions shape the regulatory framework in the global context and might extend to the issue of AML and CFT.

It is necessary to relate the experience in Hong Kong to a global context because Hong Kong is an international centre where literally every bank in the world may have a branch or at least a representative office in Hong Kong. Therefore, it is important to examine how bank regulation in Hong Kong might have been affected by global forces, and possibly vice versa. In the private banking industry, global relevance appears more important given wealth is accumulating rapidly in Asia, and Hong Kong has positioned itself to become the private banking hub in Asia. Hence a gap appears to lie in the missing link between how Hong Kong practice has been and should be affected by the global benchmarks acceptable to the clients. Similar analysis was conducted by the Swiss Banking Association (2018).

6.5.3 To test the factors of the self-corrective mechanism

Have clients burdened themselves too much to avoid dispute formation? Is this aligned with the public interest? This is an important question that may have been asked but needs further empirical studies to explain its existence, as well as whether it is a structural issue or just a private banking-only phenomenon. This would offer further empirical insights to understand in what circumstances would the grievance experiences not be perceived as injurious, when perceptions do not transform into grievances, or if grievances are only voiced to those not responsible (Felstiner et al., 1980, p. 636). In particular, legal consciousness and the effectiveness of private negotiation could benefit by incorporating possible intervention from the self-corrective mechanism with or without an existing contractual relationship, and insights can be further extended to the adoption of informal dispute resolution channels. This book suggests that the law is already embedded into everyday life in the private banking industry, and with the merge between law and society (moving on from law as a rule, then law as a tool as suggested by Merry (1985)), the self-corrective mechanism could also be extended to the study of cultural issues. This topic would benefit from both doctrinal and empirical studies (Section 6.2.3).

6.6 Final remarks – why even the wealthy don't sue

Clients are not willing to make a complaint if they do not know what to name, are unable to take control of the process, or are unlikely to win. There are three very distinct yet common clients' perceptions in resolving their disputes, directly addressing the question of whether arbitration is a viable option. First, the grievances are unlikely to come from what is being agreed upon in the written contract. Second, clients direct the banker to manage their accounts in the way they prefer. Third, regulators encourage clients to resolve their issues with banks, and banks usually cover the loss of the clients to maintain the relationship. These factors place clients in a weaker position as the disputes are unlikely to favour them in terms of a legal basis, resulting in uncertainty in adjudication. Private bankers also play a crucial role in eliminating disputes. To relate these issues to the research question on the suitability of arbitration in resolving private banking disputes, arbitration could be perceived as a suitable process from a private banking client's perspective. It may not be necessary or efficient. Private banking disputes seem to be resolved through either negotiation, litigation, or exiting the relationship. This leads to the under-utilisation of arbitration in Hong Kong, not only because private banking disputes have been excluded from the FDRC (Chapter 3, Section 3.2.4) but also because there are many exogenous factors that halt the dispute transformation process as clients perceive themselves as a weaker party.

The 'naming, blaming, claiming' model is adopted to evaluate these perspectives through a critical content review of the relevant regulatory requirements governing the private banking industry, data collected from the surveys, and feedback provided through face-to-face interviews. It appears there has been a strong force to restrict the formation of disputes. Clients are at a power disadvantage right at the contract formation stage by being willing to sign a one-sided contract and assume the responsibility of banks and bankers acting in accordance with a client's expectations and satisfaction. When a grievance is generated, it is often eliminated by either the fact that the grievance was not part of the contract or by a banker's efforts to maintain the relationship. This phenomenon has been confirmed by the survey results, which show a high awareness of clients' knowledge of relevant regulations and alignments with clients' experiences. It has arguably eliminated most of the possible disputes which make arbitration not needed in the first place and can be used to explain the under-utilisation.

With regards to the viability of arbitration, although the surveys have shown that most of the arbitration function is preferred by clients, it appears that the existing regulatory framework already incorporates an arbitration process. The bank can adjudicate their own complaints, and clients are encouraged to work with the banks on any dissatisfaction. If clients and banks are unable to resolve their dispute, clients can file a complaint to the HKMA but, arguably, the HKMA will not intervene in a bank's business decision unless there is an apparent breach of regulation from the bank's perspective. In essence, the bank has already acted as an arbitrator and the HKMA will mediate on the bank's side only. Neither the bank's internal complaint procedures nor the HKMA's complaint processes are transparent, and banks do not seem to have a duty to explain their findings or investigation results to complainants. Hence, arguably clients do not find it beneficial to file a proceeding against the bank, as confirmed by the feedback from the interviews.

It has been revealed that the regulator and private bankers can significantly impact whether a dispute is formed, as clients are encouraged to resolve their grievances internally, and clients tend to also believe that banks would not be that 'careless' in making a regulatory breach, hence the belief that their chance of winning is small. Clients rely on the banker's strong motivation to keep their business in order to get what they need; alternatively, they can leave or sue the bank. Wealth may not be the dominant concern when disputants decide to engage in a dispute resolution process; neither is the availability and features of the process. Wealthy clients don't sue, because they don't have a chance of winning under the existing contractual relationship: grievances cannot be formed or clients do not wish to explore the forest for fear of getting lost. This is particularly true in the bank–customer relationship when the rule is solely decided by the bank, and the customer can only take it or leave it.

However, it does not mean the clients will accept it. Although tight regulation makes it difficult for clients to form a dispute as there is a perception that every action performed by the bank is legal, they will try to get hold of the process to get what they need but at the same time embed the self-corrective mechanism to repress or even resist to engage in the dispute resolution process when grievances start to form. Clients with this mindset may not be desirable for Hong Kong, which aspires to be an international financial centre. It also explains why arbitration is under-utilised to resolve private banking disputes because the dispute is put off before it is formed. When the Lehman crisis emerged, neither the bank nor the regulators could handle the huge number of disputes, and the Hong Kong government had to intervene and facilitate private settlements. Nowadays, tight regulation may have made it more difficult for investors to hold banks liable for clients' grievances because banks have covered themselves well through their one-sided contracts. The HKMA does not easily intervene with complaints between clients and banks, which put clients in a weaker position in the dispute resolution process. Clients would be better off simply eliminating these grievances to avoid a bigger hassle. With this background, clients adjust themselves through a self-correction process to make sure that no dispute is necessary, instead of relying on any internal or external dispute resolution channels to resolve any dispute.

Clients need to handle disputes on their own but with the intention to eliminate them instead of resolving them. The phenomenon of dispute elimination is cultivated through carefully drafted one-side contracts. It is questionable whether the laws and regulations of banks can offer meaningful protection to individual clients. Clients have engaged themselves personally to make sure that what they need from a bank is properly fulfilled to prevent disputes. Clients also eliminate disputes because they perceive most bank activities as being regulated and hence the difficulty in using the law against a bank's conduct. It is also complicated to identify the source of regulations due to the complexity and scattered source of regulations, as well as a court's perspective, where the client's obligation to make sure they are aware of what they have engaged with the bank is confirmed.

An open court is a necessary channel for banks for discouraging complaints and for individual clients as a tool or a threat to force private negotiation. Currently, ADR seems to have been replaced by banks' internal complaint-handling procedures, where a bank seems to act as an arbitrator while the regulator acts as a mediator. This entire interaction rests solely between the banks and regulators. The clients are not involved. Even if it is the most tailor-made mechanism for banks to resolve their own disputes, without any transparency, clients might not find it suitable. The power balance between banks and clients is in favour of the bank can be seen in the following factors:

- The execution of one-sided contracts.
- The role of private bankers as non-contractual parties.
- Non-contractual behaviour in a transaction.
- Lack of transparency in a bank's internal dispute resolution mechanism.

These lead to the prerequisites of the self-corrective mechanism as stated in Section 6.2.2. The factors motivating the self-corrective mechanism to eliminate disputes show how the power imbalance created before dispute formation impacts the choice of dispute resolution mechanism. Hence, it is premature to discuss a viable and suitable arbitration or other dispute resolution mechanism to resolve civil disputes in the private banking sector. Banks would operate their businesses as if the primary goal was to avoid litigation and draft the contract just to protect themselves. In response to the one-sided contract, clients would prevent naming when using the banking service. Also, with the existing arbitration process being incorporated into existing complaint-handling processes, it requires a new logic in understanding and interpreting bank laws and regulations on top of the existing regulatory focus on scope and depth. Healthy communication between individual clients and private banks, as well as further assistance from regulators, should be provided to clients on issues that could give rise to a dispute, even if it is outside the contractual scope, such as tax reporting, cross-border rules, and AML (Consulting Technology, 2017). Clients are forced to suppress their own grievances. This self-corrective mechanism deserves regulatory attention through imposing a transparent process on how clients' complaints would be handled by the bank and providing additional support from the regulators. This is so that clients are not forced to either leave the bank or go to court to bring the public's attention to the issue and create a reputation risk for banks

Banks should be required to provide further transparency in the complaint-handling process and to engage clients in this process. Regulators might take a more active role in supervising the dispute resolution process by banks. Further support to bankers through on-the-job training and continued monitoring of their conduct is essential to ensure their conduct is in line with the industry standards and bank policies. The existing grandfathering system to professional qualification, meaning that more experienced bankers are exempted from taking examinations to get the qualification such as CPWP in Hong Kong, is less than ideal because new technical skills that bankers should be well equipped with should not be replaced by experience. It could be dangerous if we continue to rely too much on personal relationships between clients and bankers to maintain the apparent harmony in the industry, as it is difficult to regulate.

The existing bank–customer relationship might now need to be understood as the *bank–banker–customer relationship* to better reflect the actual dynamics between banks and clients. The ordinances, codes of conduct, and policies should also serve the following purposes: (a) to facilitate healthy communication between different stakeholders to help understand the business and formulate more suitable policies to protect the public interest while promoting banking and investment activities, (b) to simplify the current law and regulations, and (c) to provide a transparent framework to resolve civil disputes outside of the courtroom. The three very important pillars of the new banking world shall govern and ensure (a) trust between banks, bankers, and customers; (b) the interrelationship and dependency among banks, individual clients, and regulators; and (c) public interest to safeguard banks as the 'mother of all industries'.

It is of public interest to unveil the necessary dispute processes so that bank practices can be publicly scrutinised. Continued small fixes under public's eyes can facilitate better governance when comparing with a on e-off reform and rectification in response to one occurrence of a financial crisis causing public disruption. Tight regulation should be accompanied by transparency of banking policies and procedures in order to assist individual clients to resolve – not eliminate – disputes, as this would only encourage parties to work outside the formal law no matter how well the formal law is drafted and intended for good.

Annexes

Annex I: Sample Questions for Interview

Sample Questions of an Open-ended interview with private banking clients

[Note: some questions will involve comments from the result of the self-administered questionnaire]

Introduction

Thank you for agreeing to participate in this interview. The study will examine whether and how private banks and private banking clients handle their disputes outside the court, through the process of arbitration and through the HKMA complaint channel. Please share your opinion with us. The interview will be recorded by audio. The content will be kept private and confidential and during the conversation please refrain from mentioning your own name or name of any banks. In case such information is revealed the respective information will be redacted.

1. Have you been ever had any dispute with your private bank? Could you share some details of it?
2. How was it resolved? Do you make a complaint directly with the bank? Or go to court? Or use any other process?
3. Have you ever been involved with arbitration? If not, can you share what do you know about it?

[If interviewees have no prior knowledge about arbitration or HKMA complaint channel, researcher may provide a brief explanation before the interview continues]

In relation to the contractual relationship with the private bank

4. Do you usually read all the terms and conditions of the account opening documents?

 DOI: 10.4324/9781003407591-7

  a. If not, why not? And how do you make sure you agree with these terms?
  b. If so, have you come across with some terms and conditions that you do not agree? What did you do?

5. What would you feel about if your case is adjudicated based on the terms and conditions stated in the account opening form you signed?
6. Would you sign the account opening form if there is a mandatory clause to resolve dispute through arbitration?
7. How would you feel if it is mandatory to arbitrate your disputes with the private bank?

<u>In relation to arbitration process</u>

[Imagine you are resolving a case in front of a judge at public courtroom, or recall the time you are involved in an arbitration]

8. Would you prefer your disputes to be judged before the public courtroom or in private arbitration?
9. Would you want to design and choose the procedural rule?
10. Would you prefer to conduct the arbitration privately in person between yourself and the bank; or conduct the arbitration privately but through an institution providing dispute resolution service?
11. How do you feel about if you (and the bank) can agree to choose the arbitrator?
12. How much money would you expect yourself to pay for this service?
13. Would you prefer the judgment (award) be published or kept privately?
14. Have you been involved in arbitration process before to resolve other disputes of yours?
15. Could you describe the best process to resolve your dispute?

<u>In relation to the role of HKMA in a dispute</u>

16. Tell me what you know about the complaint channel offered by HKMA for resolving private banking disputes?
17. Have you been ever filed a complaint to HKMA?
    a. If so, please share details. (e.g., what dispute is it? Did you engage a lawyer? Satisfy with turnaround time?)
    b. If not, why not? (e.g., no dispute before, too complicated)

18. What impact do you hope HKMA will bring once your complaint is received? (e.g., act as facilitator/mediator; follow up the complaint on your behalf; guide you what to do; investigate and make a ruling; order compensation)

Annex II: The Online Survey

Part I: Understanding and experience of law/regulation governing the Private Bank / Private Banker

	A		*B*			
	You have experienced this before		*This conduct complies with the law/ regulation*			
(a) Account Opening	*Yes, I have experienced this conduct before*	*No, I have not experienced this conduct before*	*Yes, this conduct is complied with relevant regulation*	*No, this conduct does not comply with relevant regulation*	*This conduct is not regulated*	*I am not sure it this conduct is regulated*
1. You are asked to prove how you generate your wealth.						
2. The private banker explains to you the terms and conditions in the account opening forms.						
3. The bank amends the terms in the account opening forms without your consent, but simply sent you a letter and said the terms and conditions will change 1 month later.						
4. Private banker requires to see your ID card for account opening.						

(Continued)

	A		*B*			
	You have experienced this before		*This conduct complies with the law/ regulation*			
Account Opening	*Yes, I have experienced this conduct before*	*No, I have not experienced this conduct before*	*Yes, this conduct is complied with relevant regulation*	*No, this conduct does not comply with relevant regulation*	*This conduct is not regulated*	*I am not sure it this conduct is regulated*
5. You sign the blank account opening forms; the private banker fills in details after.						
(b) Product Knowledge and Risk Appetite of the Client						
6. Private bank explains the key product features and risks associated before placing an order.						
7. Private bank discloses conflict of interest before your investment order is executed.						
8. A private banker offers you his own view in an investment.						
9. You are asked to update your product knowledge and investment risk appetite regularly.						

10. You are asked to explicitly say you understand the product features before you place an investment order.

(c) Communication Channel Between Bank and Client

11. You receive a letter to inform you that your private bank account is opened.
12. Your Private Banker is registered as a Certified Private Wealth Professional (CPWP) certified by the Private Wealth Management Association (PWMA).
13. You are asked to place an investment instruction through email,
14. The bank sends you a written advice after an investment is executed.
15. The investment product brochure shows expected future performance.

(Continued)

	A		*B*			
	You have experienced this before		*This conduct complies with the law/ regulation*			
Account Opening	*Yes, I have experienced this conduct before*	*No, I have not experienced this conduct before*	*Yes, this conduct is complied with relevant regulation*	*No, this conduct does not comply with relevant regulation*	*This conduct is not regulated*	*I am not sure it this conduct is regulated*
(d) Dispute Resolution Channel						
16. You send a compliant letter to the private bank, but get no reply.						
17. Your private banker tells you that the private bank has no complaint handling department.						
18. You receive compensation directly from private banker to resolve a dispute.						
19. The private bank says they are not obliged to tell you how you can complaint against the bank internally.						
20. your private bank tells you that your complaint can only be written in a letter can be followed up.						

Part II: Your experience in private banking and arbitration

	Please indicate your choice	
1. How many private banks accounts do you have?	Less than 3	3 or above
2. On average, how much assets banked in each private bank?	Less than HK$100m	HK$100 m or above
3. How many years have you been banking with the private bank?	Less than 5 years	5 years or above
4. Have you been a disputing party in an arbitration before?	Yes	No
5. If you have been a disputant in an arbitration before, was it related to private banking dispute?	Yes: Related to: 1. Corporate action / banks act against your instruction 2. Mis-selling 3. Others (please specify)	No: Related to: 1) Commercial 2) Injury 3) Construction/ Flat Renovation 4) Family 5) Others
6. If you have a choice, will you use arbitration as a channel to resolve your dispute with the private bank?	Yes	No Key reason? (Choose one only) (i) I don't know what arbitration is. (ii) I will talk to the private bank or private banker directly. (iii) I will go to the court. (iv) It is more efficient to use other channel such as the press. (v) Others (please specify)

Part III: Your preference on Arbitration Process to resolve private banking disputes

	Please indicate your preference		
	Prefer	*Not Prefer*	*No preference*
Imagine you have a dispute with your private bank and are asked to resolve it privately (i.e., not going to the court)			
1. You argue the case directly with the bank (i.e., no judge involved).			
2. If a judge is requested, you choose your own judge.			
3. You handle the dispute directly with the bank without a lawyer.			
4. You argue the case by written submission and no need for personal hearing.			
5. You appoint a private institution to organise the arbitration for you.			
6. You organise the arbitration privately between yourself and the bank.			
7. You choose you own venue and law to hear and adjudicate your case.			
8. You design your own process (e.g., which evidence is acceptable, how to collect).			
9. You design your own schedule and timeline to process the case.			
10. You have the entire hearing process held in private.			
11. The award (i.e., the judgment) offers no reason.			
12. After the issue of award, no appeal is allowed.			

Annex III: Legal reference – Ordinances, case laws, and regulations

Regulation for banking/private banking

1. Advertising Guidelines Applicable to Collective Investment Schemes Authorized under the Product Codes
2. Code on Investment-Linked Assurance Schemes
3. Code on Pooled Retirement Funds
4. Code on Unit Trusts and Mutual Funds
5. Fund Manager Code of Conduct
6. Guideline on Anti-Money Laundering and Counter-Financing of Terrorism, HKMA
7. HKMA supervisory manual policy (IC-4)
8. Private Wealth Management Association – Code of Ethics and Conduct
9. Securities and Futures (Leveraged Foreign Exchange trading – Arbitration) Rules (HK)
10. SFC Code of Conduct
11. SFC Code on MPF Products
12. Treat Customers Fairly Charter for Private Wealth Management Industry
13. Code of Banking Practice, The DTC Association, December 2021

Statutes

1. Sections 2 and 3 of Misrepresentation Ordinance (CAP 284)
2. Sections. 7, 8, and 15 of the Control Exemption Clauses Ordinance (CAP 458)
3. Sections. 3 and 6 of Unconscionable Contracts Ordinance (CAP 458)
4. Sections 107 and 108 of Securities and Futures Ordinance (CAP 571)
5. Sections. 40/40A of Companies (Winding Up and Miscellaneous Provisions) Ordinance (CAP 32)
6. Anti-Money Laundering Ordinance (Cap 615)
7. Drug Trafficking (Recovery of Proceeds) Ordinance, (Cap 405)
8. Organized and Serious Crime Ordinance SCO (Cap 455)
9. United Nations (Anti-Terrorism Measures) Ordinance (Cap. 575)
10. Arbitration Act 1996 in the UK
11. Arbitration Ordinance CAP 609 in Hong Kong
12. Wall Street Reform and Consumer Protection Act 2010
13. Uniting and Strengthening America by Providing Appropriate Tools Required to Intercept and Obstruct Terrorism (USA PATRIOT) Act of 2001

Case Law (Tort law (duty of care, duty to advise and vicarious liability); and contract law (misrepresentation, undue influence, and non-est factum)

1. Kwok Wai Hing Selina v HSBC Private Bank (Suisse) SA HCCL 7 of 2010.
2. Field v Barber Asia, Court of first Instance of Hong Kong (HCA 7119/2000, June 17, 2003)
3. SA (2012) and DBS Bank (Hong Kong) Limited v San-Hot HK Industrial Company Limited and Hao Ting (2013).
4. Shine Grace Investment Ltd v Citibank, N.A. and Another (2008);
5. Li Kwok Heem John v Standard Chartered International (USA) Ltd (2016);
6. Chang Pui Yin v Bank of Singapore Ltd (2017).
7. Ong, C., & Hong Kong Institute of Bankers. (1995). Legal decisions affecting banks in Hong Kong: With commentary. Hong Kong: Hong Kong Institute of Bankers.
8. Belinda MacMahon, (Ed.) 'The Bank for International Settlements Arbitration Awards of 2002 and 2003', T.M.C. Asser Press
9. Ms. X v Banque Privee Edmond de Rothschild Europe (Rot; 26 Sep. 2012, Cass. Civ (1ere)
10. SEC v Goldman Sachs & Co., 790 F. Supp. 2d 147 (S.D.N.Y. 2011) (No. 10 Civ. 3229)

Key Regulations governing bank complaint procedures (other than Hong Kong)

France	Monetary And Financial Code (France)
United Kingdom	DISP 1.3 Complaints Handling Rules (UK)
China	Order No. 5 [2020] of the People's Bank of China (Implementation Measures of the People's Bank of China for Financial Consumer Protection) (China)
Singapore	Financial Advisers Act (Chapter 110) Financial Advisers (Complaints Handling and Resolution) Regulations 2021 (Singapore)

Annual Reports, other reports, and website used referenced for Table 2.4 (accessed May 2022)

Annual Reports and Other Reports

1. American Arbitration Association, Annual Reports, US, available at: www.adr.org/annual-reports
2. CIETAC 2020 Work Report and 2021 Work Plan-Work Report, available at: www.acerislaw.com/wp-content/uploads/2021/05/cietac.org-CIETAC-2020-Work-Report-and-2021-Work-Plan-Work-Report-China-International-Economic-and-Trade-Arbitra.pdf
3. CIETAC, Annual Reports, available at: https://www.cietac-eu.org/downloads/

4. FDRC, Annual Reports, HK, available at: www.fdrc.org.hk/en/html/publications/annualreport.php
5. FIDReC Annual Reports, Singapore, available at: www.fidrec.com.sg/knowledgebase/article/KA-01185/en-us
6. Financial Ombudsman Service Annual Reports, UK, available at: www.financial-ombudsman.org.uk/who-we-are/governance-funding/annual-reports-accounts
7. HKMA Annual Reports, available at: www.hkma.gov.hk/eng/data-publications-and-research/publications/annual-report/
8. Swiss Banking Ombudsman, Annual Reports and Annual Reports Summary, available at: https://bankingombudsman.ch/en/annual-reports/

Websites on arbitration institutions

1. American Arbitration Association, US, available at: https://adr.org/
2. CIETAC, available at: http://www.cietac.org/?l=en
3. FDRC, HK, available at: https://www.fdrc.org.hk/
4. FIDReC, Singapore, available at: https://www.fidrec.com.sg/ CIETAC, available at: https://www.cietac-eu.org/downloads/
5. Financial Ombudsman Service, UK, available at: https://www.financial-ombudsman.org.uk/
6. P.R.I.M.E., France, available at: https://primefinancedisputes.org/
7. Swiss Banking Ombudsman, Annual Reports and Annual Reports Summary, available at: https://bankingombudsman.ch/en/

Online Complaint Channels from Regulators

1. Federal Reserve, Consumer Help, https://forms.federalreserveconsumerhelp.gov/secure/complaint/formComplaintIntro
2. France, https://acpr.banque-france.fr/en/customer-protection/general-public/submit-claim-regarding-professional
3. HKMA, Online Complaint Form, available at: https://bankcomplaint.hkma.gov.hk/#/
4. Monetary Authority of Singapore, Reporting of Regulatory Breaches or Misconduct, available at: https://eservices.mas.gov.sg/consumerfeedback/
5. Swiss Financial Market Supervisory Authority (FINMA), Reporting an incident to FINMA or filing a complaint, https://www.finma.ch/en/finma-public/reporting-information/
6. The Autorité de contrôle prudentiel et de resolution (ACPR), Submit a claim regarding a professional

REFERENCES

Abel, R. (1982). *The politics of informal justice. Vols. 1 and 2*. Academic.

Albiston, C. R., Edelman, L. B., & Milligan, J. (2014). The dispute tree and the legal forest. *Annual Review of Law and Social Science*, *10*, 105–131.

Albiston, C. R., & Sandefur, R. L. (2013). Expanding the empirical study of access to justice. *Wisconsin Law Review*, *101*, 106.

Alexander, Nadja (2018). Hong Kong: Mediation and the future of dispute resolution. *Conflict Resolution in Asia: Mediation and Other Cultural Models*. 183–218. Research Collection School Of Law. Available at SSRN 3757372. https://ink.library.smu.edu.sg/cgi/viewcontent.cgi?article=4707&context=sol_research

Ali, S. F. (2013). *Consumer financial dispute resolution in a comparative context: Principles, systems and practice*. Cambridge University Press.

Ali, S. F., & Da Roza, A. (2012). Alternative dispute resolution design in financial markets-some more equal than others: Hong Kong's proposed financial dispute resolution center in the context of the experience in the United Kingdom, United States, Australia, and Singapore. *Pacific Rim Law & Policy Journal*, *21*, 485.

Ali, S. F., & Kwok, J. J. W. (2010). After Lehman: International response to financial disputes-A focus on Hong Kong. *Richmond Journal of Global Law and Business*, *10*, 151.

Ali, S., & Huang, H. (2012). Financial dispute resolution in China: Arbitration or court litigation? *Arbitration International*, *28*(1), 77–100.

Arner, D. W., Hsu, B. F., & Da Roza, A. M. (2010). Financial regulation in Hong Kong: Time for a change. *Asian Journal of Comparative Law*, *5*, 1–47.

Arner, D. W., & Lin, J. J. (2003). *Financial regulation: A guide to structural reform*. Sweet & Maxwell Limited.

Astor, H. (2005). Some contemporary theories of power in mediation: A primer for the puzzled practitioner. *Australasian Dispute Resolution Journal*, *16*(1), 30–39.

Astor, H., & Chinkin, C. M. (2002). *Dispute resolution in Australia (Vol. 2)*. LexisNexis Butterworths.

Auerbach, J. S. (1983). *Justice without law?: Non-legal dispute settlement in American history*. Oxford University Press.

Bakos, Y., Marotta-Wurgler, F., & Trossen, D. R. (2014a). Does anyone read the fine print? Consumer attention to standard-form contracts. *The Journal of Legal Studies*, *43*(1), 1–35.

Bakos, Y., Marotta-Wurgler, F., & Trossen, D. R. (2014b). Does anyone read the fine print? Consumer attention to standard form contracts. *The Journal of Legal Studies*, *43*(1), 1–35.

Banakar, R. (2003). *Merging law and sociology: Beyond the dichotomies of socio-legal research*. Galda and Wilch Publishing.

Bank for International Settlements. (2019, December 15). The basel framework. Retrieved September 20, 2021, from https://www.bis.org/basel_framework/index.htm?export=pdf

Banking Ordinance (Cap. 155).

Barr, M. S. (2014). Mandatory arbitration in consumer finance and investor contracts. *New York University Journal of Law & Business*, *11*, 793.

Baylis, C., & Carroll, R. (2005). Power issues in mediation. ADR Bulletin, 7(8), 1–6.

Becher, S. I. (2008). Asymmetric information in consumer contracts: The challenge that is yet to be met. *American Business Law Journal*, *45*(4), 723–774.

Berthelsen, C. B., Lindhardt, T., & Frederiksen, K. (2017). A discussion of differences in preparation, performance and postreflections in participant observations within two grounded theory approaches. *Scandinavian Journal of Caring Sciences*, *31*(2), 413–420.

Bills of Exchange Act 1882.

Boeglin, M. C. (1998). The use of arbitration clauses in the field of banking and finance–current status and preliminary conclusion. *Journal of International Arbitration*, *15*(3), 6.

Bok, D. C. (1983). A Flawed system of law practice and training. *Journal of Legal Education*, *33*, 570.

Braithwaite, J. (2002). Rules and principles: A theory of legal certainty. *Australasian Journal of Legal Philosophy*, *27*, 47–82.

Brake, D. L., & Grossman, J. L. (2007). The failure of Title VII as a rights-claiming system. *The North Carolina Law Review*, *86*, 859.

Bruce, S. (1988). *The rise and fall of the new Christian right: Conservative protestant politics in America 1978–1988*. Clarendon Press.

Buzbee, W. W. (2003). Recognizing the regulatory commons: A theory of regulatory gaps. *Iowa Law Review*, *89*, 1.

Campbell, A., & Cartwright, P. (2017). *Banks in crisis: The legal response*. Routledge.

Campos, P. F., Schlag, P., & Smith, S. D. (1996). Against the law. In Rodney A. Smolla and Neal Devins. *Against the law*. Duke University Press.

Chief Justice. (2014). Practice direction 31, mediation. Retrieved August 29, 2021, from https://legalref.judiciary.hk/lrs/common/pd/pdcontent.jsp?pdn=PD31.htm&lang=EN

Chittum, R. (2018). Diamond dealers in deep trouble as bank documents shine light on secret ways. ICIJ. Recuperado em, 14.

Civil Justice Reform. (2021a). Home: Underlying objectives. *Retrieved September 1, 2021, from* https://www.civiljustice.hk/eng/home.html

Civil Justice Reform. (2021b). Legislation. Retrieved September 1, 2021, from https://www.civiljustice.hk/eng/home.html

Consulting Technology. (2017). Top 10 trends in wealth management. Retrieved November 3, 2021, from https://www.capgemini.com/wp-content/uploads/2017/07/wealth_management_trends_2017_web_0.pdf

Consumer Council. (2021). Annual reports. Retrieved November 3, 2021, from https://www.consumer.org.hk/en/annual-report

Consumer Council. (2021a). Consumer legal action fund. Retrieved March 12, 2021, from https://www.consumer.org.hk/ws_en/legal_protection/consumer_legal_actions_fund/clafinfo.html

Consumer Council. (2021b). Mission and vision: Functions. Retrieved September 1, 2021, from https://www.consumer.org.hk/en/about-us/mission-and-vision

Crowne, C. H. (2001). The Alternative Dispute Resolution Act of 1998: Implementing a new paradigm of justice. *New York University Law Review, 76*, 1768.

Davies, H. (1998). Why regulate? *Conferencia presentada en "Henry Thornton Lecture"*. City University Business School.

Davis, A. M., & Salem, R. A. (1984). Dealing with power imbalances in the mediation of interpersonal disputes. *Mediation Quarterly, 6*, 17.

Department of Justice. (2021). 'Mediate first' pledge Signees (Companies/Organisations/Associations). Retrieved September 1, 2021, from https://www.doj.gov.hk/mediatefirst/doc/tc/pledgeSigneec.pdf

Dezalay, Y., & Garth, B. (Eds.). (2011). *Lawyers and the rule of law in an era of globalization*. Routledge.

Dezalay, Y., & Garth, B. G. (1996). *Dealing in virtue: International commercial arbitration and the construction of a transnational legal order*. University of Chicago Press.

Dugue, C. (2000). Risk control and international finance arbitration. *ICC Bulletin, Special Supplement, Arbitration, Finance and Insurance, 15*, 15–20.

Durkheim, E. (2014). *The division of labor in society*. Simon and Schuster.

Durkheim, E. (2019). The division of labor in society. In Anthony Giddens. *Social Stratification* (pp. 178–183). Routledge.

Edelman, L. B., Erlanger, H. S., & Lande, J. (2014). 11. Internal dispute resolution: The transformation of civil rights in the workplace. In *The law and society reader II* (pp. 103–110). New York University Press. https://scholarship.law.missouri.edu/cgi/viewcontent.cgi?article=1274&context=facpubs

Editors. (2008, September 15). Lehman Brothers declares bankruptcy. *History*. Retrieved September 1, 2021, from https://www.history.com/this-day-in-history/lehman-brothers-collapses

Ellickson, R. C. (1991). *Order without law*. Harvard University Press.

Ellinger, E. P., Lomnicka, E., & Hare, C. (2011). *Ellinger's modern banking law*. Oxford University Press.

Ellis, D. (2022). Evaluation of adversarial adjudication and divorce mediation as options for high-conflict parents experiencing divorce. *Gender and Women's Studies, 5*(1), 2.

Engel, D. M. (2016). The myth of the litigious society. In *The myth of the litigious society*. University of Chicago Press.

Epstein, L., & Martin, A. D. (2014). *An introduction to empirical legal research*. Oxford University Press.

Equator Principles. (2021). The equator principles. Retrieved September 20, 2021, from https://equator-principles.com/about/

Esterberg, K. G. (2002). *Qualitative methods in social research*. McGraw-Hill.

Estlund, C. (2017). The black hole of mandatory arbitration. *The North Carolina Law Review, 96*, 679.

F. A. T. F. Recommendations. (2012). *International standards on combating money laundering and the financing of terrorism & proliferation*. FATF. Retrieved May 11, 2020, from www.Fatf-gafi.Org/recommendations.html

FDRC. (2016, October). Proposals to enhance the financial dispute resolution scheme, consultation paper. Retrieved September 30, 2021, from https://www.fdrc.org.hk/en/doc/Consultation_Document_ToR_EN.pdf

FDRC. (2017, August). Proposals to enhance the financial dispute resolution scheme, consultation conclusions. Retrieved May 20, 2022, from https://www.fdrc.org.hk/en/html/publications/publications_consultation.php

FDRC. (2018). 2018 FDRC annual report. Retrieved September 30, 2021, from https://www.fdrc.org.hk/en/annualreport/2018/files/download/FDRC_annual_report.pdf

FDRC. (2019). 2019 FDRC annual report. Retrieved September 30, 2021, from https://www.fdrc.org.hk/en/annualreport/2019/files/download/FDRC_annual_report.pdf

FDRC. (2021a). What is arbitration? Retrieved September 28, 2021, from https://fdrc.org.hk/en/html/resolvingdisputes/resolvingdisputes_mediationarbitration.php?lang=en

FDRC. (2021b). Consultation – Proposals to enhance the financial dispute resolution scheme, FDRC website. Retrieved September 28, 2021, from https://www.fdrc.org.hk/en/html/publications/publications_consultation.php

FDRC. (2021c). FDRC annual report. Retrieved September 30, 2021, from https://www.fdrc.org.hk/en/html/publications/annualreport.php

Feldman, Y., & Lifshitz, S. (2011). Behind the veil of legal uncertainty. *Law and Contemporary Problems, 74*, 133.

Felstiner, W. L. F., Abel, R. L., & Sarat, A. (1980). The emergence and transformation of disputes: Naming, blaming, claiming. *Law and Society Review, 15*(3–4), 631–654.

FIDReC. (2005). FIDReC's jurisdiction. Retrieved March 23, 2021, from https://www.fidrec.com.sg/website/fidrec_jurisdiction.html

FIDReC. (2020). Reaching UP and out – Annual report 2019/2020. Retrieved March 23, 2021, from https://www.fidrec.com.sg/website/annualreports/FIDReC%20Annual%20Report%202020.pdf

Fiss, O. M. (1984). Against settlement. *Yale Law Journal, 93*(6), 1073.

Fritz-Mauer, M. (2022). Naming, blaming, and just plain giving UP. SSRN.

Galanter, M. (1974). Why the haves come out ahead: Speculations on the limits of legal change. *Law & Society Review, 9*, 95.

Galanter, M., & Cahill, M. (1993). Most cases settle: Judicial promotion and regulation of settlements. *Stanford Law Review, 46*, 1339.

Gaskell, G., & Bauer, M. (2000). *Social research design course – Mi421*. London School of Economics Methodology Institute. Unpublished lecture series cited in Relis, T. (2009).

Gilmore, G. (2015). *The ages of American law*. Yale University Press.

Gilson, R. J., Sabel, C. F., & Scott, R. E. (2010). Braiding: The interaction of formal and informal contracting in theory, practice, and doctrine. *Columbia Law Review, 110*(6), 1377–1447.

Gitchell, R. L., & Plattner, A. (1997). Mediation: A viable alternative to litigation for medical malpractice cases. *Depaul Journal of Health Care Law, 2*, 421.

Glaser, B. G., & Strauss, A. L. (2017). *Discovery of grounded theory: Strategies for qualitative research*. Routledge.

Gunningham, N. (1990). Moving the goalposts: Financial market regulation in Hong Kong and the crash of October 1987. *Law and Social Inquiry, 15*(1), 1–48.

Hamel, J., Dufour, S., & Fortin, D. (1993). *Case study methods*, Vol. 32. Sage.

Hanefeld, I. (2012). Arbitration in banking and finance. *New York University Journal of Law & Business, 9*, 917.

Harpur, P. (2014). Naming, blaming and claiming ablism: The lived experiences of lawyers and advocates with disabilities. *Disability and Society, 29*(8), 1234–1247.

Hensler, D. R. (2006). Judging arbitration: The findings of procedural justice research. In Thomas e. Carbonneau & Jeanette A. Jaeggi (Eds.), *AAA Handbook on Commercial Arbitration 41–49*. American Arbitration Association.

Hoffman, L. S. (2006). Access to information, access to justice: The role of presuit investigatory discovery. *University of Michigan Journal of Law Reform, 40*, 217.

Hong Kong Legislative Council. (2015). Panel on administration of justice and legal services meeting on 18 May 2015 background brief on the implementation of civil justice reform. LC Paper No. CB(4)964/14-15(06). Retrieved August 29, 2021, from https://www.legco.gov.hk/yr14-15/english/panels/ajls/papers/ajls20150518cb4-964-6-e.pdf

Hong Kong Monetary Authority. (2001). Comparative study on banking consumer protection and competition arrangements in the UK, Australia and Hong Kong. Retrieved from December 17, 2021, https://www.hkma.gov.hk/media/eng/doc/about-the-hkma/legislative-council-issues/20010503e1b.pdf

Hong Kong Monetary Authority. (2002, July 22). Complaint handling procedures. Retrieved July 6, 2021, from https://www.hkma.gov.hk/eng/regulatory-resources/regulatory-guides/circulars/2002/07/circu_20020722a/

Hong Kong Monetary Authority. (2008). Lehman Brothers-related products dispute mediation and arbitration scheme. Retrieved September 1, 2021, from https://www.hkma.gov.hk/eng/other-information/investment-products-related-to-lehman-brothers/explanatory_b/

Hong Kong Monetary Authority. (2009). Complaints statistics concerning Lehman-related investment products (Up to 8 Oct 2009). Retrieved May 25, 2021, from https://www.hkma.gov.hk/media/eng/doc/key-information/press-release/2009/20091009e4a1.pdf

Hong Kong Monetary Authority. (2009, July 14). Abuse and fraud prevention in private banking and wealth management. Retrieved November 3, 2021, from https://www.hkma.gov.hk/eng/regulatory-resources/regulatory-guides/circulars/2009/07/circu_20090714-2/

Hong Kong Monetary Authority. (2011, August 11). Report of the Hong Kong monetary authority on issues concerning the distribution of structured products connected to Lehman group companies. Retrieved September 28, 2021, from https://www.hkma.gov.hk/eng/other-information/investment-products-related-to-lehman-brothers/lehman-report/

Hong Kong Monetary Authority. (2012a). Selling of investment products to private banking customers. Letters Issued by HKMA on 12th June 2012. Retrieved April 30, 2021, from https://www.hkma.gov.hk/media/eng/doc/key-information/guidelines-and-circular/2012/20120612e1.pdf

Hong Kong Monetary Authority. (2012b). Norman T L Chan: Hong Kong as a private banking hub – A regulator's vision. Retrieved April 22, 2021, from https://www.bis.org/review/r120612g.pdf

Hong Kong Monetary Authority. (2015, July 31). Monetary Authority takes disciplinary action against State Bank of India, Hong Kong Branch for contraventions of specified provisions under the Anti-Money Laundering and Counter-Terrorist Financing (Financial Institutions) Ordinance, Press Release. Retrieved September 14, 2021, from https://www.hkma.gov.hk/eng/news-and-media/press-releases/2015/07/20150731-5/#Note%201

Hong Kong Monetary Authority. (2017, May 25). Frequently asked questions on customer due diligence. Retrieved December 14, 2019, from https://www.hkma.gov.hk/media/eng/doc/key-functions/banking-stability/aml-cft/faq_cdd.pdf

Hong Kong Monetary Authority. (2017, December 8). CG −6 supervisory policy manual < Competence and Ethical Behaviour >. Retrieved July 7, 2021, from https://www.hkma.gov.hk/media/eng/doc/key-functions/banking-stability/supervisory-policy-manual/CG-6.pdf

Hong Kong Monetary Authority. (2017, February 23). Guidance on selling of investment products and handling of client securities. Retrieved November 3, 2021, from https://www.hkma.gov.hk/media/eng/doc/key-information/guidelines-and-circular/2017/20170223e1.pdf

Hong Kong Monetary Authority. (2018). Guideline on anti-money laundering and counter-financing of terrorism. Retrieved April 21, 2021, from https://www.hkma.gov.hk/media/eng/doc/key-information/guidelines-and-circular/guideline/g33.pdf

Hong Kong Monetary Authority. (2021, September 17). Complaints about banks. Retrieved September 20, 2021, from https://www.hkma.gov.hk/eng/smart-consumers/complaints/complaints-about-banks /

Hong Kong Monetary Authority. (2021). The three-tier banking system. Retrieved September 8, 2021, from https://www.hkma.gov.hk/eng/key-functions/banking/banking-regulatory-and-supervisory-regime/the-three-tier-banking-system/

House Committee of Parliament of Australia. (1991). Retrieved April 15, 2021, from https://www.aph.gov.au/parliamentary_business/committees/house_of_representatives_committees?url=reports/1991/1991_pp290c.pdf

Hudson, A. (2013). *Hudson law of finance*. Sweet & Maxwell.

Hyman, D. A. (2018). Bad doctors: Naming and blaming in a world with much less claiming. *Depaul Law Review*, *68*, 263.

International Chamber of Commerce. (2018). ICC commission report, Financial institutions and international arbitration 2016. A global interview to banks in their views on arbitration, March 2019. Retrieved May 14, 2021, from https://iccwbo.org/content/uploads/sites/3/2016/11/icc-financial-institutions-and-international-arbitration-icc-arbitration-adr-commission-report.pdf

Investor Compensation Company Limited. (2022). The ICF financial statements 1 April 2020 to 31 March 2021. Retrieved May 25, 2022, from https://www.hkicc.org.hk/publications/annual_e.htm#

Johnston, R. B., & Carrington, I. (2006). Protecting the financial system from abuse: Challenges to banks in implementing AML/CFT standards. *Journal of Money Laundering Control, 9*(1), 48–61.

Joint Mediation Helpline Office. (2021). About us: Objective. Retrieved September 1, 2021, from http://www.jointmediationhelpline.org.hk/index.html

Kawulich, B. B. (2005, May). Participant observation as a data collection method. *Forum qualitative sozialforschung. Forum: Qualitative Social Research, 6*(2). https://www.qualitative-research.net/index.php/fqs/article/view/466/997

KMPG. (2014). Global anti-money laundering survey 2014. Retrieved September 14, 2021, from https://assets.kpmg/content/dam/kpmg/pdf/2014/01/global-anti-money-laundering-survey.pdf

KPMG and PWMA. (2018, September). Hong Kong private wealth management report 2018. Retrieved December 14, 2019, from https://assets.kpmg/content/dam/kpmg/cn/pdf/en/2018/09/hong-kong-private-wealth-management-report-2018.pdf

Lauren B. Edelman, Howard S. Erlanger & John Lande, Internal Dispute Resolution: The Transformation of Civil Rights in the Workplace, 27 Law & Soc'y Rev. 497 (1993)

Larson, E. (2017). Regulatory rights: Emergent indigenous peoples' rights as a locus of global regulation. In Bronwen Morgan. *The intersection of rights and regulation* (pp. 107–127). Routledge.

Law, S. W. (2019). *In search of a golden rule for private bank clients onboarding* [Unpublished manuscript]. University of Hong Kong.

LC Paper No. CB(1)113/08-09. Subcommittee to study issues arising from Lehman Brothers-related minibonds and structured financial products, background brief, 2. https://www.legco.gov.hk/yr08-09/english/hc/sub_com/hs01/papers/hs011027cb1-113-e.pdf

Lind, E. A., Greenberg, J., Scott, K. S., & Welchans, T. D. (2000). The winding road from employee to complainant: Situational and psychological determinants of wrongful-termination claims. *Administrative Science Quarterly, 45*(3), 557–590.

Luckham, R. (1981). *Law and social enquiry: Case studies of research.* Nordiska Afrikainstitutet.

Macneil, I. R. (1999). Relational contract theory: Challenges and queries. *Northwestern University Law Review, 94*, 877.

Mamdani, M. (2007). The politics of naming: Genocide, civil war, insurgency. *London Review of Books, 29*(5), 5–8.

Man, J. (2008, December 10). 60 investors get HK$30m from banks on minibonds. SCMP. Retrieved March 12, 2021, from https://www.scmp.com/article/663192/60-investors-get-hk30m-banks-minibonds

Maxwell, J. A. (2012). *Qualitative research design: An interactive approach.* Sage publications.

Mayer, B. (1987). The dynamics of power in mediation and negotiation. *Mediation Quarterly, 16*, 75.

Mayer, B. S. (2010). *The dynamics of conflict resolution: A practitioner's guide*. John Wiley & Sons.

Mayer, B. S. (2012). *The dynamics of conflict: A guide to engagement and intervention.* John Wiley & Sons.

McKinsey & Company. (2013, July). McKinsey Global private Banking survey 2013. Retrieved May 27, 2021, from http://pbwm.ru/library/global-private-banking-survey-2013-capturing-the-new-generation-of-clients/download

Menkel-Meadow, C. (1994). Ethics and the settlements of mass torts: When the rules meet the road. *Cornell Law Review, 80*, 1159.

Menkel-Meadow, C. (1996). The trouble with the adversary system in a postmodern, multicultural world. *William & Mary Law Review, 38*, 5.

Menkel-Meadow, C. (1999). Do the haves come out ahead in alternative judicial systems: Repeat players in ADR. *Ohio State Journal on Dispute Resolution, 15*, 19.

Menkel-Meadow, C. (2004). From legal disputes to conflict resolution and human problem solving: Legal dispute resolution in a multidisciplinary context. *Journal of Legal Education, 54*(1), 7–29.

Merry, S. E. (1985). Concepts of law and justice among working-class Americans: Ideology as culture. *The Legal Studies Forum, 9*, 59.

Merry, S. E. (1990). The discourses of mediation and the power of naming. *Yale Journal of Law & the Humanities, 2*, 1.

Miller, R. E., & Sarat, A. (1980). Grievances, claims, and disputes: Assessing the adversary culture. *Law and Society Review, 15*(3/4), 525–566.

Mnookin, R. H., & Kornhauser, L. (1978). Bargaining in the shadow of the law: The case of divorce. *Yale Law Journal, 88*(5), 950.

Moore, C. W. (2014). *The mediation process: Practical strategies for resolving conflict.* John Wiley & Sons.

Morgan, B. (Ed.). (2017). *The intersection of rights and regulation: New directions in sociolegal scholarship.* Routledge.

Nader, L. (1980). *No access to law: Alternatives to the American judicial system* (pp. 64–67). Academic Press.

Naheem, M. A. (2015). HSBC Swiss bank accounts-AML compliance and money laundering implications. *Journal of Financial Regulation and Compliance, 23*(3), 285–297.

Nehf, J. P. (2017). The impact of mandatory arbitration on the common law regulation of standard terms in consumer contracts. *The George Washington Law Review, 85*, 1692.

Nolan-Haley, J. (2018). Does ADR's access to Justice Come at the expense of meaningful consent. *Ohio State Journal on Dispute Resolution, 33*, 373.

Noyes, H. S. (2006). If you (re) build it, they will come: Contracts to remake the rules of litigation in arbitration's image. *Harvard Journal of Law & Public Policy, 30*, 579.

Orsini, M. (2002). The politics of naming, blaming and claiming: HIV, hepatitis C and the emergence of blood activism in Canada. *Canadian Journal of Political Science/Revue canadienne de science politique, 35*(3), 475–498.

Pakulski, J. (1995). Sidney Tarrow, power in movement: Social movements, collective action and politics. *Australian and New Zealand Journal of Sociology, 31*(2), 151–152.

Palmer, M. (1987). The revival of mediation in the People's Republic of China: (1) Extra-judicial mediation. Yearbook on Socialist Legal Systems 1987: 219–77

Park, W. W. (1990). When the borrower and the banker are at odds: The interaction of judge and arbitrator in trans-border finance. *Tulsa Law Review, 65*, 1323.

Park, W. W. (1997). Arbitration in banking and finance. *Yearbook of International Financial and Economic Law, 2*, 141.

Park, W. W. (2000). Making sense of financial arbitration. Arbitration, finance and insurance – Special supplement; ICC International Court of Arbitration bulletin.

Parra Moyano, J., & Ross, O. (2017). KYC optimization using distributed ledger technology. *Business and Information Systems Engineering, 59*(6), 411–423.

Price, B. M. (2010). Halting, altering and agreeing. *Southern University Law Review, 38*, 233.

PWMA. (2021, August). Private wealth management association code of ethics and conduct. Retrieved March 29, 2021, from https://www.pwma.org.hk/wp-content/uploads/2020/08/5bc834b39f6d4.pdf

Queen Mary University of London. (2021). Research. Retrieved September 7, 2021, from http://www.arbitration.qmul.ac.uk/research/index.html

Relis, T. (2009). *Perceptions in litigation and mediation: Lawyers, defendants, plaintiffs, and gendered parties*. Cambridge University Press.

Resnik, J. (2014). Diffusing disputes: The public in the private of arbitration, the private in courts, and the erasure of rights. *Yale Law Journal, 124*, 2804.

Resnik, J., Garlock, S., & Wang, A. J. (2020). Collective preclusion and inaccessible arbitration: Data, non-disclosure, and public knowledge. *Lewis and Clark Law Review, 24*, 611.

Reynolds, J. W. (2014). Luck v. justice: Consent Intervenes, but for Whom. *Pepperdine Dispute Resolution Law Journal, 14*, 245.

Reynolds, M. P. (2014). Arbitration and ethical codes. *Legal Ethics, 17*(3), 458–462.

Riskin, L. L., & Welsh, N. A. (2007). Is that all there is: The problem in court-oriented mediation. *The George Mason Law Review, 15*, 863.

Ruce, P. J. (2011). Anti-money laundering: The challenges of know your customer legislation for private bankers and the hidden benefits for relationship management (the bright side of knowing your customer). *Banking Law Journal, 128*, 548.

Sander, F. E. A. (1976). Varieties of dispute processing. *Federal Rules Decisions, 70*, 111–134.

Sarat, A. (1985). Legal effectiveness and social studies of law: On the unfortunate persistance of a research tradition. *Legal Studies Forum, 9*, 23.

Sarat, A. (2000). Exploring the hidden domains of civil justice: Naming, blaming, and claiming in popular culture. *Depaul Law Review, 50*, 425.

Sarat, A., & Felstiner, W. L. (1997). *Divorce lawyers and their clients: Power and meaning in the legal process*. Oxford University Press on Demand.

Sarfaty, G. A. (2017). Doing good business or just doing good: Competing human rights frameworks at the World Bank. In Bronwen Morgan. *The intersection of rights and regulation* (pp. 93–106). Routledge.

Schneider, A. K., & Honeyman, C. (2006). *The negotiator's fieldbook*. American Bar Association.

Schritt, J. (2020). Crude talking: Radio and the politics of naming, blaming and claiming in oil-age Niger. *Journal of Contemporary African Studies*, *38*(3), 415–436.

Schwartz, A. (1973). Seller unequal bargaining power and the judicial process. *Industrial Law Journal*, *49*, 367.

Schwartz, A., & Watson, J. (2004). The law and economics of costly contracting. *Journal of Law, Economics, and Organization*, *20*(1), 2–31.

Scott, R. E., & Triantis, G. G. (2005). Anticipating litigation in contract design. *Yale Law Journal*, *115*(4), 814.

Securities and Futures Commission. (2008). Issues raised by the Lehmans minibonds crisis: Report to the financial SECETARY (2008). Retrieved May 25, 2021, from https://www.sfc.hk/sfc/doc/EN/general/general/lehman/Review%20Report/Review%20Report.pdf

Securities and Futures Commission. (2010). SFC reprimands and fines HSBC $2.1 million for breaching telephone recording requirements, September 10, 2019. Retrieved March 29, 2021, from https://www.sfc.hk/edistributionWeb/gateway/EN/news-and-announcements/news/doc?refNo=19PR82

Securities and Futures Commission. (2019). Do you need a license or registration? Retrieved March 11, 2021, from https://www.sfc.hk/en/Regulatory-functions/Intermediaries/Licensing/Do-you-need-a-licence-or-registration

Securities and Futures Commission. (2020, December). Code of conduct for persons licensed by or registered with the securities and futures commission. Retrieved March 29, 2021, from https://www.sfc.hk/-/media/EN/assets/components/codes/files-current/web/codes/code-of-conduct-for-persons-licensed-by-or-registered-with-the-securities-and-futures-commission/Code_of_conduct-Dec-2020_Eng.pdf

Securities industry conference on arbitration, Uniform Code of Arbitration, ss 1(A), 31 (1994).

Shehu, A. Y. (2010). Promoting financial sector stability through an effective AML/CFT regime. *Journal of Money Laundering Control*, *13*(2), 139–154.

Silbey, S. S. (2005). After legal consciousness. *Annual Review of Law and Social Science*, *1*, 323–368.

Singer, L. R. (1979). Nonjudicial dispute resolution mechanisms: The effects on justice for the poor. *Clearinghouse Review*, *13*, 569.

Slawson, W. D. (1971). Standard form contracts and democratic control of lawmaking power. *Harvard Law Review*, *84*(3), 529–566.

Soo, G., Zhao, Y., & Cai, D. (2010). Better ways of resolving disputes in Hong Kong-some insights from the Lehman-Brothers related investment product dispute mediation and arbitration scheme. *Journal of International Business and Law*, *9*, 137.

Speidel, R. E. (1996). Contract theory and securities arbitration: Whither consent. *Brooklyn Law Review*, *62*, 1335.

Sternlight, J. R. (2002). ADR is here: Preliminary reflections on where it fits in a system of justice. *Nevada Law Journal*, *3*, 289.

Sternlight, J. R. (2004). Creeping mandatory arbitration: Is it just. *Stanford Law Review*, *57*, 1631.

Stipanowich, T., & Vasconcellos, M. (2016). The interplay between empirical studies and commercial arbitration practice. In Stavros Brekoulakis, Julian D.M. Lew and Loukas Mistelis, eds. *The Evolution and Future of International Arbitration*, 471–485. Pepperdine University Legal Studies Research Paper No. 2017/3, Available at SSRN: https://ssrn.com/abstract=2920755

The Hong Kong Association of Banks. (2021). Code of banking practice, February 2015. Retrieved November 29, 2021, from https://www.hkma.gov.hk/media/eng/doc/code_eng.pdf

The Hong Kong Association of Banks. (2021). Prevention of money laundering. Retrieved December 14, 2021, from https://www.hkab.org.hk/DisplayArticleAction.do?sid=5&ss=162019)

The Millennium Development Goals and beyond. (2015). Retrieved March 11, 2021, from https://www.un.org/millenniumgoals/global.shtml

The Swiss Banking Association. (2018, April). Swiss private banking – Regulatory competitiveness benchmarking. Retrieved May 31, 2022, from https://www.swissbanking.ch/_Resources/Persistent/6/9/6/e/696e6f09e97e4c2fcafc08d05c3deee3d89fd569/SBA_Benchmarking_Swiss_private_banking_EN.pdf

TransUnion. (2021). About us. Retrieved September 15, 2021, from https://www.transunion.hk/home

Tyler, T. R. (ed.). (2005). *Procedural justice*. Ashgate.

UBS. (2021). Hong Kong. Retrieved May 26, 2021, from https://www.ubs.com/hk/en.html#hk-private-investors

United Nations. (2016). Guidelines for consumer protection, July 2015. Retrieved Retrieved March 11, 2021, from https://unctad.org/system/files/official-document/ditccplpmisc2016d1_en.pdf

United States General Accounting Office. (1997, October 30). Private banking: Information on private banking and its vulnerabilities to money laundering. Retrieved September 8, 2021, from https://www.gao.gov/assets/ggd-98-19r.pdf

United States General Accounting Office. (1999). Money laundering: Observations on private banking and related oversight of selected offshore jurisdictions (Statement/Record, 11/09/1999, GAO/T-GGD-00-32). Retrieved September 8, 2021, from https://www.govinfo.gov/content/pkg/GAOREPORTS-T-GGD-00-32/html/GAOREPORTS-T-GGD-00-32.htm

Vidmar, N. (1984). The small claims court: A reconceptualization of disputes and an empirical investigation. *Law and Society Review*, *18*(4), 515–550.

Waldman, E. (2011). *Mediation ethics: Cases and commentaries*. John Wiley & Sons.

Weerasooria, W. S., & Wallace, N. (1994). *Banker-customer: Resolving banking disputes*. Longman Business & Professional.

Weidemaier, W. Mark C. (2010). Toward a Theory of Precedent in Arbitration, *Wm. & Mary L. Rev,51,* 1895.

Weinstein, J. B. (2009). Comments on Owen M. Fiss, against settlement (1984). *Fordham Law Review*, *78*, 1265.

Weixia, G. (2011). ADR and financial disputes in Hong Kong: The Lehman Brothers experience and the way forward. *Asian Dispute Review*, *13*, 20.

Welsh, N. A. (2001). Making deals in court-connected mediation: What's justice got to do with it. *Washington University Law Quarterly*, *79*, 787.

Welsh, N. A. (2004). Remembering the role of justice in resolution: Insights from procedural and social justice theories. *J. Legal Educ.*, *54*, 49.

Wiethoff, C. (2003). Naming, blaming, and claiming in public disputes: The 1998 Maine referendum on civil rights protection for gay men and lesbians. *Journal of Homosexuality*, *44*(1), 61–82.

Wolfsberg Group (2012). *Wolfsberg anti-money laundering principles for private banking.* available at: http://www.wolfsberg-principles.com/pdf/Wolfsberg-Private-Banking-Prinicples-May2012.pdf (accessed: 24 April 2023)

World Bank. (2019). *Complaints handling within financial service providers: Principles, practices, and regulatory approaches.* World Bank.

INDEX

Note: Page numbers in **bold** refer to tables

For Product Safety Concerns and Information please contact our EU
representative GPSR@taylorandfrancis.com
Taylor & Francis Verlag GmbH, Kaufingerstraße 24, 80331 München, Germany

www.ingramcontent.com/pod-product-compliance
Ingram Content Group UK Ltd.
Pitfield, Milton Keynes, MK11 3LW, UK
UKHW020013200926
475702UK00014B/1857
* 9 7 8 1 0 3 2 5 2 6 3 3 1 *